SOUP NIGHT

RECIPES *for* CREATING COMMUNITY AROUND A POT OF SOUP

Maggie Stuckey

Storey Publishing

To all the Stanton Street families and to darling Meg,
who first introduced me to Soup Night

The mission of Storey Publishing is to serve our customers by
publishing practical information that encourages
personal independence in harmony with the environment.

Edited by Margaret Sutherland
Art direction by Mary Winkelman Velgos
Cover design, book design, and text production by Stewart A. Williams Design

Cover photography by © Lara Ferroni
Interior photography by © Lara Ferroni, except for: Mars Vilaubi, 11, 18, 31, 66, 97, 161,
    203, 207, 221, 227, 229, 271, 289 and 290; Alethea Morrison, 251; Carolyn Eckert, 265;
    © Margaret Stuckey, 13, 235, and 237
Illustrations by © Claudia Pearson

Indexed by Christine R. Lindemer

Storey Publishing
210 MASS MoCA Way
North Adams, MA 01247
www.storey.com

Printed in the United States by Versa Press
10 9 8 7 6 5 4 3 2 1

LIBRARY OF CONGRESS CATALOGING-IN-PUBLICATION DATA
Stuckey, Maggie.
 Soup night / by Maggie Stuckey.
    pages cm
 Includes index.
 ISBN 978-1-61212-099-7 (paperback : alkaline paper)
 ISBN 978-1-60342-900-9 (ebook)
 1. Soups. 2. Seasonal cooking. I. Title.
TX757.S77 2013
641.81'3—dc23

                                        2013012589

Storey Publishing is committed to making environmentally responsible
manufacturing decisions. This book was printed on paper made from
sustainably harvested fiber.

CONTENTS

Welcome to Soup Night!

At latitude 45 degrees 30 minutes north, almost exactly halfway between the equator and the north pole, it's fully dark by 6 PM in January. In Portland, Oregon, the streetlights have been on for almost an hour. A bit before 6, in an older, sedate neighborhood on Portland's urban east side, front doors all up and down the street begin to open. For the next 10 to 15 minutes, individuals, couples, and families come out their front doors and stroll easily but with purpose in the same direction. They're all heading toward the same house, just about in the middle of the block, on the left-hand side.

Everyone is carrying something. Some of the adults have gigantic salad bowls, or warm bread wrapped in dish towels, or those familiar rectangular pans that hold the promise of homemade brownies. Some have a wineglass threaded through the fingers of one hand. Kids skip ahead, bright plastic cups firm in little fists or looped onto belts through the handle. Most people have spoons, wrapped in paper napkins and tucked into jeans pockets. One dapper fellow wears a cloth napkin folded just so in the breast pocket of his sports coat, like a fancy silk handkerchief; one soup spoon stands in the exact middle. And each person in this gentle parade carries a soup bowl. An *empty* soup bowl.

It's Soup Night on Stanton Street.

My First Soup Night

My brother and his family live on the Soup Night street. One day some months ago, my niece Meg (the most spectacular teenager in the western hemisphere) happened to mention Soup Night in the midst of telling me about something else. "Whoa," I said, "back up. What's Soup Night?"

As she started describing it, in the first five seconds I knew this was something very special. So I contacted the next host and asked if I could come as a guest. That first evening, I was totally enchanted at the sight of the parade of

people strolling down the sidewalk, carrying their empty soup bowls. When I arrived at the host house, people assumed I was new to the neighborhood. They immediately shook my hand and introduced themselves, pointing out where their house was in relation to where we were standing. It wasn't long before I was able to make it plain how I was connected (my brother lives on your street), and why I was there (I want to write about you). But it was absolutely clear that if I *had* been a new neighbor, I would have been engulfed in a very warm, very genuine welcome.

Everyone wants to live on this street. People go door to door, trying to find someone who's thinking of selling. — *Marty*

Since that first evening, I have attended more than a dozen Stanton Street Soup Nights. Over and over, I have heard the families talk about, and have observed for myself, the almost magical sense of community that they have created on their block, and the many ripples of positive benefits that flow from it. I have been happy witness to some amazing scenes and heard some great stories, and together they form the core of this book.

Neighborhoods and Neighborliness

Stanton Street runs east–west through the Irvington neighborhood in inner Northeast Portland — that is, smack in the urban core. In a city known for strong neighborhood associations and liberal politics, Irvington stands out on both scores. It is settled, sedate, and quiet — a grand old lady of a neighborhood. The streets are wide, the trees are tall, the garages (if any) are tucked away behind the house or off to the side. The houses date from the early part of the twentieth century: a mix of Craftsman bungalows, Foursquares (which in Portland are called "Old Portland"), and a few architectural styles with no specific names except "traditional."

This particular block of Stanton Street mirrors the overall look and feel of the larger Irvington neighborhood. *(By the way, I should tell you that the amazing close-knit block that started me thinking about Soup Nights is not actually on Stanton Street. It's very close by, but not on that exact street. I shifted the geography ever so slightly to give these folks a little bit of privacy protection. Besides, I quite like saying "Stanton Street Soup Night." In the interest of complete disclosure, I should also tell*

you that I played around with time, in this one way: I smooshed some scenes together, as if they had happened on the same night.)

It is completely residential and, in spite of a cheerful cacophony of kid noises, has an air of serenity. All the houses are single-family homes; large mature trees line the street on both sides; there is minimal auto traffic. Most houses boast a pretty garden or cool green lawn in front, and in every single case — this is very important — the front yard is open to the sidewalk. There are no privacy fences, no gates, nothing that walls off any one home from the rest of the block.

Urban planners, take note: By this one simple measure, a profound sense of openness, of inclusion, is created. And it perpetuates itself. There is nothing in the city ordinances or building codes that would prevent anyone from adding these features to their front yard, but on this block, no one would even think of doing such a thing. It would close them off from their neighbors.

Stanton Street is in most ways typical of the larger Irvington neighborhood of which it is a part, and Irvington in turn epitomizes many of the qualities that have put Portland on the progressive map. Portland has, for one example, developed a national reputation for its strong network of neighborhood associations and the official support structure for them within city government. Irvington has such an association, and it is one of the largest, most active, and most effective. In the Irvington neighborhood, no one need go bowling alone. So, by all accounts Portland already has in place the climate necessary for a deep and abiding sense of community among all its citizens. And yet. . . .

And yet in parts of Portland it is still possible to see scenes like this: Women and men drive home from work, climb tiredly out of the car, perhaps wave to the next-door neighbor if that neighbor is in sight, then go inside and stay there for the rest of the evening. No further contact outside the walls of their own home, not this night, or tomorrow night, maybe not even on the weekend. This kind of pattern develops before you know it, and hardens, and then it takes a deliberate strategy to break out of it. It's sort of like gaining weight — it sneaks up on you a little at a time, until you must grab hold and act with purpose to turn things around.

On Stanton Street, they did it with Soup Night.

> We make community out of the people who are right around us, right here in the neighborhood. These are not people we were already connected to, but now we are. That's the positive energy of Soup Night. — *Alex*

Everyone Is Invited

The Stanton Street Soup Night was designed from the very beginning as a way to bring neighbors together. Everyone on the block — every single person, corner to corner, on both sides of the street — is invited. The whole idea is for neighbors who might not otherwise have a natural point of contact to get to know one another. Through the simple act of sitting down to a meal together on a regular basis, even people who have very little in common build a genuine relationship.

At its core, Soup Night is a stunningly simple idea: get everybody together once a month for an informal soup supper. What is not so simple — what is in fact quite extraordinary — is what happens next.

A strong sense of community replaces social isolation.

People no longer feel like strangers.

Children thrive in a safe environment, watched over by many loving adults.

Any emergency, small or large, is met with instant assistance.

Seniors and people living alone have a new sense of security and belonging.

Life seems richer, kinder, sweeter, and more fun.

And it is healthier, in all dimensions: physical, psychological, and emotional.

On Stanton Street, when people talk about building community (which they do, a lot), they mean something very precise: creating and nurturing a way for every single person on the block to feel connected to every other person. Not just the people who already know each other, but everyone, without exception.

That connection shows itself in many different and wonderful ways. Reading their stories, we are reminded what good-neighborliness really means. But let's also take note of what it does *not* mean. It doesn't mean poking into other people's lives unwelcomed. It doesn't mean gossip. It doesn't mean comparing A to B in any manner that might diminish either one. It doesn't mean intruding, making judgments, or taking without giving.

How It Works

The mechanics of Soup Night are very simple. In fact, that's part of its genius. Once a year, usually at the annual block party in September, someone puts out a sign-up sheet, and people sign up to host each month. It isn't hard to get volunteers; the event has become so popular that people fight for the privilege. Sometimes two households go together as co-hosts, thus neatly avoiding duels at dawn.

By tradition, Soup Night happens on the last Sunday of the month, but each host has the option to change the date if need be. The host sends a reminder, usually in the form of a hand-delivered invitation or flyer, a week or so in advance. On the night itself, the host makes two huge pots of soup, one of which is vegetarian. And that's all; that is the complete limit of the host's responsibility.

One of the rules of Soup Night is that the host doesn't have to feel obligated to clean the house beforehand (although, human nature being what it is, many do). The other critical rule is that the host should not be burdened with cleanup afterward, which is why everyone brings their own bowl and spoon. It is often the case that neighbors contribute other things to the meal — a bottle of wine, a big bowl of strawberries from that day's U-Pick outing, homemade bread or cookies — but that doesn't qualify as a rule; people do that when they feel moved to do so.

There are a few other unwritten rules: It is quietly understood that some of those on the block are simply not in a position to host, and no umbrage falls to them. No one keeps score about who has hosted how often, and the idea that it's someone's "turn" would not occur to anyone. People over 70 are not expected to sit on the floor; seats at the table are reserved for them. No formal RSVP is expected, and even though the event is for a specific time period (usually 6 to 8 PM), it's okay to drop in late or leave early.

> It's really good support for Debbie, as a single mom, to know that her son is safe in the hands of people who adore him.
> — *Marty*

"Rich in Grace and Kindness"

There is something very special about this block. You can't quite put a name to it, but it is unmistakable. All you have to do is stand still on the sidewalk for five minutes, and you feel it.

The fundamental sense beneath all the interactions is a spirit of generosity, fostered by Soup Night and made tangible in countless acts of kindness. It is a powerful thing, beautifully expressed by two of the neighbors:

"Soup Night," one man says quite simply, "has created a place rich in grace and kindness."

"It's impossible to overstate how valuable it is," another says. "It fills your soul."

Any law enforcement officer will tell you that the single best safeguard against trouble is knowing your neighbors, living in an area where everyone keeps a friendly eye out. On Stanton Street, they do this as a matter of course. Every adult knows every child, and every child knows every adult, and that automatically sustains a sense of safety and security. And that can be traced directly to Soup Night.

"Because of Soup Night," explains Jessie, mother of two, "Earl knows my kids and they know him. Now, ordinarily they would have no reason for any kind of interaction. Earl is much older than most of the adults in their life, and lives a very different kind of life. But because they see him at Soup Night every month, they are comfortable with him whenever their paths cross, and vice versa. Nobody's afraid of anybody."

On this block, all the adults watch over all the kids. In a sense, the children seem to belong to everyone. It is one of the most important ways that Soup Night has enriched everyone's quality of life. And the benefits are wide-reaching.

One of the most obvious of those benefits accrues immediately to parents: they can relax. They know their kids are safe as long as they're in sight of anyone who lives on the block. They are freed from that edginess that infects so many urban families, who feel they have to watch the children every single minute lest something awful befall them.

The Splendid Soup Table

Lynne Rossetto Kasper, host of the popular NPR radio program *The Splendid Table*, was herself a guest on another NPR program, *Weekend America*, in May 2008. The news hook was a fund-raising dinner that evening, billed as a Unity Dinner, sponsored by the Democratic National Committee, which at that time was anything but unified. Kasper was asked about the power of food to bridge misunderstandings.

"Eating together is probably the second most intimate act that happens between human beings," she responded. "You're taking the nourishment of the 'other' into your body. If you think about this, that is a phenomenal occurrence." (*Weekend America*, www.publicradio.org, May 31, 2008)

Now of course we all know what the *first* most intimate act is, and no one would disagree that it is both intimate and nourishing, and sometimes quite phenomenal too. But it seems to me that since that act is generally limited to just two people at a time, both of whom are (or should be) adults, its intimacy quotient is limited.

I think even more intimacy is on view when a large group of people shares a meal together. After all, that act involves people of all ages, including some who may not already be in some sort of relationship with each other. Eating together can, in my view, create intimacy where none exists, and everybody can still respect everybody else in the morning.

Will, father of a young boy, describes it this way. "It's like going back to the way we grew up. When I was a child, it was nothing for kids to race out the front door and head down the street and play with their pals all day long. Nowadays we have to be so careful, watch them every minute. But here we don't have to. It's like the old ways again. What a special thing that is.

"It [participating in Soup Night] is more for our son than for us," Will continues. "We want to give him a sense that he's safe, protected by other adults, that people wish him well and will take care of him." And I can tell you, as an occasional visitor to the block, that this attitude of caring, of loving watchfulness, is unmissable. It fills the very air.

The Intimacy of Food

Throughout history, the sharing of food has been accorded significance far beyond simple sustenance. It is a way for enemies to acknowledge detente, for acquaintances to deepen their friendship, and for those in the uncertain middle to demonstrate the possibility of peace.

I feel strongly that with our changing society, some things get lost. Soup Night brings back the positive points of small-town living. It feels really good. — Mary

In all cultures and all religions, noteworthy moments are celebrated with food. In our country, we use food to symbolize celebration, or caring. When a friend is sick or home with a brand-new baby, we bring food so she doesn't have to cook. When a family is gathered for a funeral, we bring food to console the grieving. When a new neighbor moves in, or a new colleague starts work, we bring food to break the ice. Food honors achievements, soothes hurt feelings, and welcomes newcomers.

It is surely no accident, then, that the event that transformed a modern city block into a cohesive, caring community is built around food. Of course it's not the food per se — although the food is darned good — but the implicit message that comes with sharing it. Everyone at Soup Night feels it, and when they talk

about it they often echo each other's words. Marty says, "The idea that people would openly share their food, their home with anyone who comes … it's such a precious gift." Joy adds, "There's something about sitting down and sharing a meal that moves the whole thing to another level."

It also has a very important practical benefit. As Lisa succinctly puts it, "The simple act of eating soup together makes it easier to handle small problems."

> In parts of Africa, there is a fundamental understanding that someone who eats a meal with you will not hurt you, even if that person is from an enemy tribe. Sharing a meal is an overt act of trust.

Soup Nights around the Country

The need for community, for feeling connected to our fellow human beings, is universal and timeless. But in the modern hurry-scurry world, it's becoming harder and harder to achieve. It's a nasty kind of catch-22: the more fractured our lives become, the more we yearn for that sense of connectedness — and the more elusive it seems.

In troubled times, such as we now find ourselves in, the need is particularly acute. When people are fearful for their jobs and their homes, anxious about their family budgets, the emotional support of a strong social network means everything. Knowing you are surrounded by people who care about you goes a long way toward keeping despair at bay.

Living in a close community brings many important benefits. There is, for instance, solid evidence that cohesive neighborhoods have less crime and fewer traffic accidents, that children with a secure home environment do better in school, and that people with a strong social network have higher levels of mental and physical health. Not to mention ready access to borrowing really good lawn mowers.

All across the country thoughtful, caring, engaged people are searching for a way to build that kind of supportive community. And here's a remarkable thing: unbeknownst to each other, many of them have hit on the same solution, of hosting a Soup Night.

For, as I quickly learned, the Stanton Street Soup Night is not unique. In New York, Chicago, San Francisco, Pittsburgh, Milwaukee, Cleveland, Boston, Houston,

and many other places, neighbors are getting together regularly for their version of Soup Night. You will meet many of them in the pages ahead.

And the concept extends beyond the limits of neighborhood geography too. As I began to dig into this idea, I found many other groups all around the country that host some

Many recent studies have verified what common sense suggests: people who have a rich social network are healthier, live longer, and rank higher on the happiness index.

special event to bring people together and fulfill their goals, all while enjoying a great meal of homemade soup. (See Soup for a Good Cause, page 293.) There are countless reasons that people gather: to raise funds for a local nonprofit, to sponsor youth programs at a church, to introduce all the members of a community garden, to support cutting-edge artists with small grants, or to help a local program that's focused on alleviating hunger. What we once called a "soup kitchen" is alive and well in America, but today it takes many innovative and dynamic forms.

Originally — before I discovered all the other wonderful groups around the country — this book started out to be just about Stanton Street. Because I had the opportunity to talk at length with all the Stanton Street families (adults and children), I can share with you their very eloquent statements about what Soup Night means to them. But I know for certain that none of these good people would ever think of themselves as special, or want me to portray them that way. As you meet other Soup Nighters later in the book, you will see that, to a remarkable extent, they express the same sentiments, often in almost the exact same words. If I seem to offer more details about Stanton Street, the Soup Night that I know best, it's simply by way of presenting a model, something that can be duplicated in any town anywhere in the country. If you should be inspired to start a Soup Night in your own neighborhood — my fondest wish — the ideas described here will give you a good starting point.

Soup Night is incredibly important to the kids on the block and they don't even know it yet. Right now it's just a big party to them. But they are seeing how adults can behave cooperatively. And that's a great thing to grow up with.
— *John*

CHAPTER ONE

Soup Kettle Basics

I know you want to get right to the recipes — don't worry, this is a short chapter. Here I pulled together some general comments and tips about making soup, so I wouldn't bore you by repeating them over and over later on. Some of these ideas may already be in your repertoire, but I hope you'll find a few new things too.

The Glory of Soup

You already know many of the wonderful things about soup:

It's healthy. With a strong reliance on vegetables and protein-rich legumes like beans and lentils, relatively small amounts of meat, and almost no fat, soup is a nutrition lollapalooza. It's also a great way to sneak veggies into kids' diets.

It's inexpensive. Soup is a particularly delicious way to feed lots of people.

It's easy. Sophisticated culinary techniques are not needed. In fact, I can hardly think of any soup recipe that requires a special skill; many can be prepared by children (assuming an adult supervises the knife work).

It's versatile. Soup for lunch. Soup for supper. Soup for a crowd. Soup for a party. Soup for unexpected visitors — I'm betting you can create something delicious from your pantry and fridge in short order.

It's easy to expand. The recipes in this book are planned for 6 to 8 servings, because I know you'll want to make some for your regular family meals. But almost all of them — almost all soups, really — can easily be expanded to feed a crowd. You may not always want to double the amount of the more expensive ingredients (and it hardly ever matters), and you probably should increase the spices and herbs incrementally, tasting as you go, but in other respects, just double or triple the ingredients. In fact, even if you're not cooking for a crowd, you might want to make a double batch and freeze half. If you do, here's a tip from Sonia in Portland (page 81): "Separate the solids from the liquids before freezing.

When reheating, start with the liquids, and then add the solids. This prevents the solids from getting overcooked."

It's a great use for leftovers. A little bit of pot roast, a cupful of mashed potatoes, half a zucchini, two tomatoes that won't last another day . . . just about anything can be the start of a wonderful soup. Just add imagination, and stir.

It's forgiving. Precise measurements hardly ever matter. In fact, many great cooks don't even bother.

It's flexible. Soup nicely lends itself to improvisation. Don't have kale? Use spinach. Weather unexpectedly warm? Many hot soups are also good cold. Don't like something? Leave it out. I confess — I cannot abide the taste of cooked celery, so when it shows up in any recipe I just ignore it. And you can turn just about any vegetable into a nutritious soup in a jiffy; for example, see Cream of Anything Green Soup (page 32).

It's easy to convert for vegetarians. Leave out the meat and substitute vegetable broth or plain water for the stock.

It's delicious.

It warms your soul. For all the above reasons, plus one more: it makes tangible the many meanings of "community." Read Martha Bayne's eloquent note about the "community-built nature of soup" (page 140).

Set Up a Soup Pantry

I'm guessing that you already have on hand many of the staples — such as onions, garlic, and olive oil — for making soup on the spur of the moment. Check over this list for ingredients you might not have thought of:

- Canned beans of all kinds (and see page 27 for the alternative: dried beans)

- Lentils

- Quinoa, bulgur wheat, and other filling grains

- Canned tomatoes: diced, whole, stewed, with chiles, with basil and garlic, etc.

- Cream-style corn (if you're worried about dairy products, it doesn't contain actual cream)

- Dried pastas in small shapes: orzo, shells, elbows, radiatore, penne, rotini, alphabet

- Pesto in a jar or tube (refrigerate after opening)

- Good-quality bouillon (I am very fond of a product called Better Than Bouillon. It's a paste that comes in a jar, highly concentrated, and lasts forever. And what I especially like is that the first ingredient on the label is what you would want to see listed first: chicken, beef, vegetables, turkey, etc. — not salt! Refrigerate after opening.)

- Canned broth: chicken, beef, vegetable; search out reduced-sodium varieties

- Roasted peppers in a jar

- Bacon bits

- Canned tuna, clams, crabmeat

- Canned green chiles

- Sun-dried tomatoes

- Tomato spread intended for bruschetta (adds a strong tomato punch to soup; refrigerate after opening)

- Tapenade in a jar (refrigerate after opening)

In addition to the pantry, look to your fridge. Several staples that need refrigeration will help you make a delicious impromptu soup. Here are a few I try always to keep on hand:

○ Nonfat sour cream. It's real sour cream, but made from nonfat milk, so it's lower in calories. One big spoonful stirred in at the end adds amazing creaminess. One small container lasts a long time, even opened.

○ Fresh lemons. A splash of lemon juice brightens the flavor of many foods, and almost all soups benefit from a squeeze. I keep bottled lemon juice on hand for emergencies, but frankly it's a very poor second best.

○ Fresh limes. For many things, I like lime juice even better than lemon. It has that lovely citrus sparkle but with a slight undertone of sweetness. Wonderful in fruit soups, for instance.

○ Cheese. Any type of hard cheese, grated right on top of the soup in the bowl, adds immensely to the flavor. I especially like Parmesan, but many others work equally well.

And of course we haven't said anything about herbs and spices. But that's another book, and I'm sure you have a good selection in your cupboards, ready to explore.

Shortcuts

People who like to make soup tend to be especially ingenious and resourceful. Here are a few shortcuts, to go with the ones you no doubt have already discovered:

○ Bread cubes intended for stuffing can be croutons in a pinch.

○ Baking mix (like Bisquick) makes dumplings in a jiffy.

○ The salad bar in your supermarket is a good place to find vegetables ready to go.

○ Rotisserie chicken from the supermarket — not only for the meat but also a source for stock.

○ Frozen hash browns can take the place of russet potatoes, eliminating the peel/dice/shred steps.

Making and Freezing Stock

True to the improvisational nature of soup, the stock that serves as its liquid basis is very much a product of a cook's ingenuity and thriftiness, more than it is of a specific recipe. I know that will seem heretical to some serious chefs, those folks who purchase veal bones just for stock, for instance. Instead, let's talk about what you can easily and realistically do.

When you work with fresh vegetables, save the trimmings. Carrot scrapings, potato peels, the leafy tops of celery, the stalks of broccoli, leek tops (leaves), onion peels — all that stuff. Toss them around in a bowl with a small amount of olive oil and roast in a 400°F oven for about 10 minutes. Run the whole thing through your blender with a little water, strain, and freeze. Don't forget to label. Do this a few times, and you have the basis for a wonderful vegetarian stock.

For any entrée that starts with a cut of meat that has bones, cut away the bones first. Sauté them in vegetable oil until very well browned, then add water (or tomato juice, or wine, or a mixture) and a couple of bay leaves and simmer for at least an hour (a slow cooker works well here). Strain off and reserve the liquid, set it in the refrigerator until cool, and remove the fat after it congeals on the top.

Roasting a chicken or turkey for dinner? Not making gravy? After removing the bird, add water to the pan, scrape up the bits from the bottom, and simmer for about half an hour. Strain, cool, and skim off the congealed fat.

To release the goodness of whole spices, crush lightly with the bottom of a glass or the flat side of a knife, and then place them into one of those screw-together metal balls meant for brewing tea.

Those rotisserie chickens from the supermarket, so very handy for a quick supper, also have the makings of a great soup stock. Remove the skin, the bones, and the juices that have collected in the bottom of the container, and put them all into a soup pot with water to cover. Add some whole spices (bay leaves, cardamom, or your own favorite), a smashed clove of garlic, or a bouquet garni of fresh herbs (see below), and simmer for about an hour. Strain and discard all the solids, refrigerate, and skim off the congealed fat.

To flavor all these, add your own favorite spices and herbs. If you want stock that is completely clear when it is finished, rather than speckled with bits of green or brown, use one of the following techniques to contain the spices:

○ For fresh herbs, a simple bouquet garni is made by tying whole sprigs of herbs together with kitchen twine. Or fold fresh herbs into a square of cheesecloth, which you then tie with twine.

○ Whole spices are almost certain to be more flavorful than the ground versions that may have been in your cupboard too long. To release their goodness, crush lightly with the bottom of a glass or the flat side of a knife, and then place them into one of those screw-together metal balls meant for brewing tea.

By the way, be careful with whole spices; don't add them, intact, to soup — or any other food, for that matter — without some way to easily remove them. Some whole spices can be unpleasant to bite down on (think peppercorns), but there can be more serious problems. People can choke on whole cloves. And don't try to break bay leaves into small, edible pieces; they will stay firm and the edges are sharp: there have actually been reports of people getting cuts in their throats and even along their digestive tracts. Always leave them whole, count how many you put in, and take care to remove them all.

Reduce Your Stocks

Now for freezing. First of all, if your freezer space is limited, simmer all the prepared stocks until they are thick. This reduces the volume, so they take up less room in the freezer. It also provides you with a handy concentrate, ideal for those times when you want to add flavor but not a lot of extra liquid.

To store the concentrated stocks, you probably know the trick of freezing them into ice-cube trays, and then storing the frozen cubes in a ziplock freezer bag. If you have a large quantity of stock, another method is to place the cooled liquid into quart-size freezer bags and lay the bags flat in the freezer. Once frozen, the bags are easy to store upright in a freezer basket. Label the bags near the top, and you can easily flip through them, like those of us of a certain age used to do in record stores.

Finally, be sure to label the bags. You may think you can remember, or tell them apart by looks, but trust me, after a while you can't.

Garnishes

In many of the recipes in this book, you will find suggestions for specific garnishes that complement the flavors of the soup itself. But in fact, a garnish or two enlivens just about every kind of soup. Use your "good cook" sense to imagine which ones would go well with which soup. Think about color as well as taste: something white or creamy with dark red soup, for instance, or a bright green garnish with a pale soup. Here are several reliably delicious garnishes:

○ Crème fraîche. An alternative to sour cream and easy to make (see page 237).

○ Pesto. You can make your own, if you have a lusty crop of basil, but several commercial versions are available, and they freeze well, so you can use just a small amount.

○ Parmesan lace (see page 37)

○ Croutons (see page 248)

○ Grilled bread. If you have your outdoor grill going in the summer months, spread thick slices of a hearty artisan bread with olive oil on both sides, and grill — heavenly.

○ Herb butters. Mix softened butter with an herb that complements your soup, chill until firm, then slip a half teaspoonful into each soup bowl.

○ Red pepper purée. Dump a jar of prepared red peppers into the blender, liquid and all, and process to desired texture. Easy and delicious.

If you are lucky enough to have a vegetable garden yourself, or smart enough to make friends with someone who does, that's about as local and fresh as you can get!

○ Goat cheese. Slice crosswise into thin rounds, and float one on top of the soup in each bowl.

○ Goldfish crackers. Kids love them, but so do adults.

○ Roasted nuts. In a 350°F oven or in a dry skillet, toast whole nuts until fragrant; watch carefully, they go from fragrant to burned awfully fast. Cool, and then roughly chop.

○ Seeds, such as pumpkin, sunflower, and sesame.

○ French-fried onions. Yes, those crunchy bits your Aunt Grace uses for the green bean casserole on Thanksgiving are delicious with soup.

○ And of course, the standards: chopped chives, parsley and cilantro, scallions, sliced radishes, diced avocado, celery, tomato, cucumber, grated cheese.

Fresh or Frozen or Canned?

It's become something of a cliché in recent years: fresh and local is always better. But is it really?

Local, absolutely. Something that came from a farm seven miles from your house is bound to be fresher than something that traveled for three days in two separate refrigerated trucks halfway across the continent. Besides, those local farmers need our support. And of course, if you are lucky enough to have a vege- table garden yourself, or smart enough to make friends with someone who does, that's best of all. That's about as local and fresh as you can get!

What about "fresh"? That one's a little more complicated.

Of course, no one in their right mind would deny that the summertime wealth of fresh vegetables and fruits is a huge blessing. I happen to live in an area with a rich agricultural heritage, and I consider myself extremely fortunate to have so many family farms and U-Pick fields nearby. Every year, I start count- ing down the days until they open.

However, it is possible to get so entangled in the "fresh" mantra that we lose perspective and common sense in favor of culinary political correctness. Is "fresh" *always* best? In my opinion, not necessarily.

To grow vegetables that can withstand days of travel and handling at several stages along the way, growers have created cultivars that look great but suffer in taste. A "fresh" tomato that was picked green, then treated with gas so it turns red, can taste like cardboard. On the other hand, green beans transported to a frozen-food processing plant within hours of being picked are in fact fresher and more nutritious than their "fresh" counterparts that were trucked from someplace like California and then stored in the supermarket chain's distribution center for who knows how long before you bought them. Fresh pumpkins are great for jack-o'-lanterns, but something of a pain to cook and not appreciably better tasting than canned pumpkin.

So don't automatically reject frozen or canned vegetables. Unless you have your own garden or a nearby farmers' market, frozen or canned veggies may be your best bet for quality and nutritional value, especially in the off-season. And they're super-convenient to have on hand. Many of the recipes in this book call for canned tomatoes, for instance, and frankly I can't imagine my pantry without them. On the other hand, I've never seen frozen or canned eggplant; frozen bell peppers are very disappointing; and there's no way to preserve fresh cucumbers except as pickles, which is not always what you want in your soup. It's all a question of how to get the very best of what you need when you need it. And it's also a question of common sense.

With all that said, there is still nothing like a vine-ripened tomato that really was allowed to stay on the plant until dead ripe. You'll be hard pressed to find them anywhere except your own garden or your local farmers' market, but once you taste one, you'll never be satisfied with supermarket tomatoes again. An old country song claims that homegrown tomatoes are one of only two things in the world that money can't buy (the other being true love).

The other local treasure is fresh corn. And I mean *fresh*. The sugars in corn start to turn to starch within hours of picking, so if you don't have a big vegetable garden, try to find a farm stand or U-Pick place near home and go on the same day you're having your party. By the way, I have no real scientific evidence, but I'm quite certain that fresh corn you freeze yourself maintains its "country" taste much more than commercial frozen corn. So when you go to the farm stand, buy lots, and freeze half.

Beans: Dried or Canned?

The fresh/canned debate doesn't apply to beans as widely as some other vegetables, but it does have its own decision seesaw: should you use dried beans or the canned versions?

Here are the pros and cons.

For convenience, canned wins hands down. And since the fundamental idea of a soup pantry is to enable you to whip up a nutritious soup on short notice, you probably want some of your favorite types on hand.

On the other hand, canned beans often are high in sodium, and the liquid in the can might ruin the look and taste of your wonderful homemade stock. To deal with both these drawbacks, rinse the beans thoroughly before adding them to your soup.

Working with dried beans is the opposite of convenient, but very satisfying in other ways. You save money and feel virtuous, while completely avoiding the sodium problem. Plus, many natural food stores and food co-ops carry unusual varieties (cranberry, Anasazi, adzuki, yellow eyes, and other heirlooms, for instance) that you won't find in any can.

There are two common ways to prepare dried beans for cooking, both of which require some preplanning. Easiest is to cover your beans in about three times volume of cold water, and soak for 6 to 8 hours, even overnight. If you forgot to do that, the second method is something of a shortcut: bring the beans and water to a hard boil, remove from heat, cover, and let stand for 2 hours.

In both cases, drain off the soaking water, transfer the beans to a pot, add fresh water to cover by an inch or two, and cook, unsalted, until almost tender, so they finish cooking with the rest of the soup.

One-third cup of dried beans produces 1 cup cooked beans.

CHAPTER TWO

Fall

The leaves are turning glorious colors, the air has a little bit of a bite to it, and where I live the rains have started. It's time for soup!

Autumn brings delicious holidays — Halloween, Thanksgiving — that are opportunities for wonderful soup parties, and the grocer's shelves and late-season farmers' markets are stocked with ingredients: pumpkins, winter squashes, sweet potatoes, broccoli, cauliflower, and the many wonderful winter greens like Russian or Tuscan kale, mustard greens, or mizuna. Soup in autumn needs to be hearty, rich with vegetables, beans, and noodles — all the stuff that soothes our tummies and warms our hearts.

Soup Night on Stanton Street: October

Tonight's event is hosted by Becky and Lisa. They have lived on the block for eight years and have been together much longer. Back in 2006, when for a brief period Multnomah County allowed same-sex couples to marry, they took advantage of the opportunity. Even though the legal status was short-lived and the marriages ultimately were overturned, today both women still wear their wedding rings, and still consider themselves married. "Our certificate still hangs on the wall," Lisa says. "I don't know how you unmarry someone."

Both are in their late 40s, with the calm beauty that comes to women who know who they are, and both are professional educators (a teacher, a principal). They have one adopted son: four-year-old Sam, currently zipping around with little-boy energy and the special pride of being the host.

By 6:15 PM, the small Craftsman bungalow is bubbling with chatter. About 30 people attend this evening, a typical turnout. On the stove is a huge kettle of

---

Canadian Beef Stew (page 83), Peanut Butter–Chocolate Chip Cookies (page 96), and Onion-Bacon Rolls (page 88)

chicken noodle soup made from a recipe in the Better Homes and Gardens cookbook; on a counter, in a large slow cooker, is a creamy vegetarian soup featuring butternut squash. Both are delicious, but there is a clear favorite: in what seems like minutes, the chicken soup pot is empty.

In the living room, people sit on couches and chairs, on the piano bench, and on the floor. The dining room is a tad more formal, with eight chairs pulled up to the table. This spot is popular with the children, for the table is where the desserts are laid out. It is also where, by unspoken agreement, chairs are reserved for the block's elders. A clump of people stand chatting in the kitchen, another in the hallway. The edges of all these clusters constantly move and shift, like amoebas viewed under a microscope, as folks change seats to catch a visit with someone else.

The invitation specified 6 to 8 PM. This is standard; part of the original vision for Soup Night was that it be a definite, limited time frame, to accommodate the schedules of busy families. The two teenagers greet everyone but eat quickly and leave early — lots of homework. One couple arrives late; they have come straight from a family birthday party. Most of the adults linger way past 8, for there is big news on the block and important stuff to talk about.

All up and down the block, the word has spread quickly: Becky and Lisa just heard from the adoption agency that their application has been approved. They are definitely getting their second child. Little Sam gets to be a big brother. In a neighborhood so focused on its children, this is big news. Happy news. Grin-like-crazy news.

At tonight's Soup Night, this is the main topic of conversation. It is what has kept people talking long past the usual 8 PM ending time.

With a new baby coming, Becky and Lisa need to make some modifications to their house. As soon as they mention it, people jump in to help. One at a time or in small groups, people wander through all the rooms, thinking of possibilities. Suggestions fly thick and fast. People who've been through remodeling projects offer names of good contractors. The

experienced do-it-yourselfers, both men and women, chime in with other ideas. Substantial help is offered — contacts, tools, elbow grease. Everyone here has a stake in welcoming this baby.

On Stanton Street, it's what they do.

This sense that children are to be cherished is everywhere. Everyone talks about the kids, even those who aren't parents. At this evening's Soup Night, those with grown children fall to reminiscing about the days their children were young and all played together. Someone comments how things seem to come in waves — there's a group of young children, then they grow up and before you know it there's a new crop. Everybody smiles, nods.

The current crop of kids, meanwhile, is racing around having a grand old time. If they need reining in, any adult within grabbing range is authorized to do so.

There's a wonderful reciprocal effect at work here. Everyone has a hand in keeping the neighborhood safe for the kids, so the parents don't have to be on guard every single minute. At the same time, the children themselves are learning valuable lessons. Many of the parents have given careful thought to this. They know what it means to them, this sense of safety. But while they are grateful for the parenting support, they especially value what it means to the children.

Alex, father of two youngsters, says, "When my kids are in their 50s, sitting on their own front porch and thinking back over their life, the main thing they will remember about their childhood is Soup Night."

John, whose own children are young adults living on their own, summed it up in this poignant comment: "Soup Night is incredibly important to the kids on the block and they don't even know it yet. Right now it's just a big party to them. But they are seeing how adults can behave cooperatively. And that's a great thing to grow up with."

This is the magic of Soup Night: that something so simple and so much fun creates such wide ripples of positive effect.

Cream of Anything Green Soup

The fickleness of autumn weather means we can go from balmy Indian summer to darned cold overnight. So you might find yourself suddenly craving soup with no recipe-specific ingredients on hand. With good-quality commercial stock, a little sour cream, and just about any fresh vegetable, you can whip up something immensely satisfying. I call it "Cream of Anything Green," but in fact you could also use cauliflower, carrots, or any other non-green veggie you have at hand. True to the improvisational nature of things, no specific quantities or servings are listed. It's the only time I'll do that in this book, I promise.

An onion, 1 or 2 cloves of garlic, and enough olive oil to sauté them in

Several cups of any chopped fresh green vegetable: broccoli, spinach, kale, or any combination thereof

An equal amount of chicken broth, vegetable broth, or water — or a combination

A pinch of your favorite herbs or spices

A little bit of nonfat sour cream

Red pepper purée, for garnish

1. Heat the oil in a large soup pot over medium heat. Dice the onion and sauté until softened, about 2 minutes. Mince the garlic, add it in, and sauté 1 minute longer.

2. Cut the veggies into small chunks, tossing them into the pot and gently sautéing as you continue chopping. Add the broth along with any herbs or spices you think would complement the vegetables. I often use a spice blend called Shallot Pepper from Penzey's (www.penzeys.com). Personally, I think it's misnamed, because the main flavor is tarragon, which is a wonderful addition to this soup. Actually, it's wonderful in many things; I'm never without it.

3. Bring the soup to a boil, then simmer until the vegetables are very very tender. Transfer the soup to a blender (careful, it's hot) and purée until smooth, or use an immersion blender and purée the soup right in the pot.

4. Extra step but worth it: Strain the soup through a fine sieve to remove any stringy fibers or tough bits.

5. Return the soup to the pot, reheat gently if needed, and then whisk in the sour cream (a little goes a long way).

6. A swirl of puréed roasted red peppers (from a jar) makes the soup pretty enough for company.

Pear-Blue Cheese Soup

This luscious soup takes advantage of the so-called winter pears that are at their peak in the fall. If you can find them, use Comice pears — their juicy sweetness is like no other.

Serves 6

2 tablespoons canola oil

1 medium onion, chopped

4 pears, preferably Comice, peeled, cored, and chopped

3 cups vegetable broth

6 ounces blue cheese, such as Roquefort or Gorgonzola, crumbled

½ teaspoon paprika

Juice of ½ medium lemon (about 1½ tablespoons)

Salt and freshly ground black pepper

Chopped roasted pistachio nuts, for garnish

1. Heat the oil in a soup pot over medium heat. Add the onion and sauté until softened, about 2 minutes. Add the pears and broth. Bring to a boil, then reduce the heat and simmer for 10 minutes.

2. Add the cheese, paprika, and lemon juice, and season with salt and pepper to taste. Simmer until the cheese is melted; taste and adjust seasonings as needed.

3. Transfer the soup to a blender (careful, it's hot) and purée until smooth, or use an immersion blender and purée the soup right in the pot. Strain it through a fine sieve to remove any small fibrous bits of pear.

4. Return the soup to the pot and reheat gently until hot enough to serve. Garnish each serving with chopped pistachios.

Variation: For a dinner party, this elegant soup cries out for an elegant garnish, such as edible flowers. You should be able to find organically grown pansies or violas (which are cool-season flowers) at specialty markets, if not in your own garden.

Make ahead? Complete the soup except for the garnish; refrigerate; rewarm *slowly*.

For large crowds: Probably not the best choice for making huge quantities, since the cheese is going to be relatively expensive and you really can't do without.

Creamy Cauliflower Soup

Cauliflower gets a bad rap, in my opinion. When absolutely fresh, as it is in the fall, it offers a wonderful crispness and mild taste that melds well with other flavors. This soup takes advantage of this classic autumn vegetable, and has one other terrific trait: it's delicious either hot or cold. Of course in the fall or winter you'd probably serve it hot, but the cold version is a lot like vichyssoise except with fewer calories. Two other garnishes that offer a nice color contrast are chopped pistachios and red pepper purée (see page 24); also delicious, especially on the hot version of this soup, is Parmesan Lace (page 37).

Serves 6

8	leeks, trimmed and finely chopped, white part only (see page 186)
2	medium onions, finely chopped (about 1 cup)
1	cauliflower head, finely chopped (about 6 cups)
4	bay leaves
4	cups reduced-sodium chicken broth
2⅔	cups nonfat milk, heated
1	teaspoon salt
½	teaspoon freshly ground black pepper
	Chopped fresh chives, for garnish

1. Combine the leeks, onions, cauliflower, bay leaves, and chicken broth in a large soup pot and bring to a boil. Reduce the heat and cook, covered, until the cauliflower is tender, about 10 minutes. Remove and discard the bay leaves.

2. Add the hot milk, salt, and pepper, and transfer the soup to a blender (careful, it's hot) and purée until smooth, then return it to the pot. Or use an immersion blender and purée the soup right in the pot.

3. Serve hot with a sprinkling of chives.

Make ahead? Yes, but I would hold off on the milk and add it at reheating time. And, of course, don't add garnishes until serving.

For large crowds: With its inexpensive ingredients, this is a perfect choice for multiplying as much as you like.

Red Beans and Rice Soup

Once upon a time, I made a batch of red beans and rice for some friends, and the next day I had a little bit left over. Not enough for another meal, but too much to throw away. (Besides, have I told you about my grandmother? She would scold me from her grave if she saw me throw away good food.) So I wondered, could I turn it into soup? Sure I could, just by adding some chicken broth. It was pretty good, but I kept fiddling with it, and this version is the result. Homemade chicken broth makes a big difference here. I also learned to brown the chicken first, because when you add raw meat to simmering broth it poaches, leaving you with an unappetizing layer of foam that is hard to remove.

Serves 6

2 tablespoons olive oil

1 whole boneless, skinless chicken breast, cut into 1-inch chunks

1 medium yellow onion, chopped

1 green bell pepper, seeded and chopped

2 garlic cloves, peeled and minced

1 cup uncooked rice

4 cups chicken broth

2 (15-ounce) cans black or red beans, drained and rinsed; or about 4 cups cooked black or red beans (see page 27)

1 (15-ounce) can diced tomatoes with green chiles

Salt and freshly ground black pepper

1. Heat the oil in a large soup pot over medium heat. Add the chicken and sauté just until browned. Add the onion, bell pepper, garlic, and rice. Stir to coat the grains of rice with oil, and then sauté until the vegetables are soft and the rice begins to turn opaque, about 5 minutes.

2. Add the chicken broth. Bring to a boil, and then reduce the heat and simmer until the rice is tender and the chicken is cooked, about 15 minutes. Add the beans and tomatoes and simmer until heated through.

3. Taste, and then season with salt and pepper if needed. Serve hot.

Variations: Red beans and rice (the dish) is often flavored with some type of smoked sausage, so if you want to add some to your soup, you have my blessing. For a genuine New Orleans flavor, substitute andouille sausage for the chicken, or, better yet, use some of both.

Make ahead? Cook the chicken separately; chill. Cook the rice separately; chill. Sauté the vegetables as instructed, add the broth, beans, tomatoes, cooked chicken, and rice, and heat through.

For large crowds: Double or triple everything; if cost is a concern, you can use a smaller increase of the chicken, perhaps three half chickens, and it's still wonderful.

For vegetarians: Omit the chicken, and substitute vegetarian broth (or water) for the chicken broth.

PARMESAN LACE

In my humble opinion, Parmesan cheese makes just about anything taste better. (I haven't tried it with ice cream, but that may be next.) Of course you can sprinkle on shredded cheese from the supermarket or grate some from a block directly onto the soup, but if you have an extra few minutes, you can do something spectacular.

Heat your oven to 400°F. Line a baking sheet with a silicone mat or baker's parchment, and carefully position spoonfuls of grated (or better yet, shredded) Parmesan cheese on the baking sheet. They don't expand much during baking, so you can put them pretty close together. As a soup garnish, I like a size a little bigger than a quarter (easier to handle in a spoonful of soup), but that's up to you. With your fingers or the back of a spoon, press the cheese mounds to flatten them; otherwise, the center will still be soft when the edges are browned. Use a spoon to neaten up the edges of each round, and bake until they are nicely browned on the edges, 7 to 8 minutes.

When the cheese cools, it becomes crisp, and that crispness holds up surprisingly well in a bowl of soup. To make ahead, store in a tightly covered container — with a lock and key, if you have kids at home. (Some of you may recognize this garnish by the Italian term *frico*, but I like my name better.)

Sweet Potato Soup — Two Ways

Sweet potatoes and autumn go together nicely — something about all that orange, I think. And fortunately your favorite supermarket has a nice supply in the fall. Bonus: sweet potatoes are rich in vitamins and minerals. Here are two different ways to turn them into soup — one with a slightly spicy Southwestern twist, one rich with the aroma of roasted apples.

Santa Fe Sweet Potato and Chipotle Soup

Cumin and chipotle peppers give this version a Southwestern flavor.

Serves 6–8

1½ tablespoons olive oil

1 medium onion, chopped

2 garlic cloves, minced

2 teaspoons ground cumin

4 medium sweet potatoes, peeled and cut into 1-inch chunks

1 chipotle pepper in adobo sauce, chopped (see note)

6 cups chicken broth

Sour cream, for garnish

Note: Chipotles (pronounced chih-*poht*-lay) are jalapeño peppers that have been smoke-dried. They are most commonly sold in cans packed with adobo sauce; check the Latino section of your supermarket. One small can has several chiles, more than you will need for one recipe. Store the remainder in a glass jar, and it will keep in the refrigerator for weeks.

1. Heat the oil in a soup pot over medium-high heat. Add the onion, garlic, and cumin, and sauté until the vegetables are softened, about 5 minutes.

2. Stir in the sweet potatoes, chipotle, and broth; for a little extra punch, stir in a bit of the adobo sauce. Bring to a boil, then reduce the heat and simmer until the sweet potatoes are very soft, about 20 minutes.

3. Working in batches, transfer the soup to a blender (careful, it's hot) and purée until smooth, then return it to the pot. Or use an immersion blender and purée the soup right in the pot.

4. Bring the soup back to a simmer. Serve hot, adding a swirl of sour cream to each serving.

Variation: It's an extra step, but if you take the time to roast the sweet potato chunks before adding them to the soup, you'll get a richer flavor. (See Roasting Vegetables, below.)

Make ahead? Make the soup up to a day in advance, chill until serving.

For large crowds: This soup, with its inexpensive ingredients, is ideal for expanding. Go easy with the cumin; increase it only incrementally, and taste as you go.

ROASTING VEGETABLES

In many cases, roasting vegetables before adding them to the soup deepens and enriches the finished flavor. It does add an extra step, but the results are worth it. The general procedure is this: Preheat the oven to 400°F, peel the vegetables as desired, cut into chunks, and toss them in a little olive oil. Spread in a single layer on a baking sheet and roast. Check on the vegtables at about 5 minutes; if you want the pieces to retain their shape in the soup, remove from the oven now, while they still have some bite. If the soup will be puréed, they can go back in the oven for 5 or 6 minutes longer, until very tender.

Granny Smith's Sweet Potato Soup

Sweet potatoes and tart apples are a very appealing combination.

Serves 6–8

6 medium sweet potatoes

1 tablespoon olive oil

1 medium onion, chopped

1 celery stalk, chopped

2 tangy apples, such as Granny Smith or Braeburn, peeled, cored, and thinly sliced

6 cups water

2 teaspoons kosher salt

1 teaspoon freshly ground pepper, preferably white (see note)

Note: White pepper in this case is suggested more for appearance than taste. The soup is such a lovely color that the little black flecks of black pepper can seem visually disconcerting. But if you don't have any white pepper, black is just fine.

1. Preheat the oven to 400°F. Poke a few holes in the potatoes, place on a baking sheet, and roast until quite tender, 45 minutes or so.

2. Heat the oil in a large soup pot over medium heat. Add the onion, celery, and apple slices, and sauté until softened, about 10 minutes.

3. When the potatoes are cool enough to handle, cut them in half, scoop out the flesh, and add it to the soup pot. Stir in the water, salt, and pepper, and simmer for a few minutes, until everything is heated through.

4. Working in batches, transfer the soup to a blender (careful, it's hot) and purée until smooth, and then return it to the pot. Or use an immersion blender and purée the soup right in the pot. Check for consistency; add more water if desired.

5. Bring the soup back to a simmer. Taste and adjust seasonings; serve hot.

Make ahead? Depending on your schedule, you can do a little ahead, or a lot, or the whole thing. You can complete step 1 and store the baked potatoes in the refrigerator, in a plastic bag. Or finish through step 2 and refrigerate. Or finish the soup completely and chill until serving time.

For large crowds: This soup doubles (or triples) very nicely.

Italian Bean and Pasta Soup

Italians call this soup *pasta fagioli* (pronounced fah-*zho*-lee, or fah-zhool if you're several generations away from the old country). The combination of creamy bean soup with al dente pasta is irresistible. The flavor is so haunting and the texture so voluptuous that you'll wonder how such modest ingredients could conspire to create something so indulgent. And what makes it successful as a make-ahead main dish is that the pasta is cooked separately. I make vats of the bean soup ahead, then each time I reheat a portion, I boil up a fresh batch of dried pasta so the al dente texture balances the creaminess of the soup. If you are in the habit of buying blocks of Parmesan cheese, save the rind for this soup.

Serves 6–8

1	pound dried cranberry or pinto beans (about 3 cups), picked over and rinsed
10	cups water
½	cup plus 2 tablespoons olive oil, plus additional for drizzling
2	medium onions, chopped
1¾	teaspoons salt
2	medium carrots, chopped
2	celery stalks, chopped
5	large garlic cloves, finely chopped
¼	cup chopped fresh flat-leaf parsley
1	teaspoon dried rosemary, crumbled
¼	teaspoon black pepper
1	piece Parmigiano-Reggiano rind, roughly 2 by 3 inches (optional)
¾	pound dried small pasta

1. Bring the beans and water to a boil in a large heavy soup pot and boil for 2 minutes. Remove the pot from the heat, cover, and let stand for 1 hour. Do not drain the beans or discard the soaking liquid.

2. Heat ¼ cup of the olive oil in a wide, heavy pot over moderately high heat until hot but not smoking, and then add the onions and ½ teaspoon of the salt and sauté, stirring occasionally, until they begin to brown, 7 to 8 minutes. Add the carrots, celery, garlic, parsley, rosemary, and pepper, and sauté, stirring occasionally, for 5 minutes.

3. Add the beans with their soaking liquid and the cheese rind (if you have one on hand) and simmer, covered, stirring occasionally, until the beans are very tender. This could take 1½ to 2½ hours, depending on the age of your beans. Add more water if necessary to keep the beans covered, and stir more frequently toward the end of cooking. Remove from the heat and stir in ¼ cup of the oil and the remaining 1¼ teaspoons salt. Cool, uncovered, for 20 minutes.

recipe continues on next page

Make ahead? One of the glories of this recipe is that you cook the soup and the pasta separately; not only does that keep the pasta from getting mushy, it makes it very easy to make the entire dish ahead of time. Just refrigerate the pasta and the soup separately. Or freeze the soup for another day, and cook up a fresh batch of pasta when serving. The soup gets quite a bit thicker as it stands, so you may want to add water when reheating.

For large crowds: This recipe lends itself well to multiplying.

4. Bring a large pot of salted water to a boil for the pasta.

5. Remove and discard the cheese rind. Transfer the soup to a blender (careful, it's hot) and coarsely purée until smooth, then return it to the pot. Or use an immersion blender and purée the soup right in the pot. Reheat over moderately low heat, stirring frequently. Add water to thin if needed. Season with salt and pepper to taste.

6. While the soup is reheating, cook the pasta until al dente, and then drain in a colander and transfer to a large bowl. Toss with the remaining 2 tablespoons oil and pepper to taste.

7. Ladle the hot soup into bowls and top with spoonfuls of pasta, and then drizzle with additional olive oil.

Red Pozole

Recipe from Ann Bates, Civano Soup Supper, Tucson, Arizona (profile, page 46)

Ann says: I developed this recipe over many years and from several sources, including a Mexican friend in Sunnyside, Washington. It was one of the first things I ever made for a Civano Soup Supper. As we were all eating and talking, a young man came to ask if I was the one who had made the red pozole soup. When I responded that I had, he said, "I haven't tasted a pozole as real as this one since I used to eat my grandma's." It made my day!

Serves 6–8

3 tablespoons canola oil

8 boneless, skinless chicken thighs, cut into bite-size pieces

3 pounds boneless pork, cut into 1-inch pieces

1 onion, diced

3 garlic cloves, smashed

4 cups chicken broth

10 whole dried guajillo chiles

5 (15-ounce) cans hominy, drained

1 tablespoon fresh oregano, chopped, or 1 teaspoon dried

Garnishes

Lime wedges • Shredded cabbage • Thinly sliced radishes • Tortilla chips • Sliced jalapeños

Note: Ann adds, "These garnishes are traditional with pozole. It's also good all on its own."

1. Heat the oil in a soup pot over medium-high heat. Add the chicken and sauté until browned; remove with a slotted spoon and set aside.

2. In the same pot, brown the pork in batches. Remove with a slotted spoon and set aside with the chicken.

3. Add the onion to the soup pot and sauté over medium heat until softened, 2 to 3 minutes. Stir in the garlic and sauté until fragrant, about 1 minute.

4. Pour in the chicken broth and return the chicken and pork to the pan.

5. Leave the chiles whole but remove the seeds and membranes, to reduce the heat. The easiest way to do this is to slide the tip of a paring knife in at the stem end and slit all the way down one edge, then tease the chile open the same way you would open a book. Add the chiles to the pot and simmer, covered, for about 1 hour.

6. Remove the chiles and discard. Add the hominy and oregano and continue to simmer for 1 hour longer. Serve hot with your choice of garnishes.

Make ahead? You can make this soup in a slow cooker: Brown the chicken and pork, put them in the slow cooker, and then add the other ingredients. Simmer in the pot with the heat set on high for about 5 hours.

Alternatively, complete steps 1 and 2 and store the cooked meat in the refrigerator for as long as 24 hours. Or, if you have room in the refrigerator, make the whole thing the day ahead; like all stews, this is even better the second day.

For large crowds: Hominy is not expensive; neither are the chiles. If cost is a concern, you might increase the meats by half values and the other ingredients by full measure. Don't cut back on the chiles; the flavor they add is crucial.

POZOLE

Pozole (pronounced puh-*soh*-lee and also spelled *posole*) is the name of both the dish and its main ingredient. Pozole is another name for hominy, a food item unfamiliar to many of us (unless we grew up in the South — hominy is what grits are made from). Hominy is corn kernels that have been treated with an alkali, such as lye, which keeps them from sprouting while stored and makes the kernels expand in size. It is sold in dried form in Latino markets, or canned in most large supermarkets. Take my advice, and used the canned version; *much* easier.

Pozole the dish is an incredibly rich and flavorful stew that is very popular in the American Southwest. Often churches there host a pozole night, where volunteers prepare huge cauldrons and sell take-home containers as a fund-raiser for the church.

Civano Soup Supper

TUCSON, ARIZONA

In the southeastern corner of Tucson you will find an extraordinary neighborhood. It was conceived as a village, a place where old-fashioned neighborliness would thrive, facilitated by the design of the houses and the layout of the streets. Front porches abound, garages are hidden in back, sidewalk strolling is easy and safe, and outdoor benches placed here and there invite folks to sit a spell and visit. Today this "solar village" comprises about 650 homes, a school, a community center, a plant nursery, and other retail businesses. Best of all, that sense of community that the designers envisioned back in 1996 has taken root and grown with a vigor and richness that surpass all hopes.

"The dream of the men who built Civano," longtime resident **Judyth Willis** says, "was to create what we all had as children. That sense that you know all your neighbors, and they know you, and everyone gets along."

"It was designed from the get-go as a village," newer resident **Elizabeth Newland** adds. "A place where you can sit on your front porch and watch the world go by. And if you want to, sit out there with a bottle of wine and two glasses, and when somebody nice walks by, invite them up. The thing is, we are all conscious of deliberately working to make it a neighborhood. You know that expression, 'It takes a village to raise a child'? Well, I believe it takes a village to sustain people. We are herd animals; we're not meant to live apart."

Underscoring all of this neighborliness, and partly responsible for it, is their monthly Soup Supper. On the third Sunday of the month, from September to May, 50-some neighbors gather in the community center for soup and conversation. Often there is a program, with an invited speaker, but the real "agenda" is getting to know the neighbors.

And it works. **Ann Bates**, who has lived in Civano about five years, explains it this way. "We have a neighborhood that believes in a strong sense of community,

> **People in Civano have wildly different backgrounds, but the Soup Suppers pull us together and put us on equal ground. Hostility disappears when people sit down next to each other to eat together.**

and many friendships have emerged from that feeling. A very important part of it is the monthly Soup Suppers. These dinners are a wonderful place to learn more about our neighbors, our community, our desert, and our world."

As a testament to how significant this one event can be in fostering community, consider this story from Judyth Willis. "Those of us who were here from the beginning bought into the idea that this was a place for people who *wanted* to be neighborly. Then about year 10, the population changed a little, and that sense of community began to fade. What to do? We hit on the idea of restarting the Soup Suppers, and announced it in our newsletter. Well, we had more than 60 people show up that first night! Lots of new families with kids and babies, sitting down with older folks, people meeting each other for the first time, and having a grand time. It was marvelous, so obviously we had to continue," she says with a laugh.

In terms of logistics, having the community center is a great advantage, of course, with its full kitchen and ample table space. People sign up to contribute food on a potluck basis: five or six people offer to bring soup, enough to feed eight; then two others sign up for bread, two

for salad, and two for dessert. A few volunteers come early to set up, a few others stay for cleanup. In between, there is great food, lots of chatting, laughing, exchanging of addresses and phone numbers — all the small, sweet details of life in a close-knit neighborhood.

Elizabeth Newland eloquently summarizes: "People who live in Civano have wildly different backgrounds, income levels, political opinions, all of that. But the Soup Suppers pull us together and put us on equal ground. Some of these differences are natural points of contention that in another setting could easily lead to arguments, but hostility disappears when people sit down next to each other to eat together. This is a hugely important part of my life."

www.civano.com
www.civanoneighbors.com

FOR RECIPES FROM CIVANO SOUP SUPPER, SEE:

Sweet Corn Chowder

Recipe from Elizabeth Newland, Civano Soup Supper, Tucson, Arizona (profile, page 46)

Elizabeth says: Always a potluck favorite . . . tasty and no strange ingredient surprises!

Serves 4–6

5 bacon strips, diced

1 small leek, trimmed and thinly sliced (see page 186)

2 teaspoons fresh thyme or winter savory, or ½ teaspoon dried

Salt and freshly ground black pepper

2 large russet potatoes, peeled and cubed

2 cups milk

2 cups cream

2 cups corn kernels, fresh or frozen (preferably fresh)

1. Brown the bacon in a large soup pot over medium heat until crisp, 5 to 7 minutes. Drain off all but 2 tablespoons of the bacon fat.

2. Add the leek, thyme, and salt and pepper to taste to the pot and sauté until the leek is softened, about 5 minutes.

3. Stir in the potatoes, milk, and cream, and bring to a gentle simmer over medium heat. Simmer (do not boil) until the potatoes are tender.

4. Add the corn and continue to simmer until the corn is tender, about 4 minutes for fresh or 7 minutes for frozen.

5. Serve hot.

Variations: Elizabeth suggests, "This soup can be dressed up by adding mushrooms or shrimp." When the corn is tender, stir ½ cup sautéed mushrooms or 1 cup cooked shrimp into the soup, bring up to heat, and serve.

Make ahead? Prepare through step 3, but remove from the heat just before the potatoes are completely cooked. Refrigerate. Rewarm at serving time, simmering until the potatoes are totally tender.

For large crowds: This recipe is easily doubled or tripled. To economize, use chopped parsley or chives as garnish in place of the shrimp.

Smoky Chili

Recipe from Elizabeth Newland, Civano Soup Supper, Tucson, Arizona (profile, page 46)

Elizabeth says: I created this recipe in desperation. I can't eat any kind of fresh or canned peppers, and I spend four months of the year in the Southwest, where heated discussions of proper chili recipes can lead to blows. This in no way meets a cowboy's standards for a proper chili, but I've never had any complaints, and it always disappears on potluck nights. Best of all, I can eat it!

Serves 4–6

3	bacon strips, diced
1	small onion, chopped
1	garlic clove (or more to taste), minced
1½	pounds lean ground beef
½–2	teaspoons chili powder
1½	teaspoons ground cumin
1½	teaspoons smoked Spanish paprika
½	teaspoon cayenne pepper
1	teaspoon salt
1	(14.5-ounce) can fire-roasted crushed tomatoes
1	(8-ounce) can tomato sauce
1	cup Pilsner beer
1	teaspoon Worcestershire sauce
1	(14.5-ounce) can pinto beans, drained; or 2 cups cooked pinto beans (see page 27)

Garnishes

Grated cheese • Sour cream • Sliced scallions • Nacho chips

1. Brown the bacon in a large soup pot over medium heat until crisp, 5 to 7 minutes. Drain off some of the fat, if you like, keeping at least 1 tablespoon in the pot.

2. Add the onion and sauté until softened, 5 to 7 minutes. Add the garlic and sauté for 1 minute longer. Add the ground beef, stirring to break up the meat, and sauté until browned.

3. Add chili powder to taste, cumin, paprika, and cayenne, and season with salt to taste. Cook for 1 minute, and then add the crushed tomatoes, tomato sauce, beer, and Worcestershire. Simmer for 30 minutes.

4. Add the beans and heat through. Serve hot with any or all of the garnishes.

Make ahead? Liz says this is actually *better* if made a day ahead, refrigerated, and gently reheated.

For large crowds: You can expand this indefinitely, but for economy you might wish to increase the proportion of beans and decrease relative amounts of ground beef.

Salmon Chowder

Recipe from Maureen Ruddy, Fairfax, Virginia (profile, page 52)

Maureen says: Serve with a crusty loaf of bread and enjoy!

Serves 6–8

2 tablespoons butter

2 leeks, trimmed and chopped (see page 186)

½ sweet onion, such as Vidalia, chopped

2 tablespoons all-purpose flour

4 cups vegetable broth

3 red potatoes, cubed

⅔ cup whole milk

1 pound salmon fillet, skinned and cut into bite-size chunks

Chopped fresh dill

Salt and freshly ground black pepper

1. Melt the butter in a large soup pot over medium heat. Add the leeks and onion and cook until softened, about 5 minutes. Stir in the flour and cook for 2 minutes to make a light roux.

2. Add the vegetable broth and potatoes. Bring to a boil and cook until the potatoes are fork-tender, about 10 minutes.

3. Add the milk and return to a gentle simmer. Add the salmon and simmer until the fish is cooked through, 2 to 3 minutes.

4. Stir in dill to taste. Season with salt and pepper to taste and serve hot.

Make ahead? Prepare the chowder base, but do not add the salmon. Refrigerate, reheat, and stir in the salmon.

For large crowds: To economize while maintaining the basic idea of this soup, add other, less expensive types of fresh fish to the salmon.

Barbara Rice

CHANTILLY, VIRGINIA

I first met **Barbara Rice** through a blog post she titled "The Loveliness of Soup Night." (With her kind permission, I'm sharing some of it with you.)

Her goal: use a casual meal as a way to get the neighbors together. "It's so easy to lose track of everyone — we're all busy and not everyone has kids of bonding age."

Barbara's first Soup Night was October 2006. "I had lived in the neighborhood for 13 years," she says, "but there were some people we didn't know well, some we hardly ever saw. For that first night, I wrote up invitations and my kids and I hand-delivered them to all the neighbors, explaining the idea." (Barbara and her husband have six children, ranging from 6 to 20.) "That invitation covered three Soup Nights, so I also sent reminders a few days before each one.

"That first night, I wasn't sure what to expect. People had been very receptive when I gave them invitations, but still I had a moment of anxiety. Turns out, I need not have worried. We had a great time, and now it's a well-established neighborhood tradition. People send their kids down even if they themselves can't come! We do it once a month during soup season (usually October to April), and we have 20 or so people. The most we ever had was 40 — that was fun!"

Two of Barbara's neighbors tell us what it's like.

Maureen Ruddy has lived in the neighborhood 18 years. Her family and the Rices are original owners in the development. Barbara's Soup Night, Maureen says, is a "delightful mix of childhood chaos and adult calm. The kids range from preschool to college age, and they create this happy chaos. The kitchen, in contrast, is very orderly and calm. I don't know how she manages it.

"But even though Barbara's soups are always fantastic, it's really not about the food. She has created this lovely way for us all to connect in a community that doesn't have a natural constituency. There are many people in the neighborhood I don't know well. Or didn't. I think that's pretty common; in the modern world, it's typical not to know your neighbors. But Soup Night is a wonderful way to bring together diverse people who would not normally hang out together.

"The huge gift from Barbara is that nothing is expected in return. People don't have to do anything except come and spend time with neighbors. To give something freely with no expectations, this is so rare, and quite extraordinary."

Jan Bayer and her family have been attending Soup Nights since the beginning. When Barbara first knocked on her door with the invitation, she thought, "Oh, what a nice idea! We keep going," she adds, "because it's such a wonderful avenue to catch up with everyone in a friendly way."

Jan's two daughters, ages 10 and 13, especially love Soup Night. Jan believes the kids get as much out of the experience as the adults, and her oldest daughter, Jean, confirms it. "It's fun! You get to meet some other kids you don't know well. There's a kids' table, and the soup is really good. Then after supper we all go down to the basement and tell scary stories. Or play the piano and dance. Or dress up the littler kids in costumes." Can't you just see it?

"I'm so grateful to Barbara for doing this," Jan concludes. "It's a very nice way to get back to basics."

In chapter 6, "Start Your Own Soup Night," you will find some of Barbara's tips, learned over the years. Thanks, Barbara, for sharing.

FOR A RECIPE FROM THIS GROUP, SEE:
Salmon Chowder, page 51

Wild Rice Clam Chowder

Recipe from Albertina's Restaurant, Portland, Oregon (profile, facing page)

It's amazingly good!

Serves 6

3 cups chicken broth

1½ teaspoons lemon juice

2 bay leaves

3 medium red potatoes, cut into ½-inch cubes

2 tablespoons butter

¾ cup chopped onion

3 ounces fresh mushrooms, sliced

1 (6½-ounce) can minced clams, with juice

¼ teaspoon freshly ground black pepper

3 tablespoons all-purpose flour

1 cup half-and-half

2 cups cooked wild rice

1. Bring the broth, lemon juice, and bay leaves to a boil in a large soup pot. Add the potatoes, then reduce the heat and simmer until the potatoes are just tender, 10 to 15 minutes. Remove and discard the bay leaves.

2. While the potatoes are cooking, melt the butter in a medium skillet over medium heat, add the onion, and sauté until translucent, about 5 minutes; do not brown. Add the mushrooms and sauté until tender, 5 to 10 minutes longer.

3. Add the onion mixture to the broth in the pot, and then add the clams, clam juice, and pepper. Heat through.

4. In a small bowl, whisk the flour with ½ cup of the half-and-half to make a smooth paste. Slowly add the flour mixture to the chowder, whisking to avoid lumps.

5. Add the remaining ½ cup half-and-half and the rice. Heat to piping hot and serve immediately.

Make ahead? Cook the wild rice. Complete the recipe through step 3. Refrigerate, reheat, and complete the recipe.

For large crowds: This is a wonderful soup to expand, for the primary ingredients — canned clams and wild rice — are relatively inexpensive and easy to find year-round.

Albertina's Restaurant

PORTLAND, OREGON

In my hometown of Portland, Oregon, there is a most unusual luncheon restaurant. Housed in a beautiful historic building, it is operated almost entirely by volunteers (the only paid employees are the chef and the dishwasher). Also sharing that building are a thrift shop, gift shop, and a wonderful antiques shop.

All the proceeds from the shops and the restaurant — even the servers' tips — go to support a nonprofit organization (Albertina Kerr Centers) that provides critical services for children, adults, and families with mental health challenges and developmental disabilities.

I was one of the volunteer cooks for about 15 years, and it was one of the best experiences of my life. Everything about cooking for 100 people — the process, the equipment, the tools, the careful management of sequencing — was endlessly fascinating, and I learned a great deal about food safety and presentation. Most of all, I learned about life from the other women on my crew. They were all considerably older than me, but full of zest and sass, and taught me a lot about living a good life at that age. I'll never forget them. (Mary Steerman, my surrogate mother, I miss you every single day.)

The wonderful volunteers who cook and serve lunches are supported by many other volunteers behind the scenes. One critical group creates, tests, tweaks, and retests the recipes, paying particular attention to dishes that are suited to the kitchen's very limited space.

Over the years many of the favorites have been collected into three cookbooks; the first two are out of print, but the most recent, *Albertina's Exceptional Recipes*, is now in its fifth printing. You can find it from several online booksellers, or order direct from the restaurant (so they get all the profits). Contact theshops@albertinakerr.org for current pricing. The wonderful Albertina's recipes in *this* book, the one you are holding, are some of my personal favorites from *Exceptional Recipes*, reprinted with the board's kind permission.

And if you ever find yourself in Portland, try to have lunch at Albertina's; while you're there ask your server to tell you about Albertina herself. It's quite a story.

Albertina's Restaurant
424 NE 22nd Avenue
Portland, OR 97232
503-231-0216
www.albertinakerr.org
(reservations optional)

Creamy Chicken with Wild Rice Soup

Recipe from Julie Dahlberg, Grayslake, Illinois (profile, page 58)

Julie says: I usually make a large batch, because this is so popular at Soup Nights. If there's any left over, it's lunch the next day, or into the freezer for another night.

Serves 8–10

4 tablespoons butter

3 large carrots, cut into bite-size pieces (about 2 cups)

1 medium onion, diced

1 teaspoon ground celery seed

1 garlic clove, pressed or minced

3 (8-ounce) packages cream cheese (low-fat or nonfat work fine), softened

1 (49.5-ounce) can chicken broth

3 (6-ounce) boxes long-grain and wild rice (such as Uncle Ben's), prepared according to package directions

1 pound cooked chicken, cut into bite-size pieces

½ pound fresh mushrooms, sliced

1. Melt the butter in a large soup pot, add the carrots and onion, and sauté until the onion is softened, 5 to 7 minutes. Add the celery seed, garlic, and cream cheese, and stir constantly until the cream cheese is melted and smooth.

2. Slowly add the broth, stirring to incorporate the cream cheese; stir until all the broth is added and there are no lumps of cream cheese.

3. Add the rice, chicken, and mushrooms. Simmer for 20 minutes to blend the flavors. If the soup seems too thick, add milk or water as desired. Serve hot.

Make ahead? You can make the rice and cook the chicken as much as one day ahead.

For large crowds: Julie's recipe already makes a hefty amount, but doubles easily.

Smoked Chicken Chowder

Recipe from Suzy and Philip Poll, Houston, Texas (profile, page 61)

Suzy and Philip say: A delicious, filling chowder made easy by using a precooked rotisserie chicken from the supermarket.

Serves 6

¼ cup vegetable oil

2 cups chopped onion

3 garlic cloves, minced

1 medium baking potato, peeled and cut into ¼-inch dice

½ large fresh jalapeño or poblano chile, seeded and minced (see page 186)

3 tablespoons all-purpose flour

5 cups reduced-sodium chicken broth

1½ cups frozen corn

½ (14-ounce) can fire-roasted diced tomatoes, drained

1 tablespoon chopped fresh flat-leaf parsley

1 canned chipotle chile in adobo sauce, minced (about ½ tablespoon)

1 whole smoked chicken, skin and fat removed and meat cut into ½-inch dice

3 ounces Monterey Jack cheese, grated (about ¾ cup)

1 cup half-and-half

Salt and freshly ground black pepper

1. Heat the oil in a large heavy soup pot over medium heat. Add the onion and garlic and sauté until translucent, about 5 minutes. Add the potato and chile and stir to heat through, about 1 minute. Stir in the flour and cook over medium heat for 2 minutes, stirring constantly.

2. Whisk in the broth and bring to a boil. Add the corn, tomatoes, parsley, chipotle, and chicken, and simmer until the vegetables are tender, about 20 minutes.

3. Add cheese and stir to melt. Add the half-and-half and season with salt and pepper to taste. Reheat until hot enough to serve; do not allow to boil after adding the half-and-half.

Make ahead? Through step 2, but remove from the heat just before vegetables are tender, so that they don't overcook during reheating. Refrigerate, reheat, and complete the recipe.

For large crowds: Suzy's original recipe is double this amount, for 12 servings.

Julie and Scott Dahlberg
GRAYSLAKE, ILLINOIS

Have you ever noticed how quickly the best ideas get passed around? Julie Dahlberg and her husband Scott read a magazine article about a Soup Night in Brooklyn, and that inspired them to start one in their Illinois neighborhood. And then Julie's friend **Karen Robbins** (see page 154) liked the idea so much she started one in her own neighborhood. About the same time, Julie wrote a magazine article about her experience, which inspired Kate Allen's Soup Night (see page 107). And then Julaine Kammrath (page 266) followed Kate's example in *her* neighborhood. Same thing happened, by the way, with Claudia and Dave Darmofal (page 222), who so enjoyed the wonderful event of their Houston friends Suzy and Philip Poll (page 61) they started their own Soup Night in their Boston-area neighborhood. And believe me, everyone in this book would be totally thrilled if you copied their ideas when you start your own Soup Night.

Julie tells their story: "We are part of the Covenant Church, and had been trying to get some of our neighbors interested, without much luck. Then I read this article about a woman in Brooklyn who started a Soup Night, who invited people from her different circles and created a cohesive group. And I thought, maybe that's what we should do. Invest in our neighborhood. That could be our way to fulfill the biblical command to love our neighbors — we'd start by getting to know them!

> There's something about opening up your home that makes people open up. Our neighbors opened up, and so did we. It was wonderful to see.

"We decided to do it once a week, on Thursday evening. We created invitations and the kids helped me hand-deliver them to the neighbors; others, to Scott's coworkers and other friends, went in the mail. That very first night, I was a nervous wreck. What if nobody comes? What if all 30 families come and we run out of food? What if my soup isn't good enough?

"But of course I didn't need to worry. That first night, we had five families, and they all wanted to know where the idea came from. People introduced themselves to each other, conversation was easy, and the soup was a hit.

"We quickly figured out ways to make it manageable. It's a school night, so we started early — 5.30 PM. I did all the shopping early in the week, and always kept a loaf of garlic bread in the freezer in case we ran out.

"We set aside one drawer in the kitchen for Soup Night bowls and spoons, which made it easier to organize cleanup. I picked up bowls wherever I could, at discount stores and tag sales, so we had a big assortment of sizes and patterns, plus we kept a supply of plastic bowls and spoons just in case. I made sure the dishwasher was empty by Thursday afternoon, and people would put their dirty bowls in.

"For the children, I checked out videos from our church library. Our own children were great at helping with coats, traffic flow, and house rules.

"Some of our neighbors were hesitant at first; they thought we were trying to convert them. But we were intentionally *not* evangelizing, we didn't want the church thing to get in the way, and they saw that. They just were so eager to meet their neighbors. Years later they would say to us, 'I wasn't too sure about you at first, but now I can't imagine life without you.'"

You may have noticed that Julie is speaking in the past tense. That's because after five years the Dahlberg family has put Soup Night on hiatus for a while. "It just got too big," Julie says. "The house was rocking every week. People started inviting other people, and it became more like a party than our original purpose, which was to get to know our neighbors well enough to know how to love them, the way Jesus wants me to. Plus everybody's kids got older and were involved in other activities, and it just got harder. I think we may start up again, though."

And I think she will too, because of one final comment. "When we first started this, our friends were astonished. You mean, you just let all these people come into your house, people you don't know? What we discovered is that there's something about opening up your home that makes people open up. Our neighbors opened up, and so did we. It was wonderful to see."

FOR A RECIPE FROM THIS GROUP, SEE:
Creamy Chicken with Wild Rice Soup, page 56

Corn and Wild Rice Soup with Smoked Sausage

Recipe from Suzy and Philip Poll, Houston, Texas (profile, facing page)

Suzy and Philip say: This lusciously rich soup gets its New Orleans flavor from andouille sausage. It's a great choice for a Mardi Gras–themed event.

Serves 6

7 ounces andouille or other smoked sausage

1 tablespoon olive oil

1 cup chopped onion

½ cup diced carrots

½ cup diced celery

6 cups reduced-sodium chicken broth

1 (16-ounce) bag frozen corn kernels

2 ounces uncooked wild rice

1 sprig fresh thyme

1 bay leaf

¾ cup half-and-half

2 tablespoons minced fresh flat-leaf parsley

Salt

Make ahead? Complete through step 4; or stop at step 3, depending on your time availability. Refrigerate, reheat, and complete the recipe.

For large crowds: Suzy routinely makes twice this amount, for 12 servings.

1. Slice the andouille lengthwise into quarters, then crosswise into ¼-inch slices. Heat the oil in a large soup pot over medium heat. Add the andouille and stir to brown lightly. Remove the sausage with a slotted spoon and set aside.

2. Add the onion, carrots, and celery to the pot and sauté until the onion is translucent, about 5 minutes. Add the broth and corn, bring to a boil, and then reduce the heat and simmer for 15 minutes.

3. Using an immersion blender, lightly blend the soup to the desired consistency.

4. Add the wild rice, thyme, and bay leaf, and return the andouille to the soup. Simmer until the rice is tender, about 45 minutes. Remove the bay leaf and thyme sprig.

5. Add the half-and-half and minced parsley and reheat gently. Do not allow the soup to boil after the half-and-half has been added.

6. Taste and add salt as needed. Ladle soup into bowls and serve.

Suzy and Philip Poll
HOUSTON, TEXAS

One aspect of the Soup Nights profiled in this book that touches me deeply is how long some of these friends have been getting together. The Polls have been hosting Soup Night for six families twice a month during "soup season" (October to March) for 15 years, and in that time profound friendships have formed. I'll let some of these folks speak for themselves.

Chris Pette and her husband were part of the original group, 15 years ago. "It started as a very casual idea — 'Come have some soup with us' — and it quickly turned into a tradition. We sit around and visit, something people don't really do much these days. We stay at the table for hours, talking about everything. We solve the problems of the world at Soup Night.

"The fact that we have this wonderful sense of fellowship, and it has lasted so long, is amazing. I love the continuity of it. It's a microcosm of the whole cycle of life. We've had deaths in the family, we all went through driver's ed together, we've had the first wedding of our kids, but we've stayed together through it all. It really is like a family; we share meaning in each other's lives. One man said once,

If you don't laugh until your sides hurt, it wasn't a good night!

'I don't even like soup, but I can't imagine not coming.'

"Among our children's friends, it's a very coveted invitation; they're always asking, 'Have you started Soup Night yet? Can I come?' We can't change *anything*, the children won't let us. We *have* to have black and orange soups at Halloween, we *have* to have Cinco de Mayo. We always have Stone Soup at the last night. Suzy puts in a clean stone, and then people add whatever they brought. Tell you the truth, it's usually not all that good, but who cares? It's tradition!"

Meegan and Mike Dunlap were first invited in 1998, when Soup Night was in its second year. "It started when we all had young children," Meegan remembers. "The original idea was a way to get together and have adult conversation without having to get babysitters. But it has grown into so much more. It's almost impossible to put into words. These are now our closest friends, and there's no doubt we will be friends for life. They are our rocks. We've been through so much together — serious illnesses, deaths in the family, and good times too. We can talk about anything, bounce off any idea or problems and know we'll get honest advice. We don't always agree on things, but it's always fun and lively. If you don't laugh until your sides hurt, it wasn't a good night!

"We live in the fourth largest city in the country, yet what we have with Soup Night is a little piece of small-town America. Good fun, good food, good friends. These relationships are for life. I would be really sad if there were no more Soup Nights. I hope we'll be doing this till we die."

Mike picks up the story. "People always want to know about it. 'What's Soup Night?' That triggers a long explanation, and everybody is fascinated. They say, 'That's so neat.' And it is. It's great soup, of course, and great wine, but it's really this gathering of terrific friends. We've known these people since our children were infants; and now they're graduating college, and soon we'll be going to their weddings.

"There's not a better thing to look forward to on a Friday night. Sometimes we have friends or family who suggest going out that night, and we say, 'Sorry, that's Soup Night. We can't miss it.'"

Part of the reason this Soup Night has been so successful, it seems to me, is the careful attention that Suzy and Philip devote to all aspects of the evening. Because they have so many wonderful ideas, and because I'm pretty sure they would be happy for you to borrow them, I'll share Suzy's comments:

"Our Soup Nights often have a theme, with the soups and appetizers (and sometimes even decorations) being centered around that theme. Recurring themes we've had include Black & Orange (Halloween), Southwestern, Mardi Gras, Chinese New Year, and Classics (what that really means is that I can cook whatever I want!). I usually make two pots of soup and heavy appetizers. My husband, Philip, helps with any last-minute prep and mans the grill or the giant wok as needed. Everyone brings a bottle of wine and sometimes an appetizer or a dessert. We've even had an occasional 'guest soup.'

Among our children's friends, it's a very coveted invitation; they're always asking, 'Have you started Soup Night yet? Can I come?'

"Kids have always been welcome at Soup Night, and in the early days we typically had a houseful. Those nights were full of pillow fights, board games, and endless hours of the older kids pushing the younger kids on the swing set. We had many, many years of good rowdy fun, but the kid part of our gathering is winding down. My kids, Erica and Nathan, were four years old when we started our get-togethers — now they're going to be seniors in high school. Others have graduated from high school or even college. It's fun now to have these grown-up kids come back to visit and hear them talk about the old times."

FOR RECIPES FROM THIS GROUP, SEE:

Hot and Sour Soup

Recipe from Suzy and Philip Poll, Houston, Texas (profile, page 61)

Suzy says: For our Chinese New Year Soup Night, we have just one soup — this one.

Serves 6

6–8	ounces boneless chicken or pork, cut into bite-size chunks
4	tablespoons soy sauce
5	tablespoons water
1½	teaspoons sherry or white wine
2½	tablespoons cornstarch
½	cup dried wood ears or dried black mushrooms (optional; see note)
8	cups chicken broth
½	(12-ounce) package medium firm tofu, cut into ⅓-inch strips
½	cup canned bamboo shoots, cut into thin strips
3	eggs
¼	cup distilled white vinegar
1½	teaspoons sesame oil
1	teaspoon grated fresh ginger
1	teaspoon sugar
¼	teaspoon freshly ground black pepper
¼	teaspoon freshly ground white pepper
	Thinly sliced scallions, for garnish

Note: Wood ears are a type of dried fungus with an interesting name and chewy texture; dried mushrooms, especially shiitake, add a distinct Asian flavor. Both can be found in Asian markets, if you're lucky enough to live near one, or in the Asian section of large supermarkets.

1. In a bowl, combine the meat with 1 tablespoon of the soy sauce, 1 tablespoon of the water, and the sherry. Mix well, then add ½ tablespoon of the cornstarch. Mix again, coating the meat pieces with cornstarch. Marinate for 20 minutes on the countertop.

2. If using wood ears or dried mushrooms, soak them in a small bowl of very hot water for 10 minutes. Drain and discard the water. Slice the mushrooms into strips, discarding any tough ends.

3. Bring the broth to a boil in a large soup pot. Drain the meat and add it to the soup, stirring to separate the pieces. Return to a boil, then add the tofu, bamboo shoots, and dried mushrooms, if using. Return to a boil, and then simmer until the meat is cooked through.

4. Mix the remaining 2 tablespoons cornstarch with the remaining 4 tablespoons cold water; add to the soup and stir to thicken just a bit.

5. Lightly beat the eggs and slowly add them to the soup in a thin stream while stirring gently with a spoon. Turn off the heat.

recipe continues on next page

Make ahead? Complete steps 1 and 2; refrigerate the meat.

For large crowds: Suzy always makes twice this amount for her Soup Nights. You could easily triple it.

Note: Suzy says, "The sour flavor quickly dissipates as the soup simmers on the stove. Always taste the soup just before serving and make adjustments to the vinegar as needed."

6. Mix together the remaining 3 tablespoons soy sauce, the vinegar, sesame oil, ginger, sugar, and black and white pepper. Pour the mixture into the soup, stir to combine, and heat through.

7. Ladle the soup into bowls and serve topped with scallions.

Thanksgiving Leftover Soups

One of the main joys of the fall season is its two holidays — Halloween and Thanksgiving — and one of the main joys of both is leftovers, particularly pumpkin and turkey. The next three recipes put them to good advantage, but if you are bereft of leftovers, the ingredients are readily available in the markets this time of year.

Pumpkin Curry Soup

Recipe from Grace Martin, Aurora, Illinois (profile, page 107)

Grace Martin is a soup cook with a creative way with leftovers. You'll meet her later in this book.

Serves 6

4   tablespoons butter
1   large sweet onion, finely chopped
1   garlic clove, minced
2   teaspoons curry powder
6   cups chicken or vegetable broth
1   (29-ounce) can pumpkin purée
2   tablespoons orange juice
1   tablespoon lemon juice
1   bay leaf
⅛   teaspoon ground nutmeg
⅛   teaspoon ground ginger
    Salt and freshly ground black
      pepper
1½ cups heavy cream
    Chopped fresh chives, for
      garnish

**Make ahead? Complete soup
except for garnish; refrigerate.**

**For large crowds: This soup
doubles or triples quite nicely.**

1. Melt the butter in a large soup pot over medium heat. Add the onion and sauté until softened, about 2 minutes. Add the garlic and sauté 1 minute longer. Blend in the curry powder and cook for 1 minute. Transfer the mixture to a blender (careful, it's hot) and purée until smooth, then return it to the pot. Or use an immersion blender and purée the mixture right in the pot.

2. Add the broth and pumpkin to the mixture in the pot and stir to combine. Add the orange juice, lemon juice, bay leaf, nutmeg, ginger, and salt and pepper to taste. Bring to a boil, and then reduce the heat and simmer.

3. Stir in the cream and return to a simmer. Simmer for 10 minutes; remove and discard the bay leaf.

4. Adjust the seasonings; serve hot, topped with chives.

Pumpkin Chicken Chowder

Leftover turkey would also work in this recipe — delicious and quick.

Serves 6–8

2 tablespoons canola or vegetable oil

3 boneless, skinless chicken breast halves, cut into bite-size pieces

2 medium onions, chopped

1 red bell pepper, seeded and chopped

1 green bell pepper, seeded and chopped

3 garlic cloves, minced

6 cups chicken broth

2 (16-ounce) cans pumpkin purée

1 cup frozen corn

⅔ cup uncooked rice

1 teaspoon dried basil

½ teaspoon salt

¼ teaspoon freshly ground black pepper

1. Heat the oil in a large soup pot over medium heat. Add the chicken, onions, bell peppers, and garlic. Sauté until the chicken is no longer pink, 6 to 8 minutes.

2. Add the broth, pumpkin, corn, rice, basil, salt, and pepper. Stir well and bring the soup to a boil, then reduce the heat and simmer, covered, until the rice is tender, about 20 minutes. Serve hot.

Make ahead? Complete the soup as much as a day ahead; refrigerate.

For large crowds: This soup multiplies successfully.

Tortilla Turkey Soup

Recipe from Grace Martin, Aurora, Illinois (profile, page 107)

Serves 6

1 tablespoon olive oil

1 yellow onion, finely chopped

4 cups chicken broth

½ cup uncooked rice

1 teaspoon ground cumin

2 cups shredded cooked turkey

1 (11-ounce) can whole-kernel corn with red and green peppers, undrained

1 cup picante sauce

3 tablespoons chopped fresh cilantro leaves

2 teaspoons lime juice

2 corn tortillas

Cooking spray

Sour cream, for garnish

1. Heat the oil in a large soup pot over medium heat. Add the onion and sauté until softened, about 5 minutes. Add the broth, rice, and cumin; bring to a boil, and then reduce the heat to low. Cover and cook for 20 minutes, until the rice is almost tender. Preheat the oven to 425°F.

2. Stir in the turkey, corn, picante sauce, 1 tablespoon of the cilantro, and the lime juice. Simmer until the soup is warmed through and the rice is completely tender.

3. Meanwhile, cut the tortillas into thin strips, place the strips in a single layer on a baking sheet, and spray with cooking spray. Bake about 10 minutes, until golden brown.

4. Serve the soup topped with tortilla strips, sour cream, and the remaining 2 tablespoons chopped cilantro (1 teaspoon per serving).

Make ahead? Make the soup (steps 1 and 2); refrigerate. Make the tortilla crisps; store in an airtight container.

For large crowds: As long as you have the turkey, you can multiply this as much as you like.

The Famous Cabbage Soup

On the other hand, if you had ham for Thanksgiving (well, it could happen) and have some leftovers of that, I urge you to try this soup. The recipe came to me from the sister of a long-ago boyfriend; I've lost track of both, but I think about them every time I make this soup, which is often. In their family it was always called "the famous cabbage soup," so that is now the official name. This is one of those recipes that don't reveal their true nature on paper; just reading it, you wouldn't have any idea how delicious it is.

Serves 6–8

- 2 tablespoons butter
- ½ cup diced onion
- ½ cup diced celery
- ½ cup chopped green or red bell pepper
- 6 tablespoons all-purpose flour
- 6 cups boiling water
- 4 cups finely chopped cabbage
- 4 cups cubed ham
- 2 bay leaves
- ½ teaspoon salt
- ¼ teaspoon freshly ground black pepper
- 1½ cups sour cream
- Chopped fresh parsley, for garnish

Notes: Use real butter (it matters), but nonfat sour cream works perfectly in this soup. I left the celery in the recipe, for verisimilitude, but when I make this soup I prefer to leave it out.

1. Melt the butter in a large soup pot over medium heat. Add the onion, celery, and bell pepper, and sauté until softened, 4 to 5 minutes. Sprinkle the flour over the vegetables, stir well, and cook for 1 minute. Slowly stir in the boiling water.

2. Add the cabbage, ham, and bay leaves, and simmer until the cabbage is crisp-tender, 10 to 12 minutes. Remove and discard the bay leaves. Season with salt and pepper to taste.

3. Stir in the sour cream and simmer until heated through. Serve hot with parsley to garnish.

Make ahead? Prepare step 1. I don't much care for the texture of the cabbage when it is overcooked, so I would start with step 2 at dinnertime.

For large crowds: I have been known to make this soup for 50 people, so feel free to multiply as needed.

Lisa Fine
MONTPELIER, VERMONT

"A few weeks ago, we began a new tradition in our home: Monday Soup Night." That was my introduction to Lisa, who hosted a soup night once a week in the fall and winter months. Although this group is smaller than some of those described in these pages, the basic idea is the same: get some folks together for a simple, delicious meal of soup and bread, and watch what happens. Lisa's friends and neighbors bring a potluck collection of ingredients and they do the cooking together, which admittedly is easier with a small group, and a lot more fun.

Lisa herself picks up the story:

"A good friend of ours recently moved back to the area, and we wanted to have her over for dinner. She brought a butternut squash, which we turned into soup; last week [this was November] we made a carrot soup (we still have loads in our garden) and a potato soup; and now we've decided that these weekly soup meals are official."

I really love Lisa's thoughtful comments about the virtue of Soup Night, and am grateful for her permission to share them with you:

Why Soup Night?
Cooking together. "Making meals with friends is more fun than cooking alone. One of the main parts of the evening is making a meal from scratch together."

Potluck. "We talk during the day about what kind of soup we'll make, depending on what ingredients everyone already has. One person may have leeks, potatoes, and bread, the other may have vegetable broth, and apples for an apple crisp."

The cold. "Winter in New England lasts a long time, usually November to April. Soups are a wonderful way to warm up."

For health. "Soup broth absorbs the vitamins and minerals from its ingredients. A vegetable soup made with beans and grains is extra healthy and wholesome."

Simple living. "Living simply is about choosing experiences over stuff. Cooking the meal, sipping on a glass of wine or beer while cooking, and enjoying conversation all become an activity prior to the actual eating. I love finding new ways to spend time with the people I care about."

Low cost. "While we didn't specifically start Soup Night as part of Meatless Mondays, it's turning out to be that way. Making a hearty vegetarian soup with a homemade bread is a pretty cheap meal. Healthy can be affordable."

FOR RECIPES FROM LISA'S GROUP, SEE:
Carrot-Ginger Soup, page 73
Borscht, page 82

Carrot-Ginger Soup

Recipe from Lisa Fine, Montpelier, Vermont (profile, facing page)

This soup would be lovely with a swirl of crème fraîche (see page 237).

Serves 6

2 tablespoons olive oil

1 large onion, chopped

2 garlic cloves, minced

4 cups water or vegetable broth

1 pound carrots, sliced

1 (1-inch) piece fresh ginger, peeled and grated

Salt and freshly ground black pepper

Crème fraîche (optional)

1. Heat the oil in a large soup pot over medium heat. Add the onion and garlic and sauté until golden, about 5 minutes. Add the water and carrots and bring to a boil. Reduce the heat and simmer until the carrots can be easily pierced with a fork.

2. Transfer the soup to a blender (careful, it's hot) and purée until smooth, and return it to the pot. Or use an immersion blender and purée the soup right in the pot. Stir in the ginger.

3. Reheat and season with salt and pepper to taste. Serve hot with a dollop of crème fraîche, if desired.

Make ahead? This soup is easily made a day ahead; refrigerate.

For large crowds: Also easy to multiply.

GINGER JUICE

To get the incomparable taste of fresh ginger without adding actual pieces of ginger to your soup (some people don't like to bite into it), try making "ginger juice." Place a paper towel on a small dish and grate fresh ginger directly onto it. When you have a small mound, wrap the paper towel tightly and squeeze directly over the dish, catching the liquid.

Havana Banana–Black Bean Soup

Several folks who host soup nights have the tradition of serving an orange soup and a black soup in October, in honor of Halloween. You have several options for the orange — carrots, pumpkin, or butternut squash, all of which are represented in this book. For the black, the obvious choice is the classic black bean. You might entice your kids to try it if you call it something like Witch's Stew. Or try this version, with an unusual but delicious Latin American touch — bananas.

Serves 6–8

2 tablespoons olive oil

2 medium onions, minced

3 garlic cloves, minced

3 (15-ounce) cans black beans; or 6 cups cooked black beans with ½ cup of the cooking liquid (see page 27)

4 cups chicken broth

½ pound cooked ham, cut into bite-size pieces

1 (15-ounce) can diced tomatoes

2 tablespoons white vinegar

½ teaspoon ground cumin

Dash Tabasco

Salt and freshly ground black pepper

Ripe bananas, sliced, as garnish (4–5 slices per serving)

1. Heat the oil in a large soup pot over medium heat. Add the onions and sauté until softened, about 2 minutes. Add the garlic and sauté 1 minute longer.

2. Drain two of the cans of black beans, and then add them plus the third can with its liquid to the pot. Mash the beans lightly with a potato masher; you want a mixture of whole beans and bean pulp.

3. Add the broth, ham, tomatoes with their juice, vinegar, cumin, Tabasco, salt, and black pepper to taste. Simmer to heat everything through and allow the flavors to blend, 15 to 20 minutes, stirring occasionally to prevent sticking. Taste and adjust the seasonings if necessary.

4. Top each serving with banana slices; have extra banana slices on the table so folks can add more if they wish.

Make ahead? All the way through step 3; refrigerate.

For large crowds: Easily multiplied.

For vegetarians: Just leave out the ham, and use water or vegetable broth in place of the chicken broth.

Squash This!

Recipe from Jennifer Rollins, SE Works, Portland, Oregon (profile, page 80)

Jennifer says: This is one of my very favorites for those rainy Portland fall evenings. Add a loaf of crusty bread with sweet butter, friends, good conversation, a crisp white wine, and ideally a nice fire in the fireplace . . . and you can't go wrong!

Serves 6

1   medium butternut squash (about 2 pounds)
    Olive oil (optional)
2   tablespoons butter
1   medium onion, chopped
3   cups vegetable broth
1   cup apple cider
1   cup water, plus more as needed for consistency
1   cup heavy cream
½   teaspoon ground cinnamon
¼   teaspoon ground nutmeg
    Salt and freshly ground black pepper
1   teaspoon sherry wine vinegar, or any mild vinegar

Topping

1   tablespoon butter
1   medium apple, cored and diced
1   tablespoon fresh sage leaves, chopped or cut into pretty ribbons
    Ground cinnamon

Optional Garnishes

    More diced apple
    Crème fraîche (see page 237) or mascarpone

1. Preheat the oven to 350°F.

2. Roast the whole squash in a baking dish for 45 to 50 minutes (see box on following page) or until tender; let the squash cool, and then scoop out the flesh.

3. Melt the butter in a soup pot over medium heat. Add the onion and sauté until nice and soft. Add the broth and simmer for about 10 minutes.

4. Add the reserved squash and stir to combine. Add the cider, and then transfer the soup to a blender (careful, it's hot) and purée until smooth, then return it to the pot. Or use an immersion blender and purée the soup right in the pot. Add water as needed until you like the consistency.

5. Whisk in the cream, cinnamon, nutmeg, and salt and pepper to taste. The cream is important. You can substitute half-and-half if you must, but don't use milk. It's a mistake I made only once.

6. Stir in the vinegar; this is important to keep the soup from tasting like dessert. Heat thoroughly but gently; don't let the soup come to a boil.

7. While the soup heats up, make the topping: Melt the butter in a small skillet over medium heat. Add the apple, sage, and cinnamon to taste, and cook until everything is soft and fragrant. Remove the mixture to a bowl and set aside.

8. When the soup is hot, serve it topped with a spoonful of the apple mixture.

9. Optional but really wonderful additional toppings: uncooked diced apple (a nice little crunch and, if you use a tart apple like Granny Smith, a refreshing tang in an otherwise fairly sweet soup), and a swirl of crème fraîche. Mascarpone would work well, too.

Variations: One of the reasons for the popularity of butternut squash soup surely must be how graciously it accepts new ideas. Dennis Battles, of Long Beach, Washington, incorporates roasted pears in place of the more usual apples and always challenges his guests to name the secret ingredient (they never get it). And see Martha Bayne's version on page 140.

Make ahead? Steps 1 and 2, for sure; up through step 4 if you'll be rushed on soup day.

For large crowds: This soup is easy to multiply in the fall, when butternut squash are in such abundant supply.

ROASTING SQUASH

I hate trying to cut a tough winter squash when it's raw, so roasting it whole, with a few fork holes poked into it, is fair game as long as you don't mind getting your hands dirty removing the seeds from the roasted squash. Otherwise, lightly grease a baking dish. Cut the squash in half lengthwise and scoop out and discard the seeds. Rub oil on the cut edge, and place the halves, skin-side up, in the prepared baking dish. Bake for 45 to 50 minutes, let the squash cool, and then scoop out the flesh.
— *Jennifer Rollins*

Nona's Chicken Soup

Recipe from Sonia Montalbano, SE Works, Portland, Oregon (profile, page 80)

Sonia says: My mother came up with the original recipe for this soup, and then I changed it a little (mostly the difference is in how you deal with the chicken, see notes below). When I entered this soup in the Soup Cookoff (page 80), I had a photo of my grandmother at her wedding on the table, because nice displays always attract attention and more money for the cause. "Nona" is what Italian children call their grandmothers, and I let people draw their own conclusions; if they thought it was my grandmother's recipe, I was willing to let them! But what I didn't explain to them is that *I* am Nona, because when my friends all had kids none of them could say "Sonia" and it came out as "Nona."

Serves 6–8

2 tablespoons olive oil

1½ large yellow onions, diced

1 tablespoon dried thyme

8 cups water

1 (3- to 4-pound) chicken, giblets removed

8 ounces orzo or ancini di pepe pasta

2 large carrots, diced

2 celery stalks, including the green leaves, diced

1 (14-ounce) can corn kernels or kernels from 2 fresh corncobs

2–3 large cremini mushrooms, sliced

¼ cup chopped curly Italian parsley, plus more for garnish

2 bay leaves

1–4 cubes chicken bouillon (depending on method of preparation; see note)

   Salt and freshly ground black pepper

   Parmesan/Romano blended cheese, grated, for garnish

Note: There are two ways to prepare the chicken in this soup: the "easy" way and the "other" way. The easy way is just as flavorful, but you have to use more chicken bouillon to substitute for the flavor you get when you prepare the chicken the "other" way. They take about the same amount of time. The difference really lies in work and the cleanup.

CHICKEN PREPARATION — EASY

1. Heat the oil in a large soup pot over medium heat. Add the onions and thyme, and sauté until softened, about 3 minutes. Add the water.

2. Break the leg bones in the chicken, but do not separate the legs from the bird; this allows some marrow to be released, which is an important flavor factor. Sonia says, "Grasp the very bottom of the leg, the part you would have in your hand if you were eating the drumstick of a fried chicken, and smack the bone with something heavy. Or use pliers to crack the bone."

3. Wrap the whole chicken in cheesecloth and submerge in the water.

4. Bring to a boil, and then reduce the heat to low. Simmer until the chicken is cooked through, 30 to 40 minutes, depending on the size of the bird.

5. Remove the chicken from the pot but do not discard the water.

6. When the chicken is cool enough to handle, remove the cheesecloth and strip off the meat, discarding the skin and bones.

CHICKEN PREPARATION — OTHER

1. Separate the breast meat from the rest of the chicken. Hack the remaining chicken, including the breastbone and ribs, into pieces approximately 2 inches in size; Sonia uses a cleaver.

2. Heat the oil in a large skillet over medium heat. Add the onion and thyme, and sauté until softened, about 3 minutes. Add the breasts and sauté until nicely browned, about 5 minutes per side. Remove the chicken; when it's cool enough to handle, shred the meat and set it aside.

3. Add the chicken parts to the skillet and sauté until browned, about 5 minutes, stirring occasionally. You may need to do this in two batches, depending on the size of the chicken.

4. Place all the chicken pieces in a large soup pot, add ¼ cup of the water, and cover. Simmer on low heat for 20 minutes, stirring occasionally. This is called "sweating" the chicken; it will release the juices and makes for a richer broth.

5. Strain the chicken juices into a small bowl; remove and discard the chicken pieces that you used for sweating. Return the chicken juices to the pot and add the remaining 7¾ cups water.

NEXT

1. Add the pasta and carrots to the broth and bring to a boil. Add the celery, corn, mushrooms, parsley, and bay leaves. Reduce the heat to a simmer.

2. Add the bouillon cubes: If you used the "easy" method, add 2 or 3 cubes. If you used the "other" method, I like to add 1 cube just to boost the flavor. (Or try chicken-flavor Better Than Bouillon, a concentrated paste.) Simmer until the bouillon is dissolved, 4 to 5 minutes.

3. Add the shredded chicken. Simmer until the pasta is cooked, but still al dente (remove a sample and taste it). Remove the bay leaves. Season to taste with salt and pepper. Serve hot and pass freshly grated Parmesan and fresh parsley for garnishing.

Make ahead? Cook the chicken, whichever way you prefer, one day ahead. Refrigerate.

For large crowds: I suspect you could make this for an army, and it would still be delicious.

Soup Cookoff, SE Works

PORTLAND, OREGON

If you are involved with any nonprofit organization, or know anyone who is, or if you simply care about your community, I'm sure you have attended fundraisers built around a silent auction. And I'm also sure at some point you must have thought, "Isn't there something else we could do?"

Turns out, there is. This small agency in Portland, a grassroots organization dedicated to job training and support services, has created an innovative event built around soup. Now in its twelfth year, the Soup Cookoff is both popular and effective: in 2011, they raised $85,000 to help the families of Southeast Portland.

The agency has one big fund-raiser a year, an event with multiple layers. There is a sit-down dinner, a silent auction, and a live auction. But the part that everyone seems to enjoy the most is the Soup Cookoff. Here's how it works:

Local cooks (not professionals) are invited to enter their soup. They bring a large amount to the event, enough to serve tastings to several hundred people. The cooks are encouraged to prepare a description of their soup, and some put together an elaborate display.

As the guests arrive, they buy tickets for $1 each and vote for their favorite soup by dropping tickets into jars next to the soups they like best; if they run out of tickets, they just tuck in $1 bills. The money is part of the fund-raising, of course, but it's also a way of determining the cookoff winners. At the end of this part of the evening (before the dinner) the jars are counted and the one with the most money is deemed the People's Choice and earns the Golden Ladle award for its creator. In addition, local celebrities (chefs from local restaurants, elected officials, and community leaders) choose a second winner, and sometimes that recipe is featured in a local restaurant for a year.

The joy of it is the many conversations between tasters and cooks, and the all-in-fun competitive spirit. And in the end, the deep satisfaction of knowing that deserving people were helped.

"It was a small event at first," executive director Holly Whittleton says, "just 30 to 40 people. In 2011, we had

> **They took a typical boring event — a silent auction for charity — and turned it into something cozy and warm and welcoming. That's the power of soup.**

350 guests, but the basic idea hasn't changed. Community development is what we're all about, and this was always intended to be a grassroots event with a strong community feel. Even though we're much larger now, it still is friendly, warm, welcoming.

"Food and not-for-profits just seem to go together," she adds with a smile. "But there's something special about soup that fits with us. It creates a humble environment that just works. We don't have a lot of money to rent space, so we put a focus on affordability, on highlighting our community, on having fun."

Two recent cooks talked about their experiences — and shared their winning recipes.

Sonia Montalbano, a volunteer board member, admires this organization because "we actually get things done. We help people learn English, help people go back to school, help people get jobs." Speaking of the Soup Cookoff specifically, she says, "The first time I went, I was just blown away. It is such a clever idea. It's a very festive atmosphere, with music and people milling around talking to the chefs and checking out the auction items. People are just intrigued at the idea of trying the soups. And the cooks go all out with their presentations. They are lined up on long tables, on one side of the room, with slow cookers or restaurant-style serving pans. They have a supply of small taster cups, and people gather around to ask about the soup and to taste it. I see all kinds of neat conversations between the tasters and the chefs."

Jennifer Rollins adds, "They took a typical boring event — a silent auction for charity — and turned it into something cozy and warm and welcoming. That's the power of soup."

www.seworks.org

FOR TWO PRIZEWINNING SOUPS FROM THE SOUP COOKOFF, SEE:
Nona's Chicken Soup, page 78
Squash This!, page 76

Borscht

Recipe from Lisa Fine, Montpelier, Vermont (profile, page 72)

Lisa says: Borscht tastes especially good if you make it one day and eat it the next; the soup thickens as it absorbs the flavors of the vegetables. We make plenty for leftovers to enjoy the next day.

Serves 6

3 tablespoons olive oil

1 onion, diced

3 carrots, diced

3 red potatoes, scrubbed and sliced

3 beets, sliced

8 cups water or vegetable broth

½ cabbage, sliced

Salt and freshly ground black pepper

Sour cream or yogurt (optional), for garnish

1. Heat the olive oil in a large soup pot over medium heat. Add the onion, carrots, potatoes, and beets, and sauté until the onion is translucent, 5 to 7 minutes. Pour the water over the vegetables and bring to a boil. Reduce the heat and simmer until the vegetables begin to soften, about 30 minutes.

2. Add the cabbage and simmer until all the vegetables are cooked to your liking, about 20 minutes. Season with salt and pepper to taste.

3. Top with or mix in sour cream or yogurt, if desired, and serve hot.

Make ahead? It's even better if you do; see Lisa's note above.

For large crowds: With its inexpensive and outrageously healthy ingredients, this is an ideal soup to make in large quantities.

Canadian Beef Stew *(photo, page 29)*

Recipe from Heather Vogel Frederick, Soup and Solidarity, Portland, Oregon
(profile, page 84)

Heather says: As a young woman, my mother, Marie MacDougall, left her home in Nova Scotia for Boston, to take a position as a private-duty nurse. Her mother, my grandmother Nana Mac, packed a thermos for the train trip, filled with this beef stew. Marie made it to Boston safely, with no idea how much it would change her life. One day while working for this patient, she answered a knock on the door. Standing there was a handsome young man in uniform, an Army orderly who had cared for this same patient in an Army hospital and used his leave to come visit. Within a month, they were engaged.

Serves 6

1	tablespoon olive oil
2	pounds beef stew meat, cut into 2-inch cubes
2–3	cups water
1	teaspoon summer savory
	Salt and freshly ground black pepper
1	tablespoon butter
½	pound fresh button mushrooms, stems removed, cleaned, and cut in half
5	medium onions, chopped into large dice
10–12	good-size carrots, peeled and cut into 1-inch chunks
4–6	potatoes, peeled and chopped into large chunks
4	parsnips, peeled and cut into 1-inch slices
1	medium turnip, peeled and chopped into large chunks

1. Heat the oil in a soup pot over medium-high heat; add the meat and sear on all sides. Depending on the size of your pot, you may have to work in batches. Don't crowd the meat; if you do, it will steam rather than sear. Each batch will take about 5 minutes to develop a good sear.

2. Add water to cover and the summer savory; season with salt and pepper to taste. Bring to a boil, then reduce the heat and simmer, covered, for 30 minutes.

3. Melt the butter in a skillet over medium-high heat and sauté the mushrooms until tender, about 8 minutes.

4. Add the mushrooms, onions, carrots, potatoes, parsnips, and turnip to the soup pot. Cover with water again and simmer for several hours (or all day in the slow cooker), until the meat is fork-tender.

Make ahead? You bet. As Heather says, "It's ALWAYS best the second day!"

For large crowds: Easily multiplied.

For vegetarians? Well, it's *beef* stew.

Soup and Solidarity

PORTLAND, OREGON

My friend Heather Frederick is loaded with talent. She's a very successful author of children's books, a terrific cook, and she has a very real gift for bringing people together. I've seen her do it: whenever someone interesting crosses her path, she just swoops in and pulls them into her circle of light. So I wasn't at all surprised to learn that she had created a soup gathering, and also not surprised that it's unusual and very creative.

Any writer will tell you that writing is lonely work; they will also admit, if they are honest, that it's easy to find reasons *not* to work. Heather's clever idea tackles both those demons.

Once a month six writers gather at her house to work alone, together. Each person brings a laptop and stakes out a spot in the house to work for the morning. All are writers of books for children or young adults, and all just happen to be women.

The house is silent, except for the clicking of computer keys, as the unspoken power of peer pressure keeps everyone focused. They all agree that the very presence of other writers, hard at work, makes it impossible not to do likewise.

They also agree that simply being together adds a quality of collaboration to what is an otherwise solo occupation. "It's like a hobbit house," one member says, "all cozy and warm and productive. And knowing we'll have soup in a few hours keeps us going."

At lunchtime they gather around the table for a delicious lunch and shop talk. Sometimes their conversation turns to families or local current events, but more often it's about their work. Together they share ideas, challenges, and tips. Should I have a Twitter account? I think I need a new website designer. I'm having a contract dilemma. Can I get some suggestions for building a platform? What do you all think about this new book idea? All the "writerly" problems that you can only talk about with other writers.

Heather always makes the soup and the others alternate bringing other parts of the meal. "I always set the table with pretty linens," she says, "and flowers and candles and my mother's china." Another

> It's like a hobbit house, all cozy and warm and productive. And knowing we'll have soup in a few hours keeps us going.

member compares the lunch to a fancy tea party and points out that it's always at a round table, which she considers a crucial bit of symbolism. "That makes us all the same. It's a wonderful metaphor for our group. I love the camaraderie. It feeds the soul.

"It's rather ironic, really," she continues. "The latest modern technology [laptops] enables us to get together for this lovely, elegant lunch that feels like going back to earlier times. We sit down to savor the food, and savor the companionship.

"Afterward," Heather concludes, "we all feel refreshed and ready to go forward."

FOR RECIPES FROM SOUP AND SOLIDARITY, SEE:

Canadian Beef Stew, page 83

Nana Mac's Nova Scotia Oatmeal Bread, page 86

Vegetarian Eggplant Chili, page 260

Solidarity Salad , page 94

Nana Mac's Nova Scotia Oatmeal Bread

Recipe from Heather Vogel Frederick, Soup and Solidarity, Portland, Oregon (profile, page 84)

Heather says: This came to me from my grandmother, Eva MacDougall. I've been making it since I was 12 — make it every week for my family! And the sandwiches that my grandmother packed for my mother to take on the train with her beef stew (page 83) were made with this bread.

Makes 2 loaves

Butter (about 1 teaspoon)

1 package quick-rising yeast

1 scant teaspoon sugar

½ cup warm water (110°F)

1 cup old-fashioned rolled oats

½ cup molasses (Crosby's from Canada is my favorite)

2 tablespoons vegetable shortening

1 teaspoon salt

2 cups boiling water

6 cups unbleached all-purpose flour, approximately

1. Grease a large bowl with butter; set aside.

2. In a small bowl, dissolve the yeast and sugar in the warm water. Let stand until the mixture is foamy, 5 to 10 minutes.

3. Combine the oats, molasses, shortening, and salt in a large bowl. Pour the boiling water over all, and stir to melt the shortening. Stir in 1 cup of the flour. Add the yeast mixture, and then continue stirring in the remaining 5 cups flour to make a stiff dough.

4. Turn the dough onto a lightly floured surface and knead until it becomes smooth and stretchy. Shape the dough into a ball and place it in the greased bowl, turning to cover all surfaces of the dough with butter. Cover the bowl with a clean dishtowel and let rise in a draft-free place until doubled in size; this could take anywhere from 1 to 2 hours, depending on the conditions in your kitchen.

5. Punch the dough down so it deflates, then turn out onto a lightly floured surface and briefly knead again. It will probably feel as if the dough is pushing back against you; that's normal.

6. Generously butter two 5- by 9-inch loaf pans. Cut the dough in half and shape each half into a loaf. Place in the prepared pans, cover with clean dishtowels, and let rise again, until the dough crests the top of the pans. This might take 1 to 2 hours, again depending on the temperature and humidity in your kitchen.

7. Preheat the oven to 375°F. Bake the bread for 35 to 40 minutes. Remove the loaves from the pans, butter the tops of the loaves, and let cool on racks.

Make ahead? You almost have to, but if you want to wow your guests, time it so the bread is coming out of the oven as they arrive. You can also interrupt yourself in the middle of step 4, and set the bowl of dough in the refrigerator overnight, where it will rise patiently.

For large crowds: Make as many loaves as you can; they freeze wonderfully.

Onion-Bacon Rolls *(photo, page 29)*

Yeast rolls enjoy an extra flavor boost from bacon and caramelized onions. They are an excellent accompaniment to soups and chowders based on sweet vegetables, such as carrot, butternut squash, beet, or corn — although truth be known, anything with bacon goes beautifully with anything else.

About 3 dozen rolls

1 package active dry yeast

1 cup milk, heated to lukewarm (110–115°F)

2 tablespoons sugar

1 teaspoon salt

3 cups all-purpose flour

3 egg yolks

½ cup (1 stick) unsalted butter, softened

6 bacon strips, chopped into small bits

1 cup finely chopped onion

2 tablespoons unsalted butter, melted

Egg wash: 1 egg yolk whisked with 1 tablespoon cream

1. Make the dough: Sprinkle the yeast over ½ cup of the warm milk in a large measuring cup or medium bowl. Add the sugar and salt, and stir until dissolved. Set the yeast mixture aside in a warm spot until it bubbles. (This is called proofing the yeast, and if it doesn't happen, your yeast is dead; start over, with fresh yeast.)

2. Measure the flour carefully and place in a large mixing bowl. Make a well in the center of the flour and add the yeast mixture, egg yolks, the remaining ½ cup milk, and the softened butter. Slowly mix the flour with the wet ingredients. Beat vigorously, to form a firm dough.

3. Cover the bowl loosely with a kitchen towel or plastic wrap and place in a warm spot, such as a gas oven (the pilot light provides heat) or on top of the refrigerator, until the dough has doubled, 1 hour or more, depending on conditions in your kitchen.

4. Punch the dough down (this is the fun part — make a fist, smack the dough hard in the middle) and set it to rise a second time, covered, until doubled once again, another hour or more.

5. Make the filling: Fry the bacon in a skillet over medium heat until crisp. Remove with a slotted spoon and drain on paper towels.

6. Remove and discard about half of the bacon grease from the skillet. Add the onion and sauté over medium heat until golden brown, about 6 minutes. Remove the pan from the heat and stir the bacon into the onion.

7. Preheat the oven to 375°F. Lightly coat two baking sheets with 1 tablespoon melted butter each.

8. Assemble the rolls: Sprinkle a work surface with flour and roll out the dough to a thickness of about ¼ inch. (You may have to work in batches; if so, cover the unused dough lightly with plastic wrap while it's waiting its turn.) With a cookie cutter or a glass, cut the dough into circles about 4 inches in diameter.

9. Place 1 teaspoon of the bacon-onion mixture into the center of each circle and fold the edges inward, making a packet.

10. When all the rolls are baconed, put them, seam-side down, on the baking sheets and cover lightly with a clean towel. Set in a warm spot to rise until doubled in size, about 20 minutes.

11. Bake for 10 minutes. Remove baking sheets, paint with egg-cream wash, and bake for 10 minutes longer, or until golden brown.

Make ahead? Yes, but your guests will miss that intoxicating perfume of bacon frying. Rewarm for 5 to 10 minutes in 350°F oven.

For large crowds: Limited only by the size of your oven, or your patience, for multiple batches.

For vegetarians: Leave out the bacon and sauté the onion in oil.

Pumpkin Seed Flatbread

Recipe from Suzy and Philip Poll, Houston, Texas (profile, page 61)

Suzy and Philip say: Excellent served with Camembert cheese.

Serves 12–24

1 cup warm water (110°F)

1 teaspoon sugar

1 teaspoon active dry yeast

6 tablespoons cold unsalted butter, cut into small pieces

3 cups unbleached all-purpose flour, plus additional for sprinkling

⅓ cup cornmeal

4 teaspoons chili powder

1½ teaspoons kosher salt

Small amount of olive oil

1 cup hulled pumpkin seeds

Egg wash: 1 large egg whisked with 2 tablespoons cold water

Additional kosher salt for sprinkling

1. Combine the warm water and sugar in a large bowl and stir to dissolve the sugar. Sprinkle the yeast on top and let stand until foamy, about 5 minutes.

2. Add the butter, flour, cornmeal, chili powder, and salt to the yeast mixture and stir until a soft dough forms.

3. Turn the dough out onto a lightly floured surface and knead until it becomes smooth and elastic, 6 to 8 minutes.

4. Lightly coat a bowl with olive oil and place the dough ball in the bowl, turning to coat with oil. Cover with plastic wrap and chill for 1 hour.

5. Preheat the oven to 350°F.

6. Spread the pumpkin seeds on a baking sheet and toast in the oven until just beginning to turn golden, 3 to 4 minutes. When you can smell them, they're ready. Remove from the oven and set aside.

7. Increase the oven's temperature to 400°F. Lightly sprinkle two large baking sheets with flour.

8. Divide the dough in half and return one half to the refrigerator. On a lightly floured surface, roll out the dough to ⅛-inch thickness and sprinkle with half of the pumpkin seeds. Continue to roll the dough to ¹⁄₁₆-inch thickness, pressing the pumpkin seeds into the dough. Using a pastry brush, paint the dough with the egg wash.

9. Cut the dough into strips or wedges. Using a spatula, transfer the pieces to the prepared baking sheets and sprinkle with kosher salt. Bake until crisp, about 12 minutes, switching the position of the baking sheets halfway through baking. Transfer the flatbread to baking racks to cool. Repeat with the remaining half of dough.

Make ahead? Sure. Suzy says they keep in an airtight container up to 3 days.

For large crowds: Make as many as your appreciative friends can eat — which is a lot.

Molded Cranberry Salad with Lemon Mayonnaise

Recipe from Albertina's Restaurant, Portland, Oregon (profile, page 55)

A perfect make-ahead salad for November. Fresh cranberries are in supermarkets for only a brief period, so don't miss the opportunity.

Serves 6

1 (3-ounce) package raspberry gelatin
2 tablespoons sugar
½ cup boiling water
1 small orange, unpeeled, cut into chunks, seeds removed
½ cup sliced celery
½ cup fresh cranberries
½ cup walnut pieces (optional)
½ cup crushed pineapple, drained (reserve the juice)
½ cup reserved pineapple juice
1½ teaspoons lemon juice
Lettuce leaves

Lemon Mayonnaise
¼ cup mayonnaise
1 teaspoon freshly squeezed lemon juice

1. Dissolve the gelatin and sugar in the boiling water in a heatproof bowl. Cool to room temperature.

2. Put the orange chunks in a food processor and chop with the metal blade. Add the celery, cranberries, and walnuts, if using, and pulse until finely chopped. Add the orange mixture to the cooled gelatin. Stir in the pineapple, pineapple juice, and lemon juice.

3. Pour ½ cup of this mixture into each of six 1-cup molds. Chill overnight in the refrigerator.

4. Make the lemon mayonnaise: Whisk the mayonnaise and lemon juice together in a small bowl; chill.

5. Place a lettuce leaf on each of six small plates. Unmold the gelatin onto the lettuce and spoon a little lemon mayonnaise on top of each serving.

UNMOLDING A MOLDED SALAD

First, sprinkle a few drops of water in the bottom of the mold; you can also accomplish the same thing if you rinse the mold with cold water but don't dry it. (I know this doesn't seem logical, but it really works.) Add your gelatin mixture and chill. When the gelatin is well and truly set, run the tip of a sharp knife around the edge, between the salad and the mold itself; your goal is to break the vacuum and allow some air in.

Next, put a serving plate (or saucer, if you're using individual molds) on top, hold it tightly, and turn the whole shebang upside down. Wet a dish towel with hot water, wring it out, and hold it against the mold for about 10 seconds. Shimmy the mold gently, and lift. If the mold doesn't come off cleanly, repeat the wet dish towel for a few more seconds. But resist the temptation to go longer; if the gelatin melts, there's no fixing it.

Solidarity Salad

Recipe from Trudy Ludwig, Soup and Solidarity, Portland, Oregon (profile, page 84)

This salad has a wonderful mix of flavors — some sweet, some savory, some tangy — and textures. Plus it's packed with protein from eggs, cheese, and nuts. And Trudy's dressing is marvelous.

Serves 6

1 (10-ounce) bag mixed salad greens

⅓ cup candied pecans or walnuts (see facing page)

4–6 ounces crumbled feta cheese

1 avocado, peeled, pitted, and diced

½ English cucumber, partially peeled and diced

½ red onion, cut in half lengthwise and thinly sliced

1 yellow or orange bell pepper, seeded and diced

1 hard-cooked egg, chopped

⅓ cup mixed dried berries (I prefer Trader Joe's Golden Berry Mix of dried cherries, cranberries, blueberries, and golden raisins)

Dried tarragon leaves, crumbled (about 1 tablespoon)

Salt and freshly ground pepper

Dressing

3 tablespoons orange juice

2 tablespoons balsamic vinegar

½ teaspoon Dijon mustard

½ teaspoon sugar, or more to taste

6 tablespoons extra-virgin olive oil

1 teaspoon dried tarragon leaves

Salt and freshly ground pepper

1. Put the salad greens in a large serving bowl and add the pecans, feta, avocado, cucumber, onion, bell pepper, egg, and dried berries. Season to taste with tarragon, salt, and pepper. Toss gently.

2. Whisk the orange juice, vinegar, mustard, and sugar in a small bowl. Whisk in the oil until it is fully incorporated. Whisk in the tarragon and season to taste with salt and pepper. Take a sample taste and adjust flavors according to your personal taste.

3. Just before serving, toss the salad with dressing to taste.

Make ahead? Stash the salad (minus dressing) in the refrigerator until serving time, covered with plastic wrap. Or if your refrigerator won't hold the bowl, put all the salad ingredients into a plastic bag; it's a little more flexible when space is tight.

For large crowds: This is easily doubled or even tripled.

MAKING CANDIED NUTS

Use these approximate proportions: ½ cup sugar to 1 cup nuts. Spread the sugar evenly in a thin layer in a large skillet (cast iron, if you have one), and melt over medium heat. While that's happening, don't *touch* the pan. Don't stir, don't shake it, don't do anything but watch it. When the sugar is melted and has turned a nice caramel brown in color, take the pan off the heat, dump in the nuts all at once, and stir like mad. Try to get all the nuts coated, but work fast, and be careful — melted sugar is extremely hot. Dump the nuts onto a buttered surface, such as a baking sheet or even a section of heavy-duty aluminum foil. Spread them out as much as possible, but don't worry if some of the nuts remain clumped together. When the nuts are completely cool, break them apart with your hands or roughly chop.

Poppy Seed Dressing

Recipe from Albertina's Restaurant, Portland, Oregon (profile, page 55)

This classic dressing goes well with all green salads, especially those that have a little fruit included. If you use red onions, the dressing turns a pretty pink color.

Makes 3½ cups

1	cup sugar
⅔	cup white wine vinegar
2	teaspoons dry mustard
2	teaspoons salt
¼	cup chopped onion
2	cups salad oil
1½	tablespoons poppy seeds

1. Combine the sugar, vinegar, mustard, salt, and onion in a blender or food processor. With the motor running, slowly add the oil.

2. Transfer the dressing to an airtight container and stir in the poppy seeds. Refrigerate until ready to use.

Peanut Butter–Chocolate Chip Cookies *(photo, page 29)*

Recipe from Elizabeth Newland, Civano Soup Supper, Tucson, Arizona
(profile, page 46)

Elizabeth says: The best of both worlds — peanut butter and chocolate chips — what's not to love? I took these to a Fourth of July potluck, and they were gone before we got to the dessert part of the meal!

Makes about 4 dozen cookies

1½ cups all-purpose flour
½ teaspoon baking soda
1 cup chunky peanut butter
½ cup (1 stick) butter, softened
½ cup granulated sugar
½ cup brown sugar
1 egg
1 teaspoon vanilla extract
8–12 ounces chocolate chips

1. Preheat the oven to 375°F.

2. Whisk together the flour and baking soda in a medium bowl.

3. Beat together the peanut butter and butter in a large bowl with an electric mixer. Beat in the granulated sugar and brown sugar, mixing well. Beat in the egg and vanilla.

4. Add the flour mixture, blending thoroughly, and then stir in up to 12 ounces of chocolate chips, depending on your preference for the ratio of chocolate chips to peanut butter.

5. Shape the dough into 1-inch balls and arrange them about 2 inches apart on ungreased baking sheets. Crisscross the balls with a sugared fork, and bake for about 10 minutes, until lightly browned.

Raspberry Sherbet

Recipe from Albertina's Restaurant, Portland, Oregon (profile, page 55)

This delicious sherbet is stunningly simple; it doesn't even require the use of an ice cream maker. And because it uses frozen berries, you can enjoy it any season.

Serves 8

20 ounces frozen raspberries, thawed

2 cups buttermilk

1 cup sugar

Fresh berries, for garnish

1. Combine the raspberries, buttermilk, and sugar in a food processor or blender. Blend until well mixed, 15 to 20 seconds.

2. Transfer the mixture to an airtight container and freeze. Stir after about an hour, when partially frozen; refreeze.

3. Serve in stemmed glasses and garnish with fresh berries.

Cardamom Pavlova

Recipe from Lexa Walsh, Oakland, California; Portland Stock (profile, page 244)

Lexa is a talented chef who volunteered her services for many of the Portland Stock suppers. The Portland folks cannot forgive her for moving away. Among her many creations is this cardamom-tinged pavlova, a spectacular dessert that uses fresh seasonal fruit like jewels in a crown. Many types of fresh fruit are glorious with this dessert, which makes it a treat in any season. In fall, Lexa especially likes the brilliant color of pomegranate seeds.

4   egg whites, at room temperature
    Pinch salt
1   cup sugar
2   teaspoons cornstarch
½   teaspoon white vinegar
1   teaspoon vanilla extract
1   tablespoon plus 2 teaspoons ground cardamom
1   pint cold whipping cream
    Fresh fruit — such as kiwi, strawberries, blueberries, persimmons, or any combination. Choose with an eye to color as much as taste. Fruits that turn brown when cut, such as apples, pears, peaches, and bananas, don't work as well here. Neither do fruits with a high water content, such as citrus or melons.

1. Preheat the oven to 180°F. Line a baking sheet with baker's parchment.

2. Place the egg whites and salt in a mixing bowl and beat on high speed with an electric mixer (or by hand) until the egg whites are firm, about 1 minute. With the mixer still on high, slowly add the sugar and beat until you have firm, glossy peaks.

3. Add the cornstarch, vinegar, ½ teaspoon of the vanilla, and the 2 teaspoons ground cardamom, folding them in gently.

4. Using a pastry bag (or a sturdy plastic bag with one corner snipped off), squeeze and swirl the meringue into circles on the prepared baking sheet. Go over each one a second time, building up the sides; we are attempting to make little "bowls" of meringue.

5. Bake for about 1 hour. The meringues should be crisp on the outside and soft on the inside. They might brown a little if your oven temperature isn't precise — not ideal, but no big deal. Let cool.

6. Combine the cream, the 1 tablespoon cardamom, and the remaining ½ teaspoon vanilla, and beat until it forms soft peaks. Careful, you're not making butter. No need for extra sugar in the cream.

7. Prepare the fruit as needed: wash and dry berries but leave whole, slice strawberries in half lengthwise, peel kiwi and slice into rounds, peel persimmons and cut into bite-size chunks.

8. Top the cooled meringues with whipped cream and garnish with fresh fruit. Serve immediately; they don't last long.

Variations: Rather than individual meringues, you can make one large one, more like a cake in shape. It doesn't cut as cleanly, but it's a spectacular presentation. And many types of fresh fruit are glorious with this dessert, which makes it a treat in any season.

Make ahead? Up through step 5; the meringues themselves, without whipped cream and fruit, can be made up to several days ahead as long as you store them at room temperature in a super-airtight container.

For large crowds: Easy to multiply ingredients.

CHAPTER THREE

Winter

Winter may be the truest season for soup. Cold. Blustery winds. Icy rain, snow, sleet. Soggy mittens, wet socks, wet dogs. School closures, black ice, power outages. Broken ski poles, broken limbs — okay, enough. You know what I mean. Time for a warm fire, bread in the oven, and soup simmering on the stove.

Soup Night on Stanton Street: December

There it was, in bold letters at the bottom of the Soup Night flyer: "Let's celebrate Earl's 80th Birthday!"

It wasn't completely clear that Earl himself would be present. He and Eleanor, his new lady love, might be at the coast, someone had heard. But, no matter. The rest of the neighbors would honor their most senior member, whether he was there or not. A dozen or so birthday cards waited on the table, alongside a handsome birthday cake, courtesy of Renee and Paul, the hosts.

Suddenly, someone spotted Earl and Eleanor coming up the walk, and all conversations ceased as people rushed to gather in the front room. When the door opened, Earl and Eleanor were greeted with raucous shouts of "Surprise!" and "Happy birthday!" Earl looked stunned. He actually took a step backward, like he was trying to escape. Then, on the first notes of the birthday song, his eyes filled with tears.

Earl spent the rest of the evening hugging all the men and kissing all the women. "This is just the greatest bunch of people," he said over and over. "I'd never want to live anywhere else."

Butternut and Acorn Squash Soup (page 140), Green Salad with Mini Crab Cakes (page 174) , and Whole-Wheat Quick Bread (page 170)

One aspect of their community that the neighbors like to talk about is its diversity. That is, of course, a loaded word. Often — too often — it's a code for race. But on Stanton Street, they mean it more broadly, as it was intended. There are two gay couples. Several religious faiths are represented. One household is African-American, and out of a total of eight youngsters still living at home, three are children of color, adopted from other countries.

What's on display tonight, though, is diversity of age. The guest of honor, 80 years and 4 days old today, is deep in conversation with the 20-something son of his next-door neighbors, a graduate student who always comes back for Soup Night. Not long after, this same young man is pulled into the games of the younger children, aged 4 to 11, who glom onto him every chance they get. It's obvious the pleasure of one another's company is mutual. At the other end of the age spectrum, Dan and Ali's baby is just a few months old, and Becky and Lisa's new son is even younger.

Except he isn't here. He's still in the orphanage, and so are Becky and Lisa, on the last piece of the adoption process. They are expected back any day now.

Jessie and her son Reuben arrive a little late, but they have a very good excuse: Reuben just played at his first violin recital, and they came straight from the performance. It's a bit of a jolt to see Reuben all dressed up. The last time I saw him, he was in jeans and a T-shirt, whizzing around the block on his unicycle. He taught himself to ride, using the instructional video that came with the cycle. His current record is 24 times around the block without stopping or falling. He also taught himself to ride a pogo stick, and his current personal best is more than 150 jumps in a row without missing.

The unicycle, the pogo stick — these are typical Reuben things. A 12-year-old with enough energy to power light bulbs for a small country, he is absolutely fearless. Yet here he is, standing quietly by the fireplace in his dress-up recital clothes, ready to play for us. The conversation buzz slowly settles down, and Reuben starts to play. It's a beautiful classical piece, and he does it well.

In honor of his first recital, Reuben's grandmother is visiting from California. She's been to Soup Night before; it reminds her of her childhood in Pittsburgh, where people sat on their porches and visited while the children played in the street. On this particular evening, she had offered to take the family out to dinner, to celebrate Reuben's debut, but her son, Reuben's dad, said, "No thanks, Mom; it's Soup Night and we don't want to miss it."

Reuben finishes the short piece, to great applause and calls for an encore. So he plays it again. Then his younger sister tiptoes to the piano and starts to play. One neighbor likens this impromptu recital to the days when people knew how to entertain themselves without television. Becky, the teacher, takes advantage of the interruption to have a whispered conference with Reuben. She slips out the door, returns with her guitar, and she and Reuben, whose violin is now a bluegrass fiddle, play an unpolished but thoroughly charming rendition of "Little Burnt Potato" and "Drowsy Maggie."

Turns out, Maggie isn't the only one who's drowsy. It's getting late, and tomorrow is a school day. The parents start the process of saying their good nights, gathering up soup bowls and sorting out their own kids from the gang of youngsters. Aidan, who's five, isn't ready to leave. "But I don't WANT to go home," he wails, sobbing as though his heart is breaking. Alex (who is not his father) picks him up around the middle and holds him crosswise against his own hip (the way you would hold a gigantic bag of peat moss) and dances away with him. "OK," he says, "you don't want to go home, so let's take you somewhere else." Holding the sniffling boy sideways, he trots around a tree, around a telephone pole, halfway down the wrong street, and back again. Pretty soon the little boy is giggling, and soon after that he is safely home.

Another successful Soup Night.

Surprise Beef Stew

I've been making beef stew for a long time, and I always thought mine wasn't half bad — until I tasted the version made by my Ocean Park, Washington, neighbor, Kennette Osborn. Her part-German grandmother taught her to make the stew, and it is really good. It helps that she has access to local beef, raised organically, and the allspice lends a touch of mystery. But what really makes it extraordinary is the surprise — coleslaw. That idea came from her late husband, which makes this a true family recipe. Take a big spoonful, she said, and stir it into your bowl of hot stew. I admit, at first I was skeptical. But trust me, and give it a try. The raw cabbage adds a nice crunch, and the dressing makes the whole thing creamy, but in a nice way. I'd change only one thing: add mushrooms. And I agree with Kennette's suggestion to use a cast-iron frying pan.

Serves 4–6

---

1 cup all-purpose flour, approximately

Seasoned salt

1½ pounds beef stew meat, cut into 1-inch cubes

¼ cup olive oil (more if needed)

1 medium onion, chopped

3 garlic cloves, minced

1–2 cups beef broth

1 tablespoon sugar

½ teaspoon ground allspice

½ teaspoon paprika

3 bay leaves

Salt and freshly ground black pepper

1–2 carrots, cut into bite-size chunks

3 thin-skinned potatoes (such as red, Yukon Gold, or Yellow Finn)

1. Make the stew: Mix the flour and seasoned salt, and dredge the meat until each piece is well coated (a plastic bag makes this easy). Add the oil to a large soup pot, deep skillet, or Dutch oven and brown the meat over medium-high heat. Work in batches if needed to make sure each piece is well browned.

2. To the same pot, add the onion and garlic (add a little more oil at this point, if needed), and sauté until the onion is soft. Add enough beef broth to cover the meat, along with the sugar, allspice, paprika, bay leaves, and salt and pepper to taste. Cover the pot, and reduce the heat. Simmer until the meat is tender, about 40 to 50 minutes (longer doesn't hurt).

3. Add the carrots and potatoes and cook until the vegetables are tender, 10 to 15 minutes. If the liquid seems thin, mix a little cornstarch with cold water and add it a little at a time.

recipe continues on next page

Coleslaw

1   head green cabbage
1   cup mayonnaise
¼   cup sugar
1   tablespoon prepared mustard
¼   cup cream (or evaporated milk),
     more as needed
     Salt and freshly ground pepper

4. Make the coleslaw: Shred the cabbage (or start with a bag of coleslaw mix from the supermarket, already shredded).

5. Whisk the mayonnaise, sugar, and mustard together, and gradually add the cream until you get the consistency you like. Pour the dressing over the cabbage, mix well, and add salt and pepper; taste and adjust seasonings. Ideally, it's best to let this "brew" for an hour or two before serving.

6. Serve the stew in shallow bowls, and pass the coleslaw so that each person can take a large spoonful to stir into the stew.

Make ahead? Yes, both elements. Slow, slow cooking is best for the beef anyway, and the coleslaw needs time to meld. And, like all stews, this is better the next day.

For large crowds: If, like Kennette, you have part of a cow, custom cut, in your freezer, you can make huge batches of this. Otherwise, for expansions you might want to increase the proportion of vegetables to meat.

BOUQUET GARNI

Any dish that cooks slowly for a long time in the oven or on the stove — like beef stew — is a good candidate for a bouquet garni. It sounds fancy, but it's just a small bundle of various herbs and spices, tied together in some way and submerged in the liquid. The bundle can be created simply by tying sprigs of herbs together with twine , or by folding them into a tied packet of cheesecloth. Or use one of those screw-together metal balls meant for tea; they come in large sizes (for brewing a whole pitcher), and that's the most versatile. The whole idea is that the essence of the herbs seeps into the dish, but the herbs themselves — now soggy and with most of the flavor extracted — are easy to remove at the end.

Kate and Jimi Allen

AURORA, ILLINOIS

Back in 2003, **Kate Allen's** mother read an inspiring article about a family that started a new tradition in their neighborhood, something called Soup Night. She told her daughter, who loved the idea and decided to do the same thing in her neighborhood. That original article by Julie Dahlberg (page 58) has had many ripple effects.

Kate began her Soup Night adventure with her then-roommate Stephanie, continued by herself after Stephanie moved, and then shared host duties with her new husband Jimi. In the beginning, Kate and Stephanie hand-delivered invitations to every house on the block: 11 on one side, 11 on the other side. Word spread fast: One man hollered, "Hey, are you the soup ladies?" That might have had something to do with the invitations themselves. Kate is a very talented artist and graphic designer, and her invitations are worth saving.

The first night, only about half a dozen people came, but that quickly increased. Soon hesitancy turned into enthusiasm. By 2007, when Kate planned a visit to her parents in India, neighbors were dismayed: what will happen to Soup Night? Gently, Kate suggested someone else might do it, and that's when the hosting spread to other households. Now, each

year Kate sends out a memo to everyone, asking for volunteers for the coming Soup Night season.

The original plan was to have Soup Night every week for 13 weeks, October to March. After Stephanie moved away, Kate shortened the season to December to February. She still invites all the neighbors, and makes a point to knock on the doors of those she doesn't yet know.

Neighbor **Robert Johnson** told me, "Soup Night has become a highlight of our week. We love just getting together and chatting with the neighbors, eating some good soup and enjoying each other's company. And our two kids love it. Every Tuesday they start asking us early in the day, 'Where is Soup Night tonight?'" **Cheyenne Johnson,** Robert's wife, adds this: "Our neighborhood is like a small town, or something from the 1950s. We trust each other, we help each other. And I know it really started with Soup Night."

Lisa Parro has known Kate for many years, and has been going to Soup Night since the very beginning. "When she first told me about it, I thought, 'That's very much a Kate kind of thing. She has such a big heart.' Still, I wasn't sure how others would react. But it was terrific. That very first night, the conversations were amazing; people loved meeting their neighbors. I remember one time Kate and Jimi brought a business associate from out of town to Soup Night; he was really impressed, and pleased that he got to spend the evening with all of us instead of being by himself in a hotel."

Another neighbor, **Trula Jaffarian,** gives the perspective of newcomers. "The first time we attended Soup Night, we were new in the neighborhood. It was warm, and welcoming, and very friendly, just a phenomenal opportunity to get to know neighbors. And now that we do know everyone, it's also a great way to keep up with the news — who's sick, who's had a new baby, all that wonderful stuff. My three little granddaughters often come, and they absolutely *love* Soup Night; it means a lot to me to see them happy around all these people who know them by name. I think we're all yearning for that sense of community, and here we have it. It helps that our neighborhood is geographically defined; there are two pillars and signs at the entrance. But mostly it's because Kate made the effort and keeps us organized."

Grace Martin, another Allen neighbor, has a rich and poignant story.

"We moved to this neighborhood after 34 years in our previous neighborhood. We had good reasons, but for me, moving meant some huge changes. I left a job I loved, my church family of 37 years, the community I'd spent most of my adult life in, a house I loved, and great neighbors who were good friends as well. I didn't want to start over.

"Then, three months after we'd been here, Kate Allen came by with an invitation to Soup Night. Attending these events helped me transition my loyalties and affections from my old neighborhood to my new one. Making new

> Our neighborhood is like a small town, or something from the 1950s. We trust each other, we help each other. And I know it really started with Soup Night.

acquaintances at Soup Night put faces and names on my new neighbors and propelled me a long way into feeling like this now was home.

"At that time, Kate was the only one who hosted these events. Her soups always were delicious, and little touches like the candles in the mason jars up the steps added additional warmth along with her smiling welcome. Meeting the neighbors week by week on a regular basis helped all of us, newcomers and old-timers, establish links and make connections with each other. These folks became not just someone to nod at from down the street, but people with whom we would want to stop and chat.

"Longtime friends of ours also were downsizing and moved into the neighborhood because they liked the houses here. We immediately brought them to Soup Night, and they also felt very welcomed. They told us that they had lived in their old neighborhood for 20 years and had never been inside another neighborhood home. They moved to this neighborhood and within a few weeks had been in several homes meeting their new neighbors.

"On any given Soup Night, guests arrive looking forward to discovering what soup will be presented. Will it be an old favorite, or a new creation? No one comes thinking they can keep their diet in check. The food is too good! Neighbors are excited to see each other. The buzz in the host house is a happy music of spoons clinking on soup bowls mixed with lively conversations and raucous laughter. Guests meander in and out of sitting areas and back and forth to the soup pot and the food table, sharing and listening to the latest stories.

"We love Soup Night! It has been the foundation for community building in our neighborhood."

Grace, who clearly has given a great deal of thought to this, also put together a few tips for Soup Night success, and also for entertaining in general; you'll find them in the Start Your Own section later in the book.

www.jimiallenproductions.com
www.wemoveideas.com

FOR RECIPES FROM THIS GROUP, SEE:
Grannie's Gumbo, page 110
Pumpkin Curry Soup, page 67
Tortilla Turkey Soup, page 70

Grannie's Gumbo

Recipe from Cheyenne Johnson, Aurora, Illinois (profile, page 107)

Like many great cooks, Cheyenne Johnson's grandmother, Patricia Foster, didn't follow an exact recipe for her gumbo. She was more of a "little of this, little of that, until it looks right" kind of kitchen wizard. For her own family, Cheyenne tries to emulate her grandmother's spirit, but (luckily for us) she has developed an honest-to-Pete, written-down recipe, to which I have added a few notes.

Serves 12–14

1 whole chicken
About 4 cups water (enough to cover the chicken)
1 cup vegetable oil or bacon drippings
1 cup all-purpose flour
1½ cups diced celery
1½ cups diced scallions
1 (16-ounce) package smoked sausage, sliced into ¼-inch rounds
1 (2-pound) bag frozen, de-tailed and deveined shrimp, thawed
1 teaspoon gumbo filé powder, or more to taste
Salt and freshly ground black pepper
Tabasco (optional)
Tony Chachere's Creole Seasoning (optional)
Cooked rice

1. Cook the chicken: In a large soup pot, simmer the whole chicken in water to cover, until it is completely done and the meat falls from the bones. Remove the chicken but save the broth, straining out and discarding any solids. When the chicken is cool enough to handle, remove and discard the skin and bones, and shred the meat into small bits.

Note: A slow cooker is handy for this step, and allows you to do part of the soup in advance. Cheyenne uses plain water; you might want to pump up the flavor by adding a few whole peppercorns, dried chiles, or bay leaves.

Make ahead? You can cook the chicken and make the roux as much as one day in advance, and that will save you lots of time. Refrigerate separately.

For large crowds: Note that this recipe makes 12 to 14 servings. That's because you start with one whole chicken, and that determines the total volume of the finished dish. If you need more than that, double everything.

2. Make the roux: Heat the oil or bacon drippings (or a combination) in a large skillet over medium heat. Stir in the flour a little at a time. Cook the roux until it's chocolate brown — don't stop stirring! This can take anywhere from 30 minutes to an hour. If you smell it starting to burn, turn the heat down and prepare to stir for a longer period of time. If you see black flecks, your roux is burned and you will need to start over.

Note: Cheyenne says, "Getting the perfect roux can take some practice." Indeed it can, but you won't have authentic Cajun flavor without it. It's a skill you'll be glad you mastered, since roux in various stages of brown-ness (from blond to walnut) can be used to thicken and flavor many other dishes. See The Truth about Roux on page 112.

3. Assemble the gumbo: When the roux is done, fold in the celery and scallions. Add the roux mixture, reserved broth and chicken, sausage, shrimp, and filé powder to a large soup pot, with salt and pepper to taste. Cook over medium heat until the vegetables are tender, 8 to 10 minutes. Gumbo is supposed to be thick, but if it seems too thick, add more chicken broth. For spicy gumbo, add Tabasco and Tony Chachere's Creole Seasoning to taste. Serve over rice.

Note: Filé powder is a traditional thickener and flavor addition for gumbo; it's available in the spice section of most large supermarkets. Tony Chachere products, made in Louisiana, are available in supermarkets in the Southeastern United States and online.

Gumbo's Grannie

Every year on Christmas Eve, for as long as I can remember, my Grannie Foster made a huge pot of this fabulous gumbo for the whole family. Everybody came — aunts, uncles, all the cousins, my parents, my brother, and me. I can't imagine Christmas without it. She passed away in 2010, and that Christmas Eve, the first one without her, my aunts made the gumbo dinner for all the Louisiana relatives. We were not able to make the trip from Illinois that year, so I made the gumbo for us to enjoy here at home. I want our children to know that the tradition continues.

My grandfather was a pastor in Louisiana, which means that my grandmother was sort of an unofficial assistant pastor, doing whatever was needed to keep the church humming. At her memorial service we were asked to think of one word to describe her. The word I thought of was "gracious." She was always the epitome of graciousness, to every person who crossed her path. I like to think that she would love our neighborhood Soup Night, and would be happy to know that I shared her gumbo with our wonderful neighbors.

— Cheyenne Johnson, Aurora, Illinois

THE TRUTH ABOUT ROUX

Cheyenne Johnson's recipe for her Grannie's Gumbo (page 110) depends on a good, rich roux. So does many a Cajun dish. So, in fact, do many fine and wonderful dishes from other cuisines. It takes practice, but it is a skill well worth mastering. And, truth to tell, you really can't do gumbo without it. Or béchamel sauce. Or even a good turkey gravy.

How important is it? I once had a Mardi Gras party at my home in Oregon. Not having Cheyenne's Louisiana heritage to call on, I had no idea how to make Cajun food, so I went to the library for cookbooks. And I found one entitled *Who's Your Mama, Are You Catholic, and Can You Make a Roux?*

That's how important a good roux is in that part of the world.

But I'll tell you a secret: It's really not all that difficult. It just requires that you pay scrupulous attention.

A roux (pronounced roo) is a mixture of equal parts fat and flour, cooked until it is richly colored and fragrant. It serves as a thickener, but it is so much more. After long, slow cooking, it develops a rich, complex, smoky flavor that cannot be described in words and for which there is no substitute.

The fat can be butter, vegetable oil, bacon drippings, or a combination; traditional Cajun cooks often use rendered chicken fat. For dark Cajun roux, vegetable oil works best. Butter is not recommended for that, because the milk solids will tend to burn at high heat. Olive oil is similarly tricky, because it doesn't do well at high heat and you need reasonably high heat to make a dark roux — for reasons that will soon become clear.

This is the process:
Clear your schedule. You will be tending a Cajun roux for a half hour or more, and you don't want to be interrupted. Don't answer the phone, don't try any kind of multitasking, and don't even start if you have to go pick up anyone from anywhere anytime soon.

Melt the fat in a large skillet — cast iron, if you have one — over medium-high heat. Gradually stir in the flour, blending well.

Keep on stirring. I mean it — don't stop stirring. A good tool is a wooden spatula with a squared-off bottom that allows you to reach the very edge of the pan (which whisks, being round, do not).

Gradually the roux will become darker in color, going from blond to something resembling peanut butter, then to chocolate brown, all the way to dark walnut. Which stage you want depends on what you're using it for; see below.

If it starts to smell burned, it is. If black bits show up, it has burned. Toss it. Not kidding — throw it out. Start over.

Remove the pan from the heat when the roux is ever so slightly paler in color than you want, because it will continue to cook for a few minutes after you take it off the heat, especially if you are using cast iron like I told you to.

You can do this ahead. Store the finished roux in the refrigerator. When it cools, some of the oil will rise to the top. When you're ready to use, just stir it back in, or reheat quickly and stir a bit.

When is it ready?

The reason I want you to master this mystery of the roux is that it's used in so many dishes. And how long you cook it varies according to what you are cooking.

For sauces, 3 to 4 minutes is usually sufficient. You want the flour to cook enough to eliminate the raw taste, and fully incorporate with the oil or butter. This is a good time to use your butter; the risk of burning is lower, and its incomparable flavor works well with sauces. Then you'll add the liquid and other flavorings that make your sauce what it is and continue to cook/stir until you reach the consistency you want.

For gravies, cook the roux for 8 to 10 minutes. First, scrape from the bottom of the pan any bits left from what you were cooking: fried chicken, sausage, roast turkey, sautéed pork, whatever. Sprinkle the flour onto those little crumbs, stir them together for a few seconds, and then gradually add in the oil. Blend the oil and the flour thoroughly; if you've ever had lumpy gravy, *here* is where the damage occurred, and it's practically impossible to rectify once the liquid goes in. Cook the roux, stirring continually, until you get a rich aroma and taste, and then add your liquid gradually, stirring some more, until it's as thick as you like. Constant stirring is what makes a gravy creamy.

For Cajun or Creole dishes, you want really brown. Follow the process for making roux for gravy, but continue to cook for 30 minutes or more. And that's why you want relatively high heat, because to reach that color on low heat would take you so long you'd develop arm cramps, or you'd be tempted to crank the heat up to super-high and ruin the darned thing.

Winter Root Soup

Virginia Tackett, of Hillsboro, Oregon, called on her Iowa farm childhood to create this wonderfully rich soup, chock-full of good veggies. It can be prepared either in a slow cooker or in a large soup pot on the stove. Any or all of the optional ingredients make flavorful additions.

Serves 8

1   medium onion
1   pound carrots
1   large yam (or 2 medium)
1   large baking potato (or 2 medium)
1   large rutabaga
2   medium turnips
2   medium parsnips
3–4 cups water or broth
2   garlic cloves, minced
1–2 pounds smoked sausage (your favorite kind), cut into bite-size pieces.
1½ teaspoons kosher salt
½   teaspoon freshly ground black pepper
1   teaspoon whole mixed peppercorns
6–8 whole allspice, tied into a cheesecloth bag
3   tablespoons dried parsley, or ½ cup fresh, chopped
½   cup fresh cilantro, roughly chopped, for garnish

Optional Additions

½   teaspoon seasoned pepper
2   jalapeños, seeds and membranes removed, diced (see page 186)
2   celery stalks, sliced
1   sweet pepper, seeded and chopped (green, red, or yellow, or any combination)
2   cups chopped tomatoes
1   small jar sun-dried tomatoes

1. Prepare the onion, carrots, yam, potato, rutabaga, turnips, and parsnips: wash, peel as you wish, and cut into bite-size pieces. Place them in a large soup pot (or slow cooker), and add enough water or broth to cover all the vegetables. Add the garlic, sausage, salt, pepper, peppercorns, allspice, and parsley.

2. If using a soup pot, bring the soup to a boil and then simmer until the vegetables are tender. If using a slow cooker, cook on low for 8 hours.

3. Serve hot, sprinkled with cilantro.

Note: If you have the time for an extra step, roast the vegetables before adding them to the soup pot; see page 39 for instructions.

Variations: Virginia says this is very good just as is, but you can replace the sausage with any other kind of meat you like.

Make ahead? Sure. You might want to remove the pot from the heat a little early, so that rewarming doesn't overcook the vegetables.

For large crowds: If your pot is large enough, feel free to double everything.

For vegetarians: Use water or vegetable broth, omit the sausage, and add 2 pounds sliced cremini mushrooms.

Yellow Split-Pea Soup

I really love split-pea soup, but I've always felt that the traditional green peas produced a rather unappealing color when cooked. So when I discovered yellow split peas, I made a permanent switch. Like all foods in the yellow/orange/red range, they keep their color through long cooking. I often add other vegetables — carrots or sweet potatoes or both — and that produces an even richer color, not to mention extra nutrients.

Serves 6–8

2 tablespoons olive oil

1 medium onion, finely diced

3–4 carrots, scrubbed and thinly sliced

1 large sweet potato, peeled and cubed (optional)

2 cups yellow split peas

2 bay leaves

About 2 quarts water or broth

Black pepper

½ cup ham or smoked sausage, diced (optional; see note)

1. Heat the oil in a large soup pot, and lightly sauté the onion, carrots, and sweet potato; try not to let them brown. Add the split peas, bay leaves, and enough cooking liquid to cover well. You can use plain water, chicken broth, vegetable broth, or ham broth. Simmer the soup until the peas are thoroughly cooked, 1½ to 2 hours. (This is a great use for your slow cooker.) Check from time to time that all the liquid hasn't cooked away.

2. When the vegetables are thoroughly cooked, discard the bay leaves. Transfer the soup to a blender (in batches, if need be) and purée until very smooth, then return it to the pot. Or use an immersion blender and purée the soup right in the pot. This step is optional and purely subjective, but I think you will like the creamy texture.

3. Add pepper to taste, plus any meat you are using, and simmer until heated through. Serve hot.

Note: Whenever I have a ham for an occasion such as Easter dinner, I save the bone and simmer it for broth. Let it cool, remove the congealed fat, and snip off the bits of meat. Freeze the meat and the broth separately.

Variation: This soup is delicious as is, but if you want to add another layer of flavor, you can turn it into curry soup; see below for possibilities. If you go the simple route of adding commercial curry powder, start with 1 teaspoon, adding more to taste.

Make ahead? Sure. The soup solidifies when cold, which is startling if you've never seen it before, but returns to liquid when reheated.

For large crowds: This is one of the very best choices for making large quantities, since the ingredients are both highly nutritious and very inexpensive.

THE WORLD OF CURRY

You have several options for adding curry flavor to soup. There's commercial curry powder, of course, or you can make up your own blend. Check ethnic cookbooks or the Internet for recipes for garam masala. If there are Asian markets where you live, pick up a small jar of curry paste and add a dab to your soup. In most large supermarkets, you will find a variety of curry blends and pastes, any of which will add flavor to your soup.

I cheat: I pour in a few glugs of a bottled curry sauce that I found on sale. I won't bother you with the brand because I think it's been discontinued, but in most supermarkets you can find a selection of bottled sauces generically known as finishing or dipping sauces, and any of them with a curry flavor will do the same thing.

Big Soup,
Stephen and Melissa Neely
PITTSBURGH, PENNSYLVANIA

A fabulous once-a-year party, Big Soup was 20 years old in 2012. It has become a well-known event in the Pittsburgh area. The invitations say: "Bring a bowl. Bring a spoon. Bring a friend." People invite people they know, and those people invite others, and that's how it happens that nowadays 250 people show up at the Neelys' house for soup on the first Saturday in December.

Melissa tells how they got started. "The first year we were married, we were both 23, living in this tiny apartment, and we said to ourselves, 'Okay, we're adults now, let's have people over.' But we were poor, so it had to be something inexpensive, and we decided we needed a theme. So we said, 'We can make really good soup, and we'll have really *big* soup.' And that's how Big Soup got started.

"Later we moved to a larger house (bottom of a duplex) and by the tenth year we had 150 people come. Then three years ago we bought the house next door to the duplex, bigger still, and last year [2011] we had 250 people.

"Stephen is a music teacher and teaches at several schools around town, so he has a wide circle of contacts. We always invite people whenever we meet

them. And people just seem to hear about it. We use multiple ways to spread the word: printed invitations, which we mail and also hand out; e-mailed invitations from the guest book people sign the first year they come; and last year we used Facebook for the first time.

"A few years ago, we decided to turn it into a charity event: We have so much, let's share. It was a way to take the event away from a focus on just ourselves and give us all the opportunity to do something tangible about hunger. We put a bucket in the middle of the table and invited people to contribute. The money goes to our local food bank. In 2011 we donated $3,000. Also, in 2011 I invited a local company to sponsor our event. Pittsburgh Seltzer Works donated money and beverages.

"We have three boys, ages 8, 12, and 15. We want them to see what one family can do. I take them to the Food Bank to help out, so they can see how it works and where the money goes.

"We give out lots of little prizes: for the most unique bowl (we've had people bring a cat dish, a fireman's hat, a toy truck), the largest spoon, the farthest distance traveled. One year we had T-shirts

made. All those little things bring people together and start conversations.

"We set up a station at the door, with a guest book (that's how people get on the e-mail list) and name tags. The instructions are to put your name and how many soup parties you've been to. That one thing is a great conversation starter. People say, 'Oh, this is your first? Well, let me tell you about . . .' Or, 'Wow, you've been coming 15 years.' The guest book also lets us keep count of how many people come. I also try to take a photo of every person, so we can count how many kids, how many adults. The house is full, but people come at all different times. Also we have a big outdoor space with outdoor fire, and some people always go outside.

"We do all the cooking prep the Friday before. We have five soups, all vegetarian. Labels for each one are clipped to the soup pots with clothespins. We make super-large amounts, so over the years we've been collecting huge stockpots. For a while we used our canning kettle. A couple years ago we realized we needed a new pot, so we went to a restaurant supply store, and when we said what we were doing they donated the pot. Also two of Stephen's students come and help out as volunteers — clean up, gather garbage, etc.

"One soup we always have is Potato-Cheese Soup. It's a family recipe, and children especially like it. Then we always have one that's spicy, one ethnic, and one dessert soup. People bring things to contribute to the meal. We set up a large table for those extras: salads, breads, appetizers, and put the desserts on a separate table. Our invitations ask people to bring their own bowls, but people kept leaving them behind, so we had to put up a sign at the door: *Do you have your bowl and spoon?*"

At the Big Soup website you can see a summary of all the soups served each year since the beginning.

www.bigsoup.org

FOR A RECIPE FROM BIG SOUP, SEE:
Neelys' Potato-Cheese Soup, page 120

Neelys' Potato-Cheese Soup

Recipe from Stephen and Melissa Neely, Big Soup, Pittsburgh, Pennsylvania
(profile, page 118)

Stephen and Melissa say: We serve this every single year at Big Soup. No matter what other soups we serve, we *always* have this one, mostly because we know the kids will eat it.

Serves 6–8

8 russet potatoes, peeled and cut into small chunks

2 cups diced celery

2 cups diced onion

2 cups diced carrots

8 cups vegetable broth

½ teaspoon dried marjoram

1 teaspoon seasoned salt

8 ounces cheddar cheese, shredded (2 cups), or reserve some to add as a garnish

Freshly ground black pepper

1. Combine the potatoes, celery, onion, and carrots in a large soup pot. Pour in the broth, add the marjoram and seasoned salt, and simmer until the vegetables are very soft.

2. Purée the soup until smooth with an immersion blender.

3. Add the cheese and pepper to taste. Serve hot, with bowls of extra shredded cheese on the table for an optional garnish.

Make ahead? Yes, through step 2.

For large crowds: Double or triple or even quadruple as needed. The Neelys' recipe card shows the amounts of ingredients needed for a 9-times increase — I don't even know the word for that!

Lentil Soup Times Four

For such little bitty things, lentils pack a big punch. They are high in both protein and fiber. They contain several important minerals, particularly potassium and magnesium, which counteract sodium and thus help control blood pressure. They are extremely affordable. They cook quickly, when compared to that other common legume, dried beans. And they're cute. Of course none of that would amount to a hill of beans if they weren't also delicious. These four soup recipes will give you a good taste of the versatility of lentils.

The most familiar and most widely available are brown lentils (sometimes sold as green lentils), with a mild flavor and pleasant texture. But there are other types to explore. French lentils are smaller than the browns, and olive green in color. They retain their texture better than others, so if you're making a lentil salad, for example, this would be a good choice. Red lentils are actually red-orange in color, but turn a pale yellow when cooked. (I'm always disappointed.) They are also smaller than browns, and cook more quickly; they'll turn to mush if you're not paying attention. Of course turning to mush can be a good thing — with just a little stirring you have a soup with a wonderfully creamy texture.

One caution: whenever you cook with lentils, pick them over for tiny stones and other inedibles. The easiest way to do this is to spread a layer in something flat, like a pie tin, and check through with your fingertips. When everything is clean, dump that batch into a sieve. Then another layer into the pie tin, and so on. When you're done, rinse everything and drain.

Lentil Soup with Bacon and Orzo

There's hardly any trouble in life that isn't made better with bacon, and it sure adds a wonderful flavor to this soup. Orzo, a pasta in the shape of rice, handles long slow cooking beautifully and doesn't turn to mush like rice can.

Serves 6–8

⅔ cup olive oil

5 medium onions, chopped

8 garlic cloves, minced

½ pound bacon, chopped

3 celery stalks, chopped

5–6 carrots, peeled and chopped

3 parsnips, peeled and chopped

12 ounces red lentils, rinsed and picked over

8 cups vegetable broth

½ cup tomato paste

½ cup uncooked orzo

8 cups water

6 scallions, white and light green parts, thinly sliced

½ cup chopped parsley

1 tablespoon grated lemon zest
Parmesan cheese, for garnish

1. Heat the oil in a large soup pot. Add the onions, garlic, and bacon, and sauté over medium heat until the bacon is cooked and the onions are well browned, 6 to 8 minutes.

2. Stir in the celery, carrots, and parsnips. Cover, and cook until the vegetables are soft, about 5 minutes.

3. Add the lentils, broth, tomato paste, orzo, and water. Bring to a boil, and then reduce the heat and simmer, uncovered, until the lentils and orzo are tender, about 30 minutes.

4. Just before serving, stir in the scallions, parsley, and zest. Top each serving with grated Parmesan.

Make ahead? Yes, but stop the cooking just before the lentils and orzo are thoroughly cooked. Rewarm long enough to finish cooking. Don't add the scallions, parsley, or zest until serving time.

For large crowds: This is an ideal soup to double or triple.

For vegetarians: Skip the bacon.

A Lentil Soup Story

Sydney Stevens is an accomplished author, historian, and charismatic community leader. The community I'm speaking of is the tiny village of Oysterville at the tip of Washington State's Long Beach Peninsula. Today a national historic site, the town was founded by her great-grandfather, R. H. Espy, in 1854, when the waters of adjacent Willapa Bay were rich with native oysters. Sydney and her handsome-devil husband Nyel live in the Espy family home, and Sydney is at work on a biography of her late uncle Willard Espy, a nationally known author who loved to write about words. Sydney is a natural storyteller, and so it is no surprise that any recipe she shares comes with a great story.

"This recipe evolved from my friendship with two remarkable women. The first was Frances Sommer, wife of master photographer Frederick Sommer. Each time I went to visit her in Prescott, Arizona, I always brought a supply of liniguiça from a little butcher shop in Oakland, and sometime during my visit she would make a heavenly lentil soup. (I should note here that Frances's soup included neither oregano nor any kind of tomatoes — not diced, not sauce, nothing.)

"The second woman is Corina Santestevan, my teaching colleague. When I invited her to dinner, and mentioned we were having lentil soup, her face lit up. 'It's one of the meals I miss from home,' she said. 'Home' for Corina was Taos, where her family has lived for more than 300 years. At dinner I could tell Corina was disappointed, even though she is far too polite to complain. At my urging, she finally admitted that her family's lentil soup had a tomato base. From then on, I've always added diced tomatoes or sometimes tomato sauce, and a little oregano. Once in a while I cut down the amount of water or adjust the ratio of water to tomato sauce. Or double the amount of linguiça. But always, without fail, I think of Frances and Corina."

Southwestern Lentil Soup

Recipe from Sydney Stevens, Oysterville, Washington

Serves 8–10

2	tablespoons olive oil
2	medium yellow onions, or 1 envelope onion soup mix
1½	cups chopped celery
3	garlic cloves, minced
1	pound brown lentils, rinsed and picked over
2	quarts water
1	(28-ounce) can diced tomatoes
1	bay leaf
1	teaspoon dried oregano
¼	teaspoon freshly ground black pepper
12	ounces linguiça, sliced
⅓	cup sherry (optional)
2–3	lemons, thinly sliced

1. Heat the oil in a large soup pot and sauté the onions over medium heat until softened, about 4 minutes. Add the celery and garlic and sauté 2 minutes longer. Add the lentils, water, tomatoes, bay leaf, oregano, and pepper. Heat to boiling and simmer the soup for 1 hour.

2. Meanwhile, sauté the linguiça in a heavy skillet, pouring off as much grease as possible but being careful not to let the linguiça get rubbery.

3. Add the linguiça and sherry, if using, to the soup and heat through.

4. Just before serving the soup, add the lemon slices. Serve hot.

Variations: Sydney always uses linguiça sausage because "after living so many years among the Portuguese in California's Castro Valley and Hayward, I adore it." But other highly flavored cooked sausages (andouille, for example) would also work.

Make ahead? Absolutely. I'd hold off on the sherry until serving time, though.

For large crowds: Easily expanded.

Red Lentil Soup

My friend Diane Mermigas, a journalist who is also a great cook, has a unique way with lentil soup. "In a moment of inspiration, I once combined this red lentil soup with some leftover ratatouille I had made the day before. The result was an absolutely delicious concoction that's good hot or cold."

Serves 6

1½	tablespoons olive oil
1	large onion, chopped
3	garlic cloves, minced
2	carrots, chopped (about 1 cup)
½	cup chopped tomatoes, fresh or canned
1	celery stalk, chopped
1¼	teaspoons ground cumin
½	teaspoon salt
1	cup dried red lentils, rinsed and picked over
4	cups water
1½	cups chicken broth
2	tablespoons chopped fresh flat-leaf parsley

1. Heat the oil in a 4- to 5-quart soup pot over moderate heat, and sauté the onion until golden. Add the garlic, carrots, tomatoes, celery, cumin, and salt, and sauté 1 minute longer.

2. Add the lentils, water, and broth, and simmer, uncovered, stirring occasionally, until the lentils are tender, about 20 minutes.

3. Stir in the parsley, and season with salt and pepper. Serve hot.

Make ahead? You'd be a fool not to.

For large crowds: This is a snap to multiply.

For vegetarians? Sure. Just use vegetable broth in place of chicken.

Mulligatawny with Apple Salsa

Recipe from Renee Giroux, Stanton Street, Portland, Oregon

Renee says: The contrast of the fresh apples, crisp and tangy, with the spicy-warm lentil soup is very refreshing.

Mulligatawny — isn't that fun to say — literally means "pepper water." A spicy soup of India, it was popular with British soldiers posted there during colonial times. The turmeric brings a golden color, and the coconut milk lends that essential Asian flavor. The apple salsa makes this soup sing.

Serves 6–8

7   cups chicken broth

2   cups brown lentils, rinsed and picked over

2   medium onions, finely chopped

2   (12-ounce) cans light coconut milk

6   tablespoons tomato paste

2   teaspoons grated fresh ginger

1   teaspoon ground cumin

¼   teaspoon turmeric

2   teaspoons fresh lime juice

1   teaspoon salt

½   teaspoon freshly ground black pepper

Apple Salsa

2   tart apples, such as Granny Smith, unpeeled, cored, and finely chopped

2   celery stalks, finely chopped

2   tablespoons chopped fresh cilantro

2   tablespoons fresh lime juice

1. Combine the broth, lentils, and onions in a large soup pot and bring to a boil. Cover, reduce the heat, and simmer until the lentils are tender, about 15 minutes.

2. Add the coconut milk, tomato paste, ginger, cumin, and turmeric. Re-cover and simmer the soup 10 minutes longer.

3. Make the apple salsa: Combine all ingredients in a bowl or container and mix well, making sure all the apple pieces get limed. Cover and stash the salsa in the refrigerator until party time.

4. Turn off the heat under the soup, and add the lime juice, salt, and pepper. Top each serving with about 1 tablespoon of the salsa.

Make ahead? The salsa, for sure. The soup up to step 2, but this soup goes together so quickly you may not need to.

For large crowds: It's easy to increase, but add extra cumin a bit at a time, and taste as you go.

Soup Kitchen, Open Source Gallery

BROOKLYN, NEW YORK

For many of us, the phrase "soup kitchen" calls to mind a certain image. Whether that picture is or is not positive depends entirely on your worldview, but I'm pretty sure your mental picture looks much like mine. Unless, that is, one of us is talking about the soup kitchen at Open Source Gallery, because that one is a whole different ballgame.

The gallery is run by **Monika Wuhrer** and her husband **Michael**, both artists. It's a small space (Monika says it's "essentially a garage") in the Park Slope neighborhood of Brooklyn. They conceived the gallery as a year-round community space that would solidify their sense of being invested in the neighborhood; Monika calls it "a social art project."

Their Soup Kitchen is unique among the groups in this book. Every night in the month of December, someone volunteers to bring soup for the evening and feed whoever shows up. Monika puts out a sign-up sheet at the gallery in November, and it fills up fast. The volunteer cooks are completely responsible for their night: bring the meal, set up, help clean up.

What makes the experience unique is the entertainment aspect. Volunteers are invited to create some type of entertainment on their night and can do anything they wish: hang an art exhibit, do a poetry reading, play music, do a dance performance, anything at all. It has led to some amazing evenings.

For instance: A writer read a story, written just for the occasion, about a murder in a soup kitchen. A group of Irish cooks stuck potatoes on the wall and hung Christmas tinsel from them. An artist used pillows to create ceiling clouds and filled the walls with winter-themed ink drawings.

"One night a young man came with a pot of chicken soup and 44 paintings," Monika says. "They were portraits of the 44 presidents, all in different painting styles — cubism, expressionism, impressionism — and he hung them all in just a few minutes. He claims he had never cooked before and just called his mom for the recipe.

"Another time a young teacher for autistic kids brought all the mobiles from his classroom and hung them here for the night. Using the mobiles, he told us great stories about the kids' behaviors and his teaching methods. We had just seven people that night. One of them was a man who is homeless and very interested in art and culture. He brought his parents and friends of his parents from Germany."

The December soup suppers draw anywhere from 5 to 70 people; 20 is typical. Flyers in the neighborhood help spread the word, and special invitations are placed in nearby homeless shelters. When guests arrive at the gallery, they find two long tables set with china plates and bowls. It's a deliberate choice. The china enhances the feeling of a real sit-down dinner; the long tables mean that people sit with others they don't yet know and conversations naturally follow.

"We try to make it so people want to stay and talk with each other," Monika explains. "What we wanted to do is bring together people from many different levels and different lifestyles. I believe that people are intensely interested in other people, and we wanted a way to encourage connections."

www.opensourcegallery.org

Mussel Chowder

The Shelburne Inn, on the Long Beach Peninsula in Washington State, is more than 100 years old. Originally built in 1896, it has since been expanded, updated, and once even relocated across the street, pulled by a team of horses. It's warm, charming, and filled with beautiful antiques and stained-glass windows. David Campiche, the owner, is the quintessential innkeeper; Hollywood casting agents could not find anyone who looks the part better than David does. He's gracious, welcoming, and very funny. He's also a heck of a cook, as the following story makes clear.

Back in 1981, after some major remodeling, the inn was set to open its new fine-dining restaurant. Then, on opening night, disaster: the chef became so ill he could barely stand. David, who at the time lived at the inn with his family, jumped in to offer help. Fine, said the chef, pointing to a large bag of fresh mussels, do something with those. On the spot, David created this chowder. To his surprise, it was a hit, and has been on the menu ever since.

Serves 6

5	pounds mussels in shells
1	cup dry white wine
3	tablespoons butter
1	onion, chopped
1	celery stalk, cut into ¼-inch dice
½	sweet bell pepper, yellow or red, seeded and diced
2	teaspoons mild curry powder
1½	teaspoons dried basil
¼	teaspoon cayenne pepper
1	(28-ounce) can tomato sauce
2	cups whipping cream
1	pound thin-skinned potatoes, such as red, Yukon Gold, or Yellow Finn, peeled and cut into ½-inch cubes
	Salt and pepper

Make ahead? Not really.

For large crowds: This is probably a better choice for a small dinner party. Large amounts of fresh shellfish can get expensive.

1. Scrub the mussels in cool water and remove the byssus threads (the "beards"). Discard mussels whose shells don't close when tapped.

2. In an 8- to 10-quart soup pot, combine the mussels and the wine; bring to a boil over high heat. Cover and simmer over medium heat until the mussels open, 5 to 8 minutes. Pour the mussels and cooking liquid into a colander set in a large bowl to collect the broth. Let the mussels stand until cool enough to handle.

3. In the pot used for the mussels, melt the butter over medium heat. Add the onion, celery, and bell pepper, and sauté until the onion is limp, 6 to 8 minutes, stirring often. Stir in the curry powder, basil, and cayenne; cook until the spices become more fragrant, about 30 seconds.

4. Pour the mussel juices from the bowl into the soup pot. Add the tomato sauce, cream, and potatoes. Bring to a boil, then cover the pot, and reduce the heat to low. Simmer, stirring occasionally, until the flavors are well blended, about 30 minutes.

5. Meanwhile, remove the mussels from their shells, discarding the shells.

6. Add the mussels to the chowder; cover and simmer just until the mussels are hot, 3 to 5 minutes; do not overcook. Season with salt and pepper to taste and serve hot.

Bread and Soup,
Kathryn and Eric Meyer
CLEVELAND, OHIO

Once a year, usually on President's Day weekend, **Eric Meyer** and his wife **Kathryn** (known as Kat) host a humongous Bread and Soup party. It's famous; people come from far and wide — well, from several states — and have been doing so since 2001. With well-coordinated help, the Meyers make, from scratch, five soups and five breads, enough to serve the 100 or so people who come (the record was 150).

Eric explains: "In 2001, we had just moved into the neighborhood, and said, 'Okay, we're new on the block, let's throw a party and meet our neighbors.' Got the idea from my parents, who used to have a party every February just because you need a party in February. Not all the neighbors came, but those who did said, 'This is great; please do it again.' And so we did."

"It started as just a holiday party," Kat adds. "Then it took on a life of its own. Now we invite everybody — work colleagues, neighbors, and friends — and they bring their friends. For several weeks before the party we carry invitations around with us everywhere we go, and when we find someone interesting we give them an invitation. Sometimes they're surprised, but usually they say, 'Oh my goodness, thank you so much!'"

I first "met" the Meyers through an article Eric wrote for the family blog, and I'm so pleased he allowed me to share it with you. Here are some excerpts.

"We invite just about everyone we know, regardless of how close or far away they live. In fact, we put an invitation in the mailbox of every house on our block, so in many cases we're inviting people we *don't* know.

"Children are welcome. They were even before we had our own, but this is key if you want to draw families. Which we do.

"We use heavy paper plates and Styrofoam cups with plastic spoons for the soups. This makes cleanup a whole lot easier, plus it means we don't have to buy place settings for 128 or worry about dropped bowls shattering."

But I bet you're still wondering, how do they handle all those people? With a very efficient system, fine-tuned over the years. Kat and Eric decide on the five soups and five breads. The soups change every year, except for the Sweet Curry Soup (page 138); if it were missing, Eric says, they would have a riot on their hands. By Friday they have purchased all the ingredients, Friday night and Saturday morning they make multiple trips to the airport to pick up incoming guests, and Saturday

night there's a pizza party for the out-of-towners. Then Sunday morning, preparations click into high gear.

Kat picks up the story: "Between 8 and 10 AM, we measure out all the ingredients for each bread and each soup and put all the soup ingredients together in five soup pots. Then we have eight to ten people who work together on one soup, from start to finish. People figure out what they like to do, and just jump in to do it. One friend always makes the Sweet Curry Soup, and another is in charge of keeping everyone supplied with coffee. Our oldest daughter likes chopping, so she chops for everybody. Meanwhile, several of us work on the breads. The party starts at 4 PM, and an hour before that I have my annual breakdown — 'Nobody loves us, no one will come.' Ha. We had 115 people this year!"

The invitation says, "Don't bring anything," but people do anyway. Eric says, only half kidding, that next year he's going to put all those things on a special table and invite people to take them home with them: "'You think that looks like a nice bottle of wine? Take it, my friend. Take it.'"

The soup is kept simmering on the stove in large soup pots, and people serve themselves. The Meyers put out plates of fruit and cheese, and small dishes for bread with butter and homemade jams. Somehow it always works out, they say; "If we run out, so be it. But that hasn't happened yet."

"Our circle has changed over the years," Kat notes, "and now more families have children. This year we had a big turnout with the second-grade set. There were lots of little kids running around, and five little girls put on costumes five different times. Gradually people start leaving, and we start putting away the leftovers, if there are any. One guy is our cleanup god, bless him. By 11:30, we're sitting around the dining room table, feeling happy."

FOR RECIPES FROM THE MEYERS, SEE:

Chicken and Artichoke Soup

Recipe from Eric and Kat Meyer, Cleveland, Ohio (profile, page 132)

Eric and Kat say: This is our version of a wonderful shrimp soup we learned years ago in a New Orleans cooking school. We used chicken instead of shrimp and added the sherry. In Louisiana there's a great seasoning called Joe's Stuff, but Old Bay products are also terrific and much easier to find.

Serves 6–8

4 cups chicken broth

3 (8-ounce) packages frozen artichokes, thawed and quartered

1 cup chopped scallions, plus more for garnish

1 teaspoon dried thyme, or 1 tablespoon fresh thyme, minced

Old Bay seasoning

4 tablespoons butter

¼ cup all-purpose flour

1 pound skinless boneless chicken thighs, cut into bite-size pieces

4 cups heavy cream

Cream sherry

Salt and freshly ground black pepper

Chopped fresh flat-leaf parsley, for garnish

1. Combine the broth, artichokes, scallions, thyme, and Old Bay to taste in a large soup pot. Bring to a boil. Reduce the heat, and simmer for 10 to 12 minutes.

2. Melt the butter in a small saucepan and whisk in the flour, stirring constantly over low heat for 1 to 2 minutes to make a light roux (see page 112), then add the roux to the soup pot gradually, stirring as you go. Add the chicken and simmer for 5 to 7 minutes, until cooked through.

3. Add the cream, stir, and simmer for 10 minutes longer.

4. Reduce the heat, add sherry to taste, and season with salt and pepper to taste.

5. Garnish with the parsley and additional scallions. Serve hot.

Variations: Also wonderful made with shrimp rather than chicken.

Make ahead? Through step 2. Refrigerate.

For large crowds: Since the Meyers typically serve 100 people or more, I think it's safe to say this soup is easy to expand.

Vegetarian: Omit the chicken, and use water or vegetable broth.

Potato-Wild Rice Soup

Recipe from Elizabeth Newland, Civano Soup Supper, Tucson, Arizona (profile, page 46)

Elizabeth says: I'm lucky enough to live in two beautiful places: part of the time in Civano, part of the time in Washington State, near Seattle. Our Northwest winters are long, dark, cold, and wet. This soup is pure comfort food to warm up those nights.

Serves 6

½   cup uncooked wild rice
½   pound bacon, diced
1   pound mushrooms, sliced
4   cups peeled and diced potatoes
1½ cups chicken broth
1   medium onion, chopped
10 ounces cheddar cheese, shredded (2½ cups)
2   cups light cream, more if needed for best consistency
½   cup white wine or chicken broth
    Salt and freshly ground black pepper
½   cup chopped fresh flat-leaf parsley

Make ahead? Elizabeth often does, adding a little more light cream when reheating the soup until it is the desired consistency. If you need to divide the work between two days, do steps 1 and 2 on the first day.

For large crowds: This is just about ideal for making double or triple quantities.

For vegetarians: Skip the bacon, and use vegetable broth.

1. Bring a large pot of salted water to a boil, add the rice, and simmer for 45 minutes. Drain and set aside.

2. Heat a skillet over medium heat, add the bacon, and fry until crisp; remove and drain on paper towels. Sauté the mushrooms in the bacon fat in the same skillet. Remove with a slotted spoon and set aside.

3. Combine the potatoes, chicken broth, and onion in a large soup pot. Bring to a boil, and then reduce the heat and simmer for 30 minutes. Transfer the potato mixture to a blender (careful, it's hot) and purée until smooth.

4. Return the potato purée to the soup pot, and add the reserved rice, bacon, mushrooms, cheese, cream, and wine. Heat the soup gently until heated through. Adjust the consistency, if needed, by adding a little more light cream. Season with salt and pepper to taste.

5. Sprinkle parsley over the top of the soup just before serving.

Ham and Red Bean Soup

The sweetness from the pineapple and cinnamon takes this familiar favorite to a new level. Serve with a warm pan of the Carolina Cornbread on page 171.

Serves 6

1 tablespoon olive oil

1 medium onion, finely chopped

1 garlic clove, minced

½ cup chopped green pepper

2 (16-ounce) cans red kidney beans, drained; or 3–4 cups cooked kidney beans (see page 27)

1 (16-ounce) can diced tomatoes

½ cup diced cooked ham

1 bay leaf

¼ teaspoon ground cinnamon

¼ teaspoon ground cumin

¼ teaspoon dried oregano

1 (8-ounce) can crushed pineapple

1. Heat the olive oil in a large soup pot over medium-high heat. Add the onion and sauté until softened, about 4 minutes. Add the garlic and green pepper, and sauté 1 to 2 minutes longer.

2. Add the beans, tomatoes, ham, bay leaf, cinnamon, cumin, and oregano. Reduce the heat under the pot, cover, and simmer 30 minutes. Remove the bay leaf.

3. Stir in the pineapple and its juice, and heat through. Serve hot.

Make ahead? Through step 2.

For large crowds: Easy to expand.

For vegetarians: Just leave out the ham.

Sweet Curry Soup

Recipe from Eric and Kat Meyer, Cleveland, Ohio (profile, page 132)

Eric and Kat say: If we don't have this soup each and every time, we face a mutiny. It's that good.

Serves 6–8

4 cups chicken broth

1 (20- to 24-ounce) bag frozen peas and carrots

2 sweet potatoes, peeled and diced

12–14 ounces smoked sausage, cut into bite-size pieces

1 tablespoon curry powder

1 (14-ounce) can sweetened condensed milk

½ (12-ounce) can evaporated milk (more if needed)

½ cup raisins

1. Combine the broth, peas and carrots, and sweet potatoes in a large soup pot. Bring to a boil over medium-high heat, then reduce the heat and simmer for 5 minutes.

2. Add the sausage (we use chicken sausage) and the curry powder, and simmer for 15 minutes longer.

3. Lower the heat, making sure it's reduced below a simmer before adding the sweetened condensed milk, evaporated milk, and raisins. Stir well. Watch this like a hawk. Don't let the soup boil; if you do, it will separate.

4. Taste the soup and add more curry powder, evaporated milk, and/or raisins if desired. Serve hot.

Make ahead? Probably not a good idea. You will risk the ingredients separating during reheating. Besides, it only takes about 20 minutes from start to end.

For large crowds: The Meyers feed more than 100 people, so obviously this soup can be expanded!

Chicago Soup and Bread, Martha Bayne

CHICAGO, ILLINOIS

Martha Bayne is the Queen Mother of soup in Chicago. Starting with one simple idea, she has had a major impact on hunger awareness, first in her hometown, and now in other cities too.

The basic format is straightforward: Once a week, from early January to mid-April, she coordinates a soup supper in the back room of a bar called The Hideout, where she works as a bartender. She sweet-talks local cooks (both professionals and home cooks) to contribute the soup and bread. Each night, six cooks bring soup already hot in slow cookers, and stay to serve it. Small tables set with candles and compostable bowls and spoons welcome the diners, who are asked to contribute what they can afford.

The volunteer cooks help spread word of the event through their own networks, and each supper usually draws between 100 and 150 people. On a typical evening, the donation bucket totals $350, although it has been as much as $1,000. All the proceeds are donated to local nonprofits working on hunger relief.

> Small tables set with candles and compostable bowls and spoons welcome the diners, who are asked to contribute what they can afford.

After four years in Chicago, Martha took her act on the road, hosting Soup and Bread Suppers in Brooklyn, Philadelphia, Detroit, Seattle, and Madison, Wisconsin, which now has its own Soup and Bread event.

And then, in 2011, this very energetic woman took her passion to a new level, by publishing a book about soup and soup-based community events: *Soup & Bread Cookbook: Building Community One Pot at a Time*. It's a small book but filled to the brim with wonderful stories about many community efforts to address hunger, anecdotes about the volunteer chefs, and delicious recipes. Reading it will warm your soul.

www.soupandbread.net

FOR A RECIPE FROM CHICAGO SOUP AND BREAD, SEE:

Butternut and Acorn Squash Soup, page 140

Butternut and Acorn Squash Soup

Recipe from Martha Bayne, Chicago Soup and Bread (profile, page 139)

Martha says: This soup is adapted from one found in the *Soup & Bread Cookbook*. It was created for Soup & Bread by a Chicago filmmaker named Jack Newell, who in turn adapted it from a recipe in Eric Ripert and Michael Ruhlman's *A Return to Cooking*. Such is the mutable — and community-built — nature of soup.

Try adjusting the proportions of acorn to butternut squash — or swap in a cup of sweet kuri squash. Or roast an apple in the oven and then throw that in the mix as well. If you are *really* lazy, you can roast the squash in its skin first (see page 77) and then just scoop out the innards and add the squash to the sauté mix.

Serves 6–8

6 tablespoons unsalted butter

1 cup sliced yellow onion

2 cups peeled and diced acorn squash

2 cups peeled and diced butternut squash

Sea salt

Freshly ground white pepper (fresh and white are important)

5 cups chicken broth

1 cup heavy cream or half-and-half

3 sprigs fresh thyme

3 ounces sharp cheddar cheese, grated (¾ cup)

Optional seasonings: ground nutmeg, honey, cayenne, and/or minced fresh ginger

Make ahead? Absolutely.

For large crowds: This soup could be expanded almost indefinitely.

1. Melt 2 tablespoons of the butter in a large soup pot over medium heat. Add the onion and sauté until translucent, 3 to 5 minutes. Add the acorn and butternut squash and sauté until soft, maybe 10 minutes.

2. Season the squash mixture with salt and pepper, add the broth, and bring to a simmer. Cook until the squash is tender, about 30 minutes.

3. Transfer the soup to a blender and purée until smooth. For extra-satiny smoothness, pass the soup through a fine sieve after it's puréed.

4. Return the soup to the pot, and add the cream and the remaining 4 tablespoons butter. Simmer.

5. Wrap the thyme in a piece of cheese-cloth and tie with string to make a little bundle. Add it to the simmering soup and let it infuse for 10 minutes, then remove.

6. Add the cheese and mix gently until incorporated. Add optional seasonings as desired and serve hot.

Winter Sausage Soup

This hearty soup is rich with Southwestern flavors, and it's a very warming option for a cold evening.

Serves 6

1   (14½-ounce) can Mexican-style stewed tomatoes, broken up

2   cups beef broth

½   cup salsa

1   teaspoon dried oregano

12   ounces bulk-style pork sausage, spicy or mild, as you prefer

2   teaspoons olive oil

1   cup frozen whole-kernel corn

1   tablespoon finely chopped fresh cilantro

1. Combine the tomatoes, broth, salsa, and oregano in a soup pot. Bring to a boil over medium heat, and then reduce the heat to low.

2. Shape the sausage into small patties, about 1 inch in diameter. Heat the oil in a skillet over medium heat and add the sausage patties. Cook the patties until no longer pink in the center, 10 to 12 minutes. You may have to do this in two batches. Drain on paper towels.

3. Add the corn to the soup, cook for 3 to 4 minutes, and then add the sausage. Continue to simmer until everything is heated through.

4. Sprinkle with cilantro and serve hot.

Variation: To reduce fat and sodium, substitute ground chicken or turkey for the sausage. Cook in the same spoon-size rounds.

Make ahead? Of course. I suggest you cook the sausage and refrigerate it separately from the tomato mixture.

For large crowds: Double or triple the basic soup, maybe using proportionately a little less of the meat. Increase the oregano gradually, tasting as you go.

Red Bean and Red Pepper Soup

With the maroon-colored beans, bright crimson peppers, and red wine in the stock, this soup becomes a study in red. Artistic and also delicious.

Serves 6–8

1 pound dried red kidney beans
Water
2 onions, coarsely chopped
3 celery stalks, coarsely chopped
2 bay leaves
Salt and freshly ground black pepper
3 large red bell peppers, seeded and finely chopped
¼ cup red wine
10 cups chicken broth
4 hard-cooked eggs, chopped, for garnish
2 lemons, cut into wedges, for garnish

1. Cover the beans with water and soak overnight. Or, if you forgot to do it the night before, here's a quick alternative: cover the beans with water, bring them to a boil, boil rapidly for 2 minutes, then leave to stand for 1 hour.

2. Drain off the cooking liquid and add the onions, celery, bay leaves, salt and pepper to taste, bell peppers, wine, and broth. Bring to a boil over high heat, stirring occasionally.

3. Reduce the heat and simmer, partially covered, for about 3 hours, or until the beans are completely tender.

4. Remove the bay leaves. Transfer the soup to a blender (careful, it's hot) and purée until smooth, then return it to the pot. Or use an immersion blender and purée the soup right in the pot.

5. Bring the soup up to heat and serve hot. Garnish each serving with chopped egg, and serve lemon wedges on the side.

Variation: There's something quite satisfying (not to mention economical) about starting with dried beans, but you may prefer to take advantage of the convenience of canned beans. You'll need 4 or 5 cans; drain and rinse well.

Make ahead? Up through step 4.

For large crowds: Expands easily.

Leftover Yellow Split-Pea Soup

Elsewhere (see page 175) I describe my friend Andrea Pedolsky as a cook who uses her editorial talent to create new dishes from old recipes. Here's another example, created from leftovers (hence the name). Andrea says the final soup should be slightly chunky.

Serves 6–8

1   medium russet potato, chopped (but not fine-diced)
2   tablespoons olive oil
    Salt
1   pound yellow split peas
6   cups water
1   small onion, chopped
1   celery stalk, chopped
1   garlic clove, smashed
1   teaspoon chopped fresh thyme
    Freshly ground black pepper
¼   cup heavy cream

Make ahead? You bet.

For large crowds: Easy to multiply, and very economical for a crowd.

1. Preheat the oven to 400°F.

2. Toss the potato in 1 tablespoon of the oil, place on a baking sheet, sprinkle with salt, and roast until browned, about 30 minutes. Open the oven occasionally and stir the potato pieces so they don't stick to the pan.

3. Wash the split peas and put them in a large soup pot. Add the water, stir well, and bring to a boil. Reduce the heat, and then simmer, stirring occasionally, until the peas have softened, about 1 hour.

4. Heat the remaining 1 tablespoon oil in a skillet over medium heat. Add the onion and sauté until just past translucent, about 3 minutes. Add the celery and sauté until soft, 1 to 2 minutes; add the garlic and sauté until softened and well blended with onion and celery, about 1 minute. Add the thyme and salt and pepper to taste.

5. When the split peas have softened (some of the water will have been absorbed), add the onion mixture to the soup pot and stir to combine. Add the roasted potato and stir; then stir in the cream.

6. Cook the soup for at least 30 minutes longer to allow the ingredients to soften and blend a bit more. Serve hot.

Elizabeth Schellberg
PORTLAND, OREGON

Liz Schellberg loves her Soup Night so much, she organized her wedding around the same theme!

"Our wedding in 2006 was a Soup Party. The whole event was at our house, both the ceremony and then the celebration. It was a second wedding for both of us, and we didn't want anything formal. A soup celebration seemed just the right thing: let's just open our house to our families and friends, and serve them soup. Family came from Seattle, Idaho, and California, and I made four gallons of split pea soup (this was February). The ceremony itself lasted about 10 minutes, and then we just ate and laughed and hugged."

Liz has been doing Soup Nights for more than 20 years, and has lots of good ideas to share. One that particularly captured my heart is her table covering: she puts down brown butcher paper, with crayons nearby, and everyone — kids and grownups alike — has fun doodling. I'll let her tell you the whole story.

"In my former neighborhood, another family was hosting Soup Nights every other week. I went several times and found it a great way to meet interesting people and have interesting conversations. It was like an instant welcome to the neighborhood. Then that family

moved away and I thought I'd just start doing it. So I bought myself a big canning pot and started the tradition at my home. That was in 1990, I think, and I have continued doing them through kids, kids growing up, divorce, moving and remarriage . . . that is to say, life.

"About 10 years ago we moved to a new neighborhood and started all over again. It was my way of introducing myself to the neighbors.

"I invite everyone I meet, everyone in the neighborhood, everyone I work with, and everyone I have ever known. I still do printed invitations, on a half-sheet of paper. I put all the dates for the whole season, and take it around the neighborhood. Then, before each one, I give people reminders. I have an e-mail list, and I distribute flyer reminders around the neighborhood; recently I've added Facebook announcements, though I am a neophyte at social media. I encourage people to bring friends, and some who first came that way have come back multiple times.

"My formula has been pretty constant from the start: Soup Night once a month, on Sunday night; it's usually the second Sunday, though I am not a slave to a particular week, if something like the Super Bowl or Mother's Day gets in the way. I usually start in September, and then go through May or June. Pretty much the school year. I have learned over the years to just skip December, there's too much going on. And then sometimes I do extras, on a spontaneous basis — like when we have an ice storm or those rare times when we're snowed in. I just walk around the neighborhood and knock on doors and invite people.

"When I'm inviting people who are new to neighborhood, they usually say something like 'It's really wonderful to move into a neighborhood where people know each other.' No one has ever said, 'Go away and don't bother me.' For me, a big part of it is walking around the neighborhood each month, passing out invitations and talking to people. Soup Night takes us back to earlier times, to a gentler way of doing things.

"Some folks come almost all the time, some never. It makes no difference to me. I have had as many as 50 and as few as 1; most often there will be between 10 and 20. The large crowds are fun, but if it is a small group, I get to talk and relax more. Somehow, I have never run out of soup, and any excess goes in the freezer for another day.

"I make the soup and others bring salad, bread, or dessert — and friends, although I really have to encourage them to bring other people and assure them that it is not presumptuous or intrusive.

That's one of the things about Soup Night, it pulls people back from being overprogrammed and automated. Simple things like dominoes have a great appeal. I look at the mix of ages we have here, and I know it's the simple things that capture people.

"Some soups are traditional. In November, I always do some kind of savory squash. In February, split pea (because of our wedding). In April, some sort of carrot soup. I usually make everything vegan, and set out separate bowls of milk products. So if it's a soup that in other settings would usually be a cream soup, then people can add that. Same with meat — I marinate it and cook it ahead, and set up separate bowls.

"I put paper down to serve as a tablecloth, with crayons for doodling. I will often get thematic with fall leaves on the table, or paper to cut snowflakes, or whatever. This gives both kids and adults entertainment and conversation,

and makes for easy cleanup. It also lets parents with younger kids relax, less worried about spills.

"Putting the brown paper down on the table is such a simple thing, but it really draws people together. One year Soup Night was close to my birthday, 50-something, and that time we didn't have any kids. I had drawn candles all around the edges of the paper, and the adults took the crayons and started coloring them in. It was really beautiful — a work of art. I hated to have to get rid of it.

"I have a coffee table with three sets of dominoes out for the little kids. You would think that kids these days would get bored with dominoes, but they play with them endlessly — all ages. If for some reason I don't put them out, they all ask me, Where are the dominoes? I think that's one of the things about Soup Night, it pulls people back — back from being overprogrammed and automated. Simple things like dominoes have a great appeal. I look at the mix of ages we have here, and I know it's the simple things that capture people.

"I think I probably will do Soup Nights until I can't any more. They are human. They are easy. They force me to clean my house once a month. They make our neighborhood a friendly place where people know and relate to each other. They bring many parts of my life together."

FOR A RECIPE FROM ELIZABETH, SEE:
Liz's Award-Winning Chili, page 148

Liz's Award-Winning Chili

Recipe from Elizabeth Schellberg, Portland, Oregon (profile, page 145)

Elizabeth says: One of the best cookbooks around, in my opinion, is *The Best of Cooking Light Soups and Stews*. That's where I originally found the recipe that I have over time adapted into my own version. I believe the combination of the chipotle chiles, Marion-Blackberry Chipotle Sauce, chocolate, and Korean hot bean paste is what gives my version of this chili its unique taste.

And I really did win an award with it. A few years ago, I was working temporarily in Seattle, consulting with a company that designs cutting-edge medical equipment. The head of the department I was working with decided it would be fun to have a chili cook-off, and invited everyone to enter, including me. Because of the timing of this event, I had to make the chili at my home in Portland and transport it to Seattle, which meant making it a day ahead. And I'm pretty sure that's why I won, because as we all know, chili is always better the next day!

Serves 6–8

1 pound beef sirloin stew meat

1 cup fruit-flavored chipotle hot sauce, plus more for serving

2 tablespoons olive oil

1 cup chopped onion

2 garlic cloves, minced

2½ tablespoons Korean hot bean paste (see note)

2 teaspoons unsweetened cocoa

2 teaspoons dried oregano

2 teaspoons ground cumin

1 teaspoon salt

1 chipotle chile in adobo sauce, minced

1 cup water

1 cup cherry tomatoes, halved

1 (28-ounce) can whole tomatoes, chopped, juice reserved

1. Cut the meat into small ½- to 1-inch chunks and marinate at least an hour in the fruit-flavored chipotle sauce. It is a major contribution to the flavor. In the past I have used Marion-Blackberry Chipotle Sauce, a wonderful local product from a well-known Portland restaurant called Jake's. Alas, I haven't been able to find it recently, so I make my own version: bottled chipotle sauce mixed about half and half with marionberry jam. (See page 282 for the marionberry story. If you aren't lucky enough to live in marionberry country, substitute any blackberry jam.) If you can, find a fruity chipotle sauce or concoct one.

1 (15-ounce) can black beans,
  drained; or 2 cups cooked
  black beans (see page 27)

1 (15-oounce) can kidney beans,
  drained; or 2 cups cooked
  kidney beans (see page 27)

1 (7-ounce) can diced mild green
  chiles, drained

8 ounces frozen corn (half a bag)

1 (7-ounce) jar roasted red bell
  peppers, chopped

1½ tablespoons red wine vinegar

Garnishes

Sour cream or plain yogurt

Shredded cheddar cheese

Diced avocado

Note: I use Korean hot bean paste or
"goh-chu-chong" (there are many variations on the spelling) instead of chili powder in *any* recipe. Find it in Asian markets.
It is very hot and spicy but with a sweetness that softens the heat.

2. Drain the beef and discard the marinade. Heat 1 tablespoon of the olive oil in
a skillet, and fry the meat, along with the
onion and garlic, over medium-high heat
until the meat is browned on all sides.
Remove the meat mixture with a slotted
spoon and set aside in a bowl. Cooking the
beef separately prevents it from becoming
overcooked, and it retains the flavor of the
marinade better.

3. Heat the remaining 1 tablespoon olive
oil in a soup pot over medium heat; add the
Korean bean paste, cocoa, oregano, cumin,
and salt. Cook the mixture for 1 minute,
stirring constantly. Stir in the chipotle
chile, water, cherry tomatoes, and canned
tomatoes with their juice. Bring this mixture to a boil; cover, reduce the heat, and
simmer for 15 minutes.

4. Stir in the reserved meat mixture, the
beans, green chiles, and corn; simmer for
10 minutes.

5. Stir in the roasted peppers and vinegar, and cook for 3 minutes or until the
chili is thoroughly heated. If the mixture
is too thick for your taste, add more water,
tomato juice, or some beef broth.

6. Set out bowls of the garnishes and
extra chipotle sauce, and let everyone help
themselves.

Make ahead? Liz says, "It is always better the next day, so make it ahead
if you can."

For large crowds: "For Soup Night, I always make double or triple this
recipe," Liz says. "I figure if some is good, more is better."

For vegetarians: Skip the sirloin altogether. Sauté the onion and garlic
along with the spices (step 3). Be sure to add some of the fruit-flavored
chipotle sauce at step 3.

Taco Soup

There are lots of versions of taco soup floating around in cyberspace, and I'm sure they're all good, but this one, the creation of my book-group buddy Marilyn Katz, is extremely easy, delicious, and — thanks to using four different types of beans — very colorful.

Serves 6–8

2 pounds ground beef

3 (15-ounce) cans stewed tomatoes

1 (15-ounce) can black beans, drained and rinsed

1 (15-ounce) can navy beans, drained and rinsed

1 (15-ounce) can kidney beans, drained and rinsed

1 (15-ounce) can pinto beans, drained and rinsed

1 (16-ounce) bag frozen corn

4 celery stalks, chopped

2 large onions, finely chopped

2 packets taco seasoning

2 teaspoons garlic powder

2 teaspoons chili powder

2 (15-ounce) cans beef broth

Salt and freshly ground black pepper

Garnishes

Grated cheddar cheese • Sour cream • Tortilla chips, lightly crushed • Sliced scallions • Sliced black olives

1. Brown the ground beef in a large soup pot over medium-high heat until thoroughly cooked; drain away any fat.

2. Add the tomatoes, all the beans, the corn, celery, onions, taco seasoning, garlic powder, chili powder, and broth, and simmer for 30 minutes. Season with salt and pepper to taste.

3. Set out the garnishes in bowls, and serve the soup hot.

Make ahead? Sure. It improves with age.

For large crowds: Easy to multiply, and not expensive.

For vegetarians: Leave out the meat. It won't be authentically taco-like, but still good. Also, check out Jeni Sammons's Tortilla Soup, page 152.

Tortilla Soup

Heather Frederick, of Soup and Solidarity (page 84) credits her friend Jennifer Sammons with this soup, which is very popular with the writing group. But Jennifer adds that it's a real hit for any occasion where friends and family gather, and she suggests serving it with corn chips and a complementary jalapeño slaw.

Serves 6–8

1 tablespoon olive oil

⅓ cup chopped onion

3 cloves garlic, chopped

¾ teaspoon ground cumin

¾ teaspoon dried oregano

¼ teaspoon chili powder

¼ teaspoon black pepper

8 cups veggie broth, more to thin if needed

1 (14-ounce) can diced tomatoes, undrained

1 (4-ounce) can diced green chiles

1½ cups corn kernels (frozen or canned)

1 cup cooked black beans (canned or homemade), drained and rinsed

10 (6-inch) corn tortillas

2–3 teaspoons salt

Garnishes

Avocado, sliced or diced • Shredded sharp cheddar cheese • Sour cream • Sliced black olives • Chopped fresh cilantro

1. Heat the oil in a large soup pot over medium heat and sauté the onion for about 1 minute. Add the garlic, cumin, oregano, chili powder, and pepper, and cook 1 to 2 minutes longer, until the spices are fragrant.

2. Add the broth, tomatoes (including juice), and green chiles. Cover and bring to a boil over high heat. Add the corn and black beans.

3. Stack and cut the tortillas in ⅛-inch-wide strips and add them to the boiling broth. Reduce the heat, cover, and simmer for 10 minutes, stirring occasionally. The tortilla pieces disintegrate during cooking, thickening the soup in the process. Simmer until the soup is heated through and the tortilla strips have fallen apart. Season with salt and pepper to taste.

4. Set out the garnishes in bowls, and serve the soup hot.

Variation: This can easily be turned into a chicken-tortilla soup, with all the flavors of chicken fajitas. As a first step, cut 1 or 2 chicken breasts into ½-inch strips and sauté in vegetable or olive oil over medium-high heat until nicely browned and no longer pink inside, about 5 minutes. Remove with a slotted spoon and set aside. Add the chicken strips to the soup pot at step 2.

Make ahead? Of course. If you're making the chicken version, I would cook the chicken and refrigerate it separately, then add at step 2.

For large crowds: This is perfect for a crowd, but go easy multiplying the cumin. It's a strong taste, and you might not need a full double or triple measure. Add increases in tiny increments and taste as you go.

Karen Robbins
GRAYSLAKE, ILLINOIS

The Robbins family is friends with the Dahlbergs (they live in the same town but different neighborhoods), and loved going to their Soup Nights (page 58). So when the Robbinses moved into their new home, they decided to start a Soup Night too. Their usual pattern is once a week, from early January to late February or early March.

"One thing I wanted to do," Karen says, "was share what God has given me. I love to share my home. When I mentioned Soup Night to people, they were completely shocked that I would have people in my house that I didn't know. But I never thought of it as work. The big payoff was getting to see everyone, especially in winter."

The first year, Karen made handwritten invitations and delivered them to all the neighbors; they also invited about 30 friends from church and 20 other friends from their daughters' school. From a slow start the first year, they now sometimes have as many as 60 people.

The Robbinses agreed to do this as a family. Their two teenage daughters have specific jobs, and Karen has developed a checklist to simplify the preparations; thanks to her for allowing me to share it with you (see page 292). Some other logistics they have developed over the years:

- A mix-match collection of bowls picked up at sales, stacked beside the stove where two big soup pots are kept simmering.
- Spoons, napkins, and whatever food contributions others bring (breads, appetizers) are laid out on the dining room table. The desserts are on a separate table so the kids don't grab them first.
- They now send invitations by e-mail, with a reminder the day before. Everyone is asked to sign a guest book, so new people can be added to the list. The invitations specify no RSVP is needed, just come if you can.

"I love to see the connections develop," Karen says. "Once I watched two women start chatting, and pretty soon they were crying. Turns out they were talking about adoptions, which can be pretty emotional."

The Robbinses found, after five years of Soup Nights, that families have more complicated schedules as their children get older. So they took a break in 2012, only to find that people were always asking about it. But when I think about Karen's last comment to me, I have a feeling they will start up again: "People used to sit on their front porches and visit with whoever walked by. Now we don't even know our neighbors, much less visit with them. We're all too busy to socialize. It's not healthy. It's just not healthy."

Madras Chicken Soup

A "soupy" version of traditional chicken curry, this versatile soup is delicious both hot and cold; see serving suggestions below. If you have time, simmer a whole chicken for richly flavored homemade broth, then cut the chicken meat into small chunks for the soup.

Serves 6

4   tablespoons butter

2   medium onions, chopped

3   celery stalks, chopped

2   tablespoons Madras curry powder

1   bay leaf

6   cups chicken broth

2   tart apples, such as Granny Smith, cored, peeled, and chopped

1   cup light cream

1   cup cooked chicken, in strips

Garnishes

Shredded coconut, toasted (see note) • Sliced almonds, toasted (see note) • Raisins or dried cranberries

1. Melt the butter in a large soup pot and sauté the onions and celery over medium heat until softened, about 4 minutes. Reduce the heat and stir in the curry powder; cook for 5 minutes.

2. Add the bay leaf, chicken broth, and apples. Simmer until the apples start to fall apart, about 10 minutes.

3. Working in batches, transfer the soup to a blender (careful, it's hot) and purée until smooth, then return it to the pot. Or use an immersion blender.

4. Stir in the cream and the chicken, and heat through. Serve with bowls of garnishes alongside.

Notes: To toast the almonds, spread them in a thin layer on a metal baking sheet, and toast in a 300°F oven for a few minutes until golden brown. Stir occasionally so they toast evenly. Set aside. The coconut is more easily toasted in a dry skillet on the stovetop; watch closely, it only takes a couple of minutes.

Variation: For cold soup, refrigerate after step 3. Then proceed to step 4 when ready to serve.

Make ahead? Prepare the chicken and broth, either from scratch or using purchased cooked chicken. Make the soup through step 3; refrigerate. At party time, complete step 4 and reheat *slowly.*

For large crowds: Since chicken is among the least expensive meats, this is appropriate for groups.

Chicken Soup with Lentils and Barley

Here's another soup that starts with cooked chicken, perhaps a rotisserie bird from the supermarket. This is also a great way to use leftover turkey.

Serves 6

2 tablespoons butter or margarine

1 cup sliced leeks (see page 186) or chopped onion

½ cup chopped red or green bell pepper

1 garlic clove, minced

5 cups chicken broth

1½ teaspoons snipped fresh basil, or ½ teaspoon dried basil, crushed

1 teaspoon snipped fresh oregano, or ¼ teaspoon dried oregano, crushed

¾ teaspoon snipped fresh rosemary, or ¼ teaspoons dried rosemary, crushed

¼ teaspoon freshly ground black pepper

½ cup brown lentils, rinsed and drained

1½ cups chopped cooked chicken or turkey

1½ cups sliced carrots

½ cup quick-cooking barley

1 (15-ounce) can tomatoes, cut up, juices reserved

1. Melt the butter in a large soup pot over medium heat. Add the leeks or onion, bell pepper, and garlic, and sauté until tender but not brown, about 4 minutes.

2. Carefully stir in the broth, basil, oregano, rosemary, pepper, and the lentils; bring to a boil. Reduce the heat and simmer, covered, for 20 minutes.

3. Stir in the chicken or turkey, carrots, and barley. Simmer, covered, about 20 minutes longer or just until carrots and barley are tender.

4. Stir in the tomatoes and reserved juices; heat through. Serve hot.

Make ahead? Get the chicken ready: either cook 1 or 2 chicken breasts, or pick up a supermarket chicken and cut up enough to make 1½ cups meat. If you need to, you can also do the entire recipe ahead; stop step 4 a few minutes early, so that the reheating doesn't overcook the carrots.

For large crowds: This is a good candidate for making large quantities.

For vegetarians? You could leave out the chicken, of course, but you'd have to come up with another name for the soup.

Toni Kelly

ERIE, PENNSYLVANIA

For the past 14 years, Toni has been serving up soup once a week to family and friends. "When my youngest son moved out of the home, he was in his early 20s and not eating like he should. So I started to have him over for soup one night a week. It proved to be a winner for him and for me, knowing that at least one night he was getting something warm and nutritious, and we could stay in touch.

"What I didn't realize was how much he appreciated it too. It was one hour we could sit together just to talk about our week without criticism. We have continued to have our Soup Night during the fall and winter months for years now. He got married this past year, and he and his bride still want to come for Soup Night.

"I also didn't realize what an influence this has had on others until one of the wives at my husband's office Christmas party thanked me for telling her about Soup Night. They now have Soup Night once a week at their house too, and love it."

FOR RECIPES FROM TONI, SEE:

Cheeseburger Soup, page 159

Broccoli, Cheese, and Cauliflower Soup, page 160

Whole-Wheat Peanut Butter Cookies, page 176

Cheeseburger Soup

Recipe from Toni Kelly, Erie, Pennsylvania (profile, page 158)

Toni says: I've seen other recipes for soup with the flavor of cheeseburgers, but most of them use Velveeta cheese, which I don't really like. Mine has cheddar and my own spice combination. This is a soup all your kids will like!

Serves 6–8

4	tablespoons butter
1	pound ground beef
1	cup chopped onion
1	cup shredded carrots
1	cup chopped celery
1	teaspoon dried basil
1	teaspoon dried parsley
4	cups chicken broth
4	cups cubed potatoes
¼	cup all-purpose flour
2	cups milk
8–10	ounces cheddar cheese, grated (about 2 cups)
⅓	cup sour cream

Make ahead? Steps 1 and 2. But the whole soup assembles so quickly, you may not need to.

For large crowds: Double or triple, especially if you're expecting lots of children.

1. Melt 1 tablespoon of the butter in a large soup pot over medium heat. Add the ground beef, onion, carrots, and celery, and cook, stirring and breaking up the beef, until the beef is browned. Stir in the basil and parsley. Add the broth and potatoes. Bring to a boil, then reduce the heat and simmer until the potatoes are tender, 10 to 12 minutes.

2. Melt the remaining 3 tablespoons butter in a small saucepan and then stir in the flour and cook for a few minutes to make a light roux. Slowly add the milk, whisking until smooth.

3. Gradually add the milk mixture to the soup, stirring constantly. Bring to a boil, and then reduce the heat to a simmer.

4. Stir in the cheese, and heat gently, until the cheese is melted. Add the sour cream and heat gently; do not boil. Serve hot.

Broccoli, Cheese, and Cauliflower Soup

Recipe from Toni Kelly, Erie, Pennsylvania (profile, page 158)

Chock-full of good-for-you veggies and lusciously rich with sharp cheddar — a perfect combination for a cold winter night.

Serves 6–8

1	large head broccoli (about ¾ pound)
1	cup water, lightly salted
3	cups cauliflower florets
5	tablespoons butter or margarine
2	cups chopped onions
8	cups chicken broth
1	teaspoon dried oregano, crumbled
¼	cup all-purpose flour
2	tablespoons Dijon mustard
⅛	teaspoon freshly ground black pepper
1½	cups milk
8	ounces sharp cheddar cheese, shredded (2 cups); more if you like your soup cheesy
	Salt

1. Wash the broccoli and cut off the florets, reserving the stalk. You should have about 3 cups florets; set aside 1 cup. Cut the florets in the remaining 2 cups into small pieces, a good spoonable size. Bring the water to a boil in a medium saucepan, add the 2 cups broccoli, and simmer for 2 minutes. Use a slotted spoon to remove the florets and immerse them in cold water to stop the cooking. Save the cooking water.

2. Chop the remaining 1 cup broccoli florets, all the broccoli stalks, and the cauliflower into small pieces. Melt 3 tablespoons of the butter in a large soup pot over medium heat. Add the onions and sauté for 5 minutes, or until golden. Add the chopped broccoli and cauliflower, 4 cups of the chicken broth, and the oregano; simmer for 20 to 30 minutes, until the vegetables are tender.

3. Working in batches, transfer the soup to a blender (careful, it's hot) and purée until smooth, then return it to the pot. Or use an immersion blender and purée the soup right in the pot.

4. Melt the remaining 2 tablespoons butter in a small saucepan; stir in the flour and cook, stirring constantly, until smooth and bubbly. (You're making a light roux.) Stir in the mustard and pepper, and then gradually add the milk and whisk until thickened.

5. Stir the milk mixture into the soup; add the remaining 4 cups chicken broth and the cooking water from the simmered broccoli florets. Continue to cook, stirring, until the mixture begins to bubble.

6. Add the cheese; stir until the soup is smooth and the cheese is melted. Season to taste with salt and additional pepper. Add the reserved broccoli florets and heat through. Serve hot.

Make ahead? You can certainly do steps 2 and 3 ahead of time, but I would save the broccoli florets uncooked, and finish up just before serving, so you don't lose that beautiful color.

For large crowds: Easy to multiply, although you might not want the full extra measure of cheese.

Three Winter Chowders

Chowder, in a dictionary sense, means a chunky soup with a dairy base (milk or cream or a combination) and usually some kind of shellfish. The name comes from the French word *chaudière* (pronounced show-dee-*air*), which is the name of the three-legged kettle that Mediterranean fishermen used to brew up supper over an open fire from the day's catch. Like all foods that originated in this "whatever we have on hand" way, there are many versions and passionate but usually friendly rivalry among proponents of each one. Today our sense of what makes a chowder a chowder and not a soup has also expanded — to include corn, for instance. However we define it, a chowder, hearty and rich with solid chunks of good stuff, is perfect for winter. Here are three wonderful versions.

Clam and Corn Chowder

Here's a good way to compromise between the "clam" and the "corn" chowder factions — combine the two!

Serves 6

4   bacon strips, diced

1   medium onion, chopped

2   tablespoons all-purpose flour

2   cups milk

2   (7-ounce) cans minced clams

1   (15-ounce) can cream-style corn

½   teaspoon salt

¼   teaspoon freshly ground black
      pepper

Make ahead? Yes, up through step 2.

For large crowds: Doubles easily.

1. In a large soup pot, cook the bacon over medium heat until browned and crisp, 5 to 6 minutes. With a slotted spoon, transfer the bacon to paper towels to drain. Pour off all but 1 tablespoon fat.

2. Sauté the onion in the bacon fat until softened, about 2 minutes. Sprinkle the flour over the onion, and cook 1 minute, stirring constantly. Reduce the heat and stir in the milk; blend well, and simmer until thick, about 5 minutes.

3. Stir in the clams with their liquid, the corn, salt, and pepper. Heat through.

4. Add the reserved bacon just before serving.

Two-Rice Chowder

In this tasty chowder, the chewiness of wild rice replaces the more commonly used potatoes.

Serves 6

½   pound bacon, chopped

1   tablespoon vegetable oil

½   cup chopped onion

⅓   cup all-purpose flour

½   cup uncooked wild rice

½   cup uncooked brown rice

4½   cups water

2   cups chicken broth

1   (12-ounce) can evaporated milk, undiluted

2   cups grated cheddar cheese

1–2   tablespoons chopped fresh parsley

1. In a large skillet, cook the bacon pieces over medium heat until browned and crisp, 5 to 6 minutes. With a slotted spoon, transfer the bacon to paper towels to drain.

2. Heat the oil in a large soup pot over medium-high heat; add the onion and sauté until translucent, about 2 minutes. Reduce the heat and sprinkle the flour evenly over the onion, and cook for 1 minute, stirring constantly.

3. Add the wild rice, brown rice, water, and broth. Increase the heat to high, bring the soup to a boil, and then reduce the heat and simmer, stirring often, until the rice is tender, 40 to 45 minutes.

4. Stir in the evaporated milk, reserved bacon, and cheese. Heat gently until the cheese is melted.

5. Sprinkle the parsley into the chowder, and serve hot.

Make ahead? Get the time-consuming parts of the recipe out of the way the day before: Cook the two rices separately; cook bacon; refrigerate. Finishing the soup is now a matter of completing steps 2 through 5, reducing the simmering time in step 3 to 4 to 5 minutes.

For large crowds: An easy and economical choice for expansion.

Edamame Corn Chowder

Edamame is the Japanese name for soybeans harvested when young, still at the "shelling" stage. Outside of Asian markets, you are most likely to find them in the freezer compartment of your supermarket, either shelled or still in the pods. This creamy chowder is lower in fat content than many, because the cream-style corn replaces some of the usual quantity of half-and-half.

Serves 6–8

6   bacon strips, diced
2   medium onions, chopped
7½   cups reduced-sodium chicken broth
2   red potatoes, cut into small cubes
1   teaspoon dried Italian seasoning
4   cups frozen shelled edamame
2   (15-ounce) cans cream-style corn
1   cup half-and-half
     Salt and freshly ground pepper

Make ahead? Up through step 3.

For large crowds: Unless you have guests who're afraid to try edamame, this is perfect for a big group.

1. In a large soup pot, cook the bacon over medium heat until browned and crisp, 5 to 6 minutes. With a slotted spoon, transfer the bacon to paper towels to drain. Pour off all but 1 tablespoon fat.

2. Add the onions to the bacon fat and cook, stirring occasionally, until soft, 4 to 5 minutes. Add the broth, potatoes, and Italian seasoning. Simmer until the potatoes are just tender, about 6 minutes.

3. Stir in the edamame, corn, and half-and-half. Season with salt and pepper to taste. Simmer until the edamame are tender, about 8 minutes.

4. Serve the chowder sprinkled with the reserved bacon.

Boiled Peanuts versus Edamame

My siblings and I, who grew up in the South, absolutely *love* boiled peanuts. It's a quintessentially Southern snack, and definitely an acquired taste. A few years ago, on a family vacation in the South, I tried to convince my Oregon-born niece and nephew to try it by telling them boiled peanuts are quite similar to edamame, which they like (they didn't buy it). On that same trip, out to dinner with South Carolina cousins, I tried to get them to share my edamame appetizer by telling them it tasted a lot like boiled peanuts. They would have none of it.

Ice Storm Stone Soup

In a major storm, an impromptu version of this soup was a literal lifesaver (see story next page). It began with an existing recipe for a fairly generic vegetable soup, the sort that lends itself to endless variations. The original recipe card, from 1972, is heavily splattered and barely legible, testament to long use.

Serves 6, or a multitude

2 tablespoons butter

3 onions, chopped

1 pound lean ground beef

3 garlic cloves, minced

3 cups beef broth

2 (15-ounce) cans tomatoes, diced or stewed or whole, whatever you have on hand

1 cup diced potatoes

1 cup diced celery

1 cup chopped green beans

1 cup diced carrots

1 cup sliced mushrooms

1 cup red wine

2 teaspoons chopped fresh parsley

½ teaspoon dried basil

¼ teaspoon dried thyme

1 teaspoon salt

½ teaspoon pepper

1. Melt the butter in a large soup pot and sauté the onions until soft and golden, about 5 minutes. Add the ground beef and garlic to the onions, and cook until the meat is browned. Add the beef broth and tomatoes to the soup pot, bring to a boil, and then reduce the heat.

2. Add the potatoes, celery, green beans, carrots, mushrooms, wine, parsley, basil, and thyme, and then simmer for 1 hour.

3. Season with salt and pepper to taste and serve hot.

Make ahead? Certainly. It does well the second day. In an ice storm, you can always burn the furniture and use that fire to reheat the soup.

For large crowds: This is a very dense soup, packed with vegetables. To make large quantities under non-emergency conditions, double or triple the veggies, use a lower proportion of meat, and increase the herbs a little at a time, tasting first. Unless you, like my friends, actually face a power outage — in which case, throw in all the meat that has defrosted. And don't bother adding extra wine to the soup — just drink it.

Stone Soup: A Fable for Modern Times

The classic fable about stone soup is really a story about cooperation, and the virtue of sharing in times of adversity. It has taken different forms in different parts of the world and different times, but the essential story is this: A stranger, or a group of strangers (sometimes soldiers, sometimes gypsies, sometimes a traveling monk, sometimes a hobo) arrive in a village and beg for food. The villagers, themselves destitute, protest that they have none to share. And then, slowly, people realize that they do, in fact, have a little something extra: a few carrots, a potato or two, a scrap of meat not big enough to serve any other purpose. All these offerings are added to a big soup kettle filled with water, and soon they have created a huge cauldron of delicious, nourishing soup, enough for all.

Several years ago, friends of mine here in Portland found themselves in a jam, and found their solution in a modern-day version of Stone Soup.

Their neighborhood is at a slightly higher elevation than the rest of the city, and filled with steep, narrow, twisty streets. Because of the elevation, they are especially hard hit in times of icy weather, which we always seem to get in early January. The steep streets, when covered with ice, are next to impossible to navigate. Back in 1979, a particularly ferocious ice storm shut the whole city down. It was especially hard on this hilly neighborhood. Overnight, the streets were thickly coated with black ice, making travel extremely hazardous. Then things got worse.

"All the power went out and stayed out for days," my dear friend Mary Ella Kuster remembers. "I did not have so much as a working flashlight. Two other neighbors had elderly mothers visiting (probably staying on as part of Christmas visits). Food in our refrigerators started going bad, so we combined what we had, used one guy's camping stove, and actually produced quite a nice supper. Somehow we got soup down the street to another neighbor's house, and I remember them being especially grateful, as her mother was ill and the warm food was needed.

"To me, it was an example of real (by that I mean authentic) 'community' — people coming together to help out, share, take care of each other. We all remember, with great fondness, the night we made what we have come to call Ice Storm Stone Soup."

I hope you never have to struggle through a power outage, but in case you do — or even if you don't — the recipe is included here (on the facing page) to honor this event that brought this close neighborhood even closer.

Pita Crisps

This is just about as easy as opening a bag of commercial pita crisps — and about a thousand times better tasting.

Makes 64 crisps

8 pita breads, 6- or 8-inch
1 cup (2 sticks) butter, melted

Variation: Before baking, sprinkle the buttered pita pieces with salt and/or your favorite herb (crumbled to dust) or ground spice.

Make ahead? Yes, rewarm at 350°F for a few minutes. Watch that they don't burn.

For large crowds: I suggest you make a lot; I've known people to put away a dozen each without even trying hard.

1. Preheat the oven to 350°F.

2. Cut each pita into wedges about 2 inches wide at the bottom end, as if cutting a pie. Depending on the original uncut size of your pitas, you will make quarters or sixths or eighths. (The suggested quantity is based on cutting a pita into fourths.) Kitchen scissors work well here.

3. Gently separate each wedge into a top and a bottom. If you want your finished crisps to be perfect, keep the tops separate from the bottoms, since one is usually much thinner than the other and therefore will brown more quickly. If baked all together, some will be almost burnt while others not fully done.

4. Place the pita pieces, inner side up, on a baking sheet, trying not to overlap, and brush the top sides with melted butter. Toast until the wedges are brown and crisp, about 10 minutes.

Cheddar Drop Biscuits

Recipe from Albertina's Restaurant, Portland, Oregon (profile, page 55)

Easy and delicious. Don't skip the flour-sifting step; it helps keep the biscuits light.

Makes 20–24 medium biscuits

2 cups sifted all-purpose flour	**1.** Preheat the oven to 400°F. Grease a baking sheet.
1 tablespoon baking powder	
½ teaspoon salt	**2.** Sift together the flour, baking powder, and salt. Rub the butter into the flour mixture, then add the cheese (or use a food processor). Stir in the milk to form a soft, sticky dough.
4 tablespoons cold butter, cut into bits	
12 ounces cheddar cheese, grated (3 cups)	
1 cup milk	**3.** Drop the biscuit dough by rounded spoonfuls onto the prepared baking sheet.
	4. Bake for 12 to 15 minutes, or until the biscuits are pale golden brown. Serve hot or warm.

Make ahead? If you really need to, you could make the batter ahead and store it in the refrigerator, but wait until dinnertime to do the baking, so that everyone enjoys the wonderful smells.

For large crowds: This recipe is infinitely expandable.

Whole-Wheat Quick Bread (photo, page 101)

Whole-wheat buttermilk goodness without the kneading; the nuts add extra protein and an extra depth to the flavor.

Makes 1 loaf

2¼	cups whole-wheat flour
2½	teaspoons baking powder
1	teaspoon baking soda
¾	teaspoon salt
¾	cup brown sugar
1	cup ground nuts (your choice)
1½	cups buttermilk

1. Preheat the oven to 350°F. Butter an 8- by 4- by 4-inch loaf pan.

2. Combine the flour, baking powder, baking soda, salt, sugar, and nuts in a large mixing bowl. Stir in the buttermilk, mixing well.

3. Scrape the batter into the prepared pan. Bake for 1 hour, or until the top and sides of the loaf are golden brown and a toothpick inserted in the center tests clean. Cool on a baking rack before serving.

Carolina Cornbread

Cornbread is the classic accompaniment to chili, but it also pairs gloriously with many hearty wintertime soups and stews. Actually, it tastes wonderful with just about anything.

Makes 9 (1-inch) squares

1   cup cornmeal
1   cup all-purpose flour
⅓   cup sugar
1   tablespoon baking powder
1   teaspoon salt
1   egg
1   cup milk or buttermilk
⅓   cup vegetable oil

1. Preheat the oven to 400°F. Lightly oil a 9-inch-square baking pan.

2. Combine the cornmeal, flour, sugar, baking powder, and salt in a large mixing bowl.

3. In a small bowl, beat the egg well, add the milk and oil, then combine with the dry mixture.

4. Pour the batter into the prepared pan, and bake for 20 to 25 minutes, or until the top has formed a golden crust and a toothpick inserted in the center tests clean. Serve the cornbread hot, if at all possible.

Variations: There are lots of ways to personalize your cornbread: Substitute sour cream for half of the milk. Add 1 can cream-style corn (reduce the milk to ½ cup). Fold grated cheese into the batter or sprinkle on top. Roast garlic cloves, finely chop, and add to the batter. Add a small can of diced green chiles (drain first). And by the way, if you're short on time, there's absolutely nothing wrong with using cornbread mix, especially if you gussy it up with corn, chiles, or cheese.

Salad Coquille

Recipe from Albertina's Restaurant, Portland, Oregon (profile, page 55)

This is a classic salad that can be served with almost any soup.

Serves 10–12

Dressing

2½	tablespoons white wine vinegar
1½	teaspoons lemon juice
½	teaspoon dry mustard powder
½	teaspoon paprika
2½	tablespoons honey
⅓	cup sugar
½	teaspoon celery salt
½	teaspoon grated onion
½	cup salad oil

Salad

½	cup slivered almonds
1	head iceberg lettuce, torn into bite-size pieces
1	head leaf lettuce, torn into bite-size pieces
1	cup canned mandarin oranges, drained
½	red onion, sliced and separated into rings

1. Preheat the oven to 350°F.

2. Make the dressing: Combine the vinegar, lemon juice, mustard, paprika, honey, sugar, celery salt, and grated onion in a saucepan and heat until the sugar dissolves. Add the oil, and let the mixture cool. Before serving, whisk or blend the dressing thoroughly.

3. Toast the almonds: Spread the almonds in a thin layer on an ungreased baking sheet and bake for about 3 minutes or until golden brown. Stir occasionally so they toast evenly; and watch carefully, for they can burn quickly. Or do the same on top of the stove in an ungreased frying pan, preferably cast iron.

4. Layer the iceberg lettuce, leaf lettuce, oranges, and onion in a salad bowl, toss with the dressing, then sprinkle with toasted almonds.

Asian Noodle Salad

Patty and Bruce Wood, of Ocean Park, Washington, owned a small café that featured picnic-ready sandwiches, soups, and salads. This was one of their creations, popular with both vacationers and locals.

Serves 8

1 pound vermicelli or Asian noodles

4–6 scallions, chopped

3 celery stalks, sliced on the diagonal

3 cups sweet bell peppers, thinly sliced — red, orange, green, or any combination

1½ cups water chestnuts, sliced thinly

Sauce

½ cup peanut oil

⅓ cup sesame oil

⅔ cup orange juice

¼ cup soy sauce or tamari

¼ cup rice wine vinegar

3 garlic cloves, crushed

¾ teaspoon red pepper flakes

1–2 tablespoons freshly grated ginger

1. Bring a large pot of salted water to a boil and cook the noodles according to the package instructions. Drain, rinse with cold water, and set aside.

2. Make the sauce: Combine the peanut oil, sesame oil, orange juice, tamari, vinegar, garlic, red pepper, and ginger in a small bowl.

3. Combine the scallions, celery, peppers, and water chestnuts with the chilled noodles. Add the sauce to the noodles, mixing well. Chill in the refrigerator for at least 1 hour.

4. Before serving, let the salad warm up to room temperature.

Variations: Other salad options include snow peas, snap peas, fresh bean sprouts, and pineapple chunks. Two classic Asian touches: chopped cilantro and chopped peanuts, added at the last minute.

This same salad, made with rice instead of noodles, is also delicious. Use all brown rice, or a mixture of brown and white rice. Toss with the sauce while the rice is still warm, and then refrigerate. At serving time, fold in the vegetables and a little more sauce, if needed.

Green Salad with Mini Crab Cakes

(photo, page 101)

My friend Nancy Allen, of Long Beach, Washington, has one great advantage over the rest of us — her husband Phil. He loves to catch crabs in the waters off the Long Beach Peninsula, where they are rich and sweet, and only a skip away from their home. From that bounty she has created many wonderful recipes, including this original version of crab cakes.

Serves 8–10

Crab Cakes

1	pound Dungeness crabmeat
½	cup plus 2 tablespoons mayonnaise
3	scallions, finely chopped
¼	cup finely chopped parsley or cilantro
1	tablespoon Dijon mustard
1	teaspoon sea salt or kosher salt
¼	teaspoon freshly ground black pepper
	Panko crumbs, or fine plain dry breadcrumbs
2	tablespoons butter

Optional Additions

	Grated lemon zest
	Lemon juice
1	teaspoon apple cider vinegar or balsamic vinegar
1	teaspoon Tabasco sauce
1	teaspoon dill weed, fresh or dried
2	teaspoons chili powder
½	teaspoon chopped garlic
1	tablespoon diced red pepper
1	tablespoon diced celery

Salad

10–12	ounces mixed salad greens
1	red onion, thinly sliced
4	scallions, diced
	Vinaigrette

PANKO CRUMBS

Originally from Japan, panko crumbs have become widely popular in the United States in recent years, and with good reason: they are unbelievably crisp and crunchy, and retain that crispness through baking, oven frying, or frying. They are especially appropriate for delicately flavored items like shellfish, when you want crunch without any extra flavor.

1. Make the crab cakes: Combine the crabmeat, mayonnaise, scallions, parsley or cilantro, mustard, salt, and pepper, plus any optional additions, according to your preferences. Form the mixture into small patties about the size and shape of a flattened ping-pong ball.

2. Coat each crab cake thoroughly with panko crumbs (or, if you can't find panko, with plain finely grated bread crumbs, such as Progresso brand). Place the patties on a plate or tray, cover with plastic wrap, and refrigerate at least 1 hour (longer is fine).

3. Just before serving time, assemble the salad: Layer the salad greens, red onion slices, and scallions into a bowl. If possible, include some bitter greens (such as arugula, watercress, or endive) along with several types of lettuces; their tangy taste is a nice complement to the sweetness of the crab. Don't add any dressing yet.

4. Cook the crab cakes: Melt the butter in a large skillet over medium-high heat. Arrange the crab cakes in the pan with room to spare; if you crowd them, they'll steam rather than fry — you don't want that. Set your timer for 4 minutes. Don't touch them until the 4 minutes are up. Turn them over and set the timer for another 4 minutes.

5. While the crab cakes are cooking on their second side, toss the salad with your favorite vinaigrette and place servings on individual salad plates.

6. Place 3 or 4 crab cakes on each salad plate and serve at once.

White Salad Dressing

My friend Andrea Pedolsky, of Washington, D.C., is a wonderfully creative vegetarian cook. I've had the pleasure of eating at her table and admiring what she can do with the simplest ingredients. She is a wizard with salads and created this dressing in that improvisational way that so many great cooks favor: by combining several ideas and then finalizing the results into something new and unique. In her day job, Andrea is a talented editor, which may help explain her skill at combining, adapting, and reshaping disparate parts into something wonderful. Check out her Leftover Split-Pea Soup (page 144) for another example of her "editorial" work.

Makes ½ cup

⅓ cup extra-virgin olive oil	Combine all of the ingredients in a small bowl and whisk until emulsified. Serve on a fresh, green salad.
2 tablespoons white balsamic vinegar	
2 tablespoons plain yogurt	
1 teaspoon Dijon mustard	

Whole-Wheat Peanut Butter Cookies

Recipe from Toni Kelly, Erie, Pennsylvania (profile, page 158)

A more wholesome version of the classic favorite.

Makes 4 dozen cookies

- ½ cup (1 stick) unsalted butter
- ½ cup natural peanut butter, either creamy or crunchy
- ½ cup brown sugar, packed
- 1 cup granulated sugar
- 1 egg
- 2 tablespoons milk
- 1 teaspoon vanilla extract
- ¾ cup unbleached all-purpose flour
- 1 cup whole-wheat flour
- 1 teaspoon baking soda
- ½ teaspoon sea salt

1. Preheat the oven to 375°F.

2. Cream the butter, peanut butter, brown sugar, and ½ cup of the granulated sugar together in large mixing bowl. Add the egg, milk, and vanilla, beating well after each addition. Add the all-purpose flour, whole-wheat flour, baking soda, and salt, and mix well.

3. Shape the dough into 1-inch balls and roll in the remaining ½ cup sugar.

4. Arrange the balls on baking sheets and flatten slightly with a fork in a criss-cross pattern. Bake until set and lightly browned, 8 to 10 minutes.

5. Allow the cookies to cool on the baking sheets for a minute before moving them to a cooling rack.

Desserts for Winter

Lemon Ice Cream

Recipe from Albertina's Restaurant, Portland, Oregon (profile, page 55)

This is incredibly rich, incredibly easy (you don't need an ice cream maker), and incredibly good. I have known folks to lick their dessert bowls, to get the very last drop. Seriously.

Serves 6

1 cup sugar
1 cup whole milk
⅓ cup freshly squeezed lemon juice
1 cup whipping cream
½ teaspoon vanilla extract
Mint leaves, for garnish
1 lemon, sliced paper thin, for garnish

1. Mix the sugar, milk, and lemon juice in a medium bowl.

2. Whip the cream until stiff, then fold it into the milk mixture. Add the vanilla, and mix well. Pour into a shallow container to freeze.

3. Stir the ice cream at least once when partially frozen.

4. Garnish with fresh mint leaves or lemon slices.

Mimi's Double Chocolate Brownies

For most of the first decade of the twenty-first century, David Kenworthy, Episcopal minister and unpretentious gourmet cook, prepared a wonderful holiday gift for his friends — a compilation of a dozen or so recipes that he had especially enjoyed during the year, including some from his mother, Mimi. He chose the best of the best, lovingly printed them out on holiday-themed paper, and bound them together with a holiday letter filled with gentle wit and good wishes. His many friends miss him greatly. I like to think he would have loved the idea of Soup Nights.

Makes about 50 brownies

¾ cup (1½ sticks) butter, at room temperature, plus more for greasing the pan

4 ounces unsweetened chocolate, chopped, the best you can afford

1 cup granulated sugar

3 eggs, room temperature

1 teaspoon vanilla

½ teaspoon salt

1 cup all-purpose flour, plus more for the pan

½ cup walnut halves (optional)

4–5 ounces good-quality chocolate chips (optional)

1. Preheat the oven to 350°F. Lightly butter a 10- by 13-inch baking pan, dust with flour, then tap out the excess flour.

2. Melt 4 tablespoons of the butter and the chopped chocolate in a small saucepan over low heat.

3. In a mixing bowl, cream the remaining ½ cup butter with the sugar until light and fluffy, scraping down the bowl occasionally. Add the eggs one at a time, mixing after each one. Stir in the vanilla and salt. Add melted butter–chocolate mixture, stirring to combine well.

4. Sift 1 cup flour and then spoon it back into the measuring cup. Sifting will add air to the flour; level the measuring cup with a spoon. Add the flour to the batter one-third at a time, mixing well after each addition.

5. Add the walnuts and chocolate chips. Both are optional, but adding the chocolate chips is what makes these brownies "double chocolate."

6. Pour the batter into the prepared pan and bake for 25 minutes. Check the brownies after 20 minutes; if the top is cracking, whisk the pan out of oven, because they're getting too done. To be sure they're done, insert a toothpick in the center; if it comes out clean and the sides are beginning to shrink from the pan, cool the brownies to room temperature and cut. If the brownies are not done, put them back in the oven for a few more minutes.

In memoriam: David G. P. Kenworthy

Dave's recipes came to me, and now to you, from his longtime friend Connie West. They were high school pals in the small town of The Dalles, Oregon, but, as these things often go, lost track after graduation. When they ran into each other a few years later, Dave was on leave from his mission work in St. Croix, Virgin Islands. He happened to mention that a new school, under construction, was in need of teachers. Connie, a woman with a bold heart, didn't hesitate. Off she went to St. Croix and to an amazing adventure that would change her life. The teaching job led to a position as private tutor to one of her students, which meant traveling the world, and eventually led her to the man she would marry.

CHAPTER FOUR

Spring

Spring brings many good things. The first flowers, the first tantalizing warm days, the first farmers' markets. And asparagus, the quintessential spring vegetable. At its peak, there's nothing like it, and anyone can be forgiven for gorging themselves.

In fact, I once read a story in a cooking magazine (this was years ago, and I no longer remember which publication) about a woman who was tired of her friends complaining that they never got enough fresh asparagus because the season was so short, so she decided to do something about it. She prepared an elegant dinner party of just asparagus — nothing more. At several critical points along the table, she placed small bowls of drawn butter, butter with lemon, and hollandaise sauce, but otherwise the only thing on the table was a half dozen big white platters mounded with beautifully steamed asparagus spears, bright green and tender-crisp. Her friends thought it was magnificent.

In honor of this wonderful treat that truly is only worth eating when it's fresh, let's start the recipes with two versions of asparagus soup.

Soup Night on Stanton Street: March

It's about 6:30 PM, and everyone has settled in with their full soup bowls when Milo stands up and taps his wine glass with his spoon. Most of the conversations continue uninterrupted, but Milo teaches middle school and he is not about to let a bunch of unruly adults get the best of him. Over good-natured protests, he finally gets everyone to stop talking.

Pot Sticker–Spinach Soup (page 187), Spinach-Almond Salad (page 228), and Wonder Bars (page 230)

His announcement is simple, but his excitement is plain to all: He and Joy have just learned that they are about to welcome their first grandchild. The room erupts in cheers.

Milo is generally one of the quiet ones, but this evening he was bubbling over. "He was on cloud nine," Alex remembers. "Soup Night gave him a way to share his good news with all of us, all at one time. I didn't know Milo very well at that point, but ever since then I think about him differently."

That simple comment opens a window onto one of the most significant effects of Soup Night — whenever people share something of themselves, they get something back. This is no small thing.

Soup Night has really opened my eyes to what a relationship with neighbors can be about. There's no anxiety, not like at work, say, where you're always worried that you're being judged. With your neighbors, you are just accepted for who you are. No pretensions. People say, "There's Will, going out to get the paper in his socks, with holes in them." — *Will*

At tonight's gathering, Milo and Joy brought a special cake in honor of the new grandchild. They have lived on the block a long time, and so some of the neighbors remember the new dad-to-be from when he was a kid himself. It's a sweet example of what one neighbor calls "the big cycle."

"First we had lots of little kids," Fred says, ticking items off on his fingers. "Then we had the fun of watching them grow up and then there's a new surge of little kids. We all remember buying lemonade from little Meg when she set up her sidewalk stand, and now she's a teenager learning to drive." This evening the lemonade entrepreneur is on self-assigned kid duty, watching to make sure five-year-old Aidan, who doesn't like soup but loves bread, has butter to go with it.

And then there is baby Isaac, with the big brown eyes and chubby cheeks. Becky and Lisa's new son has been here for just a few weeks but has been thoroughly introduced to everyone on the block. At supper tonight, he spends the entire evening being cooed over and passed from one set of adult arms to another. Alex is taking a turn when both the baby's parents are called into a conversation outside. "Alex," Lisa asks as she moves to leave the room, "are you okay there?" Alex, whose own son is way past lap-baby size, looks down and says with a soft smile, "We're just fine."

Asparagus and Pea Soup

This soup pairs fresh asparagus with another seasonal delicacy, freshly shelled peas.

Serves 6–8

1½ pounds asparagus
2 tablespoons butter
3 tablespoons olive oil
1 minced shallot (about 1 tablespoon)
2 garlic cloves, minced
½ pound fresh garden peas, shelled
4 small red potatoes, diced
8 cups chicken broth
Pinch cayenne pepper
Pinch ground nutmeg

Make ahead? Certainly. Up through step 5. Reheat when ready.

For large crowds: As much as your budget will permit.

For vegetarians: Substitute vegetable broth for the chicken.

1. Snap off the tough ends of the asparagus spears. Cut the first 2 or 3 inches from about half the spears, and simmer the tips in salted water until crisp-tender; then immediately drain and cover them with ice-cold water. When they are completely cool, drain and set the tips aside for a garnish.

2. Heat the butter and olive oil in a large soup pot over medium heat and sauté the shallot and garlic until softened, about 4 minutes.

3. Cut the rest of the asparagus into 1- to 2-inch pieces and add them to the soup pot along with the peas and potatoes. Sauté the vegetables for 2 minutes, until softened.

4. Add the chicken broth, cayenne, and nutmeg, and bring the soup to a boil. Reduce the heat and simmer until the vegetables are very tender, about 15 minutes.

5. Working in batches, transfer the soup to a blender (careful, it's hot) and purée until smooth. Perfectionists may want to strain the soup through a large sieve, to remove any asparagus "strings." Return the soup to the pot and heat through.

6. Garnish each serving with a few reserved asparagus tips and serve hot.

Asparagus-Leek Chowder

Recipe from Albertina's Restaurant, Portland, Oregon (profile, page 55)

Chowders don't necessarily have to include clams; this delicious version takes good advantage of two springtime treats: asparagus and leeks.

Serves 6–8

6 tablespoons butter

½ pound mushrooms, sliced

2 large leeks, trimmed and sliced (see page 186)

¾ pound fresh asparagus, trimmed and chopped

3 tablespoons all-purpose flour

½ teaspoon salt

⅛ teaspoon freshly ground black pepper

2 cups chicken broth

2 cups half-and-half

1 (12-ounce) can white whole-kernel corn, undrained

2 tablespoons chopped pimientos

1. Melt the butter in a large soup pot over low heat. Add the mushrooms, leeks, and asparagus and cook until almost tender, about 10 minutes.

2. Sprinkle the flour, salt, and pepper evenly over all the vegetables; sauté for 3 to 4 minutes.

3. Add the chicken broth gradually, stirring to prevent lumps, and simmer for 10 minutes. Add the half-and-half and heat, stirring constantly, until the soup is hot and bubbly.

4. Stir in the corn and pimientos and heat through, being careful not to boil. Season to taste with additional salt and pepper, if needed, and serve hot.

Make ahead? Yes; when reheating, be careful not to let soup boil.

For large crowds: Go ahead and splurge — asparagus season is short.

For vegetarians: Use vegetable broth rather than chicken.

DEALING WITH LEEKS

This member of the onion family, which looks a gigantic scallion, has a mild, almost soft taste that beautifully complements many dishes; it's especially nice with potatoes and asparagus.

Because of the way they grow underground, leeks often have sand or dirt trapped between the layers, and if you simply slice the whole leek horizontally into rounds (which seems the natural thing to do), the sand will still be there.

There is an easier way to deal with this: First cut the entire leek into two big pieces, right where the green leaves start. Discard most of the green leaves; they're usually rather tough, especially the nearer you get to the tops. But keep a bit of the lowest edge of the leaves (nearest where you cut), because they have a nice color when cooked. Cut the white part lengthwise into halves (even quarters, if the leek is very fat), and swish them vigorously in a large bowl of water. You may need to do this more than once. Now drain, and proceed to chop, dice, or cut the leeks however you need for your recipe.

WORKING WITH HOT CHILES

Hot chiles need to be handled carefully, because they can burn your skin, especially if you happen to have a small cut on a finger. The "heat" is in the seeds and, even more, in the ribs that attach the seeds to the inner walls. Slice the chile open and remove the seeds and ribs, and then slice or chop the chile flesh as needed. You may prefer to wear gloves, but if you do not, be sure not to rub your eyes or mouth, and wash hands thoroughly afterward.

Pot Sticker–Spinach Soup (photo, page 181)

Pot stickers are small Asian dumplings, half-moon-shaped and stuffed with either a mixture of finely chopped vegetables or a meat and vegetable blend. As an appetizer, they are pan-fried on the flat side until golden brown (sometimes they stick to the pan, hence the name) and served with a soy-sesame-chili dipping sauce. These tidbits are now so popular in Asian restaurants that several brands are available in the frozen food section of most supermarkets. I especially like the ones sold at Trader Joe's. Here they are used, straight from the package, to add flavor and heft to a delicious soup.

Serves 6

4   (15-ounce) cans reduced-sodium chicken broth

4   garlic cloves, minced

2   jalapeño chiles, seeded and minced (see page 186)

30–35   frozen pot stickers

3   cups fresh baby spinach or regular spinach, torn into pieces

Hot chili oil (optional)

1. Simmer the broth, garlic, and jalapeños in a large soup pot over low heat until the peppers are tender, about 5 minutes.

2. Add the frozen pot stickers (no need to thaw) and simmer for 5 minutes longer.

3. Add the spinach and simmer until the leaves are just wilted but still bright green.

4. Serve hot, with chili oil on the table for those who prefer it.

Make ahead? Not really; the pot stickers and the spinach don't hold up well to long reheating. On the other hand, this comes together very quickly.

For large crowds: Very easy to make large batches.

For vegetarians: Use vegetable broth instead of chicken; be sure to choose vegetarian pot stickers.

Avgolemono (Greek Chicken-Rice Soup)

Diane Mermigas, a second-generation Greek-American in Chicago, grew up loving the delicious aromas and flavors of avgolemono, the classic lemon-chicken Greek soup that she calls "comfort food for all seasons."

Serves 6

2 quarts chicken broth
½ cup uncooked long-grain white rice
2 whole eggs or egg yolks
Juice of 2 medium lemons, strained (about 6 tablespoons)
2 tablespoons butter
Salt

Make ahead? Do steps 1 and 2, refrigerate separately.

For large crowds: Easy and economical to make large batches.

For vegetarians? Sorry, can't have avgolemono without chicken.

1. Bring the broth to a full boil in a large soup pot. Gradually add the rice, stirring constantly until the broth boils again. Reduce the heat, cover, and simmer until the rice is tender, 12 to 14 minutes. Remove the pot from the heat and keep warm.

2. Prepare the avgolemono sauce: In a mixing bowl, beat the eggs for 2 minutes. Gradually add the lemon juice, continuing to beat.

3. Add a cup of the hot broth to the egg-lemon mixture, then gradually stir it all into the soup pot, beating steadily until all has been added. Simmer over very low heat (don't let it boil) until the soup thickens enough to coat a spoon.

4. Swirl in the butter, taste for salt, and serve immediately, or keep the soup warm in a double boiler over hot water until ready to serve.

Spinach and Lentil Soup

If there's any reason to complain about lentils, an otherwise noble food-stuff, it's that their color is a tad boring. Combining them with bright green spinach — a seasonal fresh favorite now available year-round — is a nifty, tasty solution.

Serves 6–8

½ cup brown lentils, picked over and rinsed (see page 121)

1 tablespoon olive oil

1 medium onion, chopped

1 celery stalk, chopped

1 leek, trimmed and chopped (see page 186)

1 pound russet potatoes, peeled and diced

4 cups chicken broth

8 ounces fresh spinach, chopped

Make ahead? Yes, up through step 3. You want the spinach to retain its beautiful color as much as possible.

For large crowds: Soup can easily (and economically) be multiplied for a crowd, but try to add the spinach as late as possible. Kept simmering on the stove, it will lose some of its bright color.

For vegetarians? Absolutely. Just switch out the chicken broth for vegetarian broth.

1. Cover the lentils with water in a saucepan and bring to a boil, then reduce the heat, cover, and simmer until the lentils are tender, about 20 minutes. Drain and set aside.

2. Heat the olive oil in a large soup pot over medium heat, and sauté the onion, celery, and leek until softened, about 5 minutes.

3. Add the potatoes and broth, bring to a good strong simmer, and cook until the vegetables are tender and the potatoes have started to fall apart, about 20 minutes.

4. Add the spinach and cook for 1 to 2 minutes longer.

5. Working in batches, transfer the soup to a blender (careful, it's hot) and purée until smooth, then return it to the pot. Or use an immersion blender and purée the soup right in the pot. Stir in the lentils and reheat. Serve hot.

Paul and Lori Fredrich

MILWAUKEE, WISCONSIN

Soup is a very democratic food: It equally warms the hearts and stomachs of cooks and eaters, and since it is so forgiving, even very inexperienced cooks can make it successfully. And then there are folks like Paul and Lori and their friends, who happily describe themselves as "foodies." Even these serious cooks enjoy making and sharing soup.

In 2008, Paul and Lori said to each other, "What if we took a Sunday evening, invited family and friends, people we don't see on a regular basis?" They settled on Sundays, 4:30 to 7:30, because "Sunday is a quiet evening, and we set the time early for people with little kids." Invitations went to about 30 different families: "We'll make soup, you just show up, no need to RSVP."

Now they have settled into a pattern: once a month for three months — January, February, and March — on

Sunday evenings. They make three soups, one of which is vegetarian, and set them out in slow cookers. Various toppings are in separate bowls, so any allergies can be managed. Someone always brings bread, someone always brings dessert. No one goes home hungry.

"At World Market," Lori explains, "we found sets of oversized mugs, so we bought two sets, each with 24 mugs in a rack. Newbies always make the mistake of filling up the mug with their first soup, then they're too full to try the others. They learn fast — just take a sample of each one. Soup Night is a way to experience new recipes; everybody wants to try everything."

One year, when Paul's job was eliminated, they put Soup Night on hiatus. Everybody understood the reasons, but they sorely missed coming. Paul says, "I came to realize that when times are

tight, that's the very point you need your friends around you, and soup seems just right. In retrospect, I would never stop in hard times."

The original goal, inspired by a magazine article, was to encourage a feeling of community in the neighborhood. That didn't work as well as they had hoped. So the following year they expanded the invite pool to people interested in food. That upped the invitation list to 60 people. "I was a little worried we might run out of soup," Lori says. "Didn't happen." They continue to invite the neighbors and sometimes a few new people do come, but mostly their focus has shifted to something bigger than the neighborhood, to people who are seriously interested in food.

I know it's simple, but I can't help thinking: maybe all the world *really* needs is another Soup Night.

"The community aspect really clicked in the second year," Lori says. "We invited people who didn't know each other except in virtual connections, then they discovered they were friends and neighbors but didn't know it. So the virtual connections turned into real-time connections.

"What happens now is that people who come run into people they already know but didn't realize they were neighbors. When we started inviting food bloggers, we had people come who had met online but didn't know each other in real life. They love getting to meet in person. We just stand back and watch it happen. People look forward to this in a way that I never would have imagined."

Several of those who attend Paul and Lori's Soup Night echo that sentiment.

Rebecca Gagnon writes a food blog about cooking from scratch with whole foods. She "met" Paul and Lori by reading their blog, which includes an open invitation to Soup Night.

"The first time I went," Rebecca remembers, "I was nervous. Didn't know anybody, totally out of my comfort zone. Paul and Lori are very good at social networking, using Facebook and Twitter, but we'd never actually met, so I was walking into a house full of strangers. I was thinking, 'Oh my, should I go in?' But at that very first visit I was warmly welcomed and quickly felt at ease. They have gathered together lots of people with common interests."

Bryan and Jen Peters moved to Milwaukee in 2007, and found the Soup Night a wonderful way to meet people. They are part of the "local food movement." Bryan, a computer network specialist by day, works a booth at a farmers' market on the weekends, and that's how he met Paul.

Bryan continues: "Food is a central theme in our home — local, organic, sustainable. Paul and I have gone foraging for morels, also found fiddleheads and wild onions. So I would say Soup Night has led to a great friendship with Paul and Lori, and also with other people. Our son Oliver was two when we first went, so he has grown up with Soup Night; he thinks it's normal. If our children don't come with us, everybody asks, Where are the kids?"

Jen speaks for both of them: "We *really* enjoy Soup Night. At first we didn't know anybody except the hosts; now it has created lasting friendships that might not have happened otherwise."

Nicole Adrian and Nathan Huitt, fellow food bloggers, started attending Soup Night as a way to meet other people interested in the same things: good food and good beer (Nathan brews his own). "The food is always delicious," Nicole says. "And it's a great way to get feedback on a new recipe. We invite others to taste the home-brewed beer. But the main thing is, we've become good friends with others who share our interests."

Paul and Lori host a food blog called Burp: Where Food Happens (www.eatatburp.com), and often write about Soup Night. The titles of the blog articles are quite revealing:

- The Power of Soup
- Soup Night: Why Size Really Doesn't Matter
- Seventy-Five Degrees with a Chance of Soup (April 2010)
- Blue Flower Soup and Lessons on Friendship

In one post, Lori talked about the beginnings: "Paul thought I was completely nuts, but I insisted that I really wanted to open up my home to others, to build community and really give myself a chance to get to know people who might otherwise remain strangers. . . . And now [that vision] is really coming to fruition. Everyone takes part in this amazing community of nourishment, both physical and spiritual. There's adventure. And sharing. And somehow, regardless of how many people show up, there's always enough. It's like nothing I've ever seen before."

Paul talks about the hiatus year. "After a year's break, we both wondered if we'd have the nerve to start up again. [But we did], and gosh, it was like coming home. Soup Night is really more about the company than the soup. It's about that feeling you get when you're surrounded by the people who really count. I know it's simple, but I can't help thinking: maybe all the world *really* needs is another Soup Night."

FOR RECIPES FROM PAUL AND LORI, SEE:
Blue Flower Soup, page 193
Tuna Chowder, page 196
Slow-Cooker Chili, page 194
Skillet Flatbread, page 218

Blue Flower Soup

Recipe from Lori and Paul Fredrich, Milwaukee, Wisconsin (profile, page 190)

Lori and Paul say: A creamy cauliflower soup with cracked anise and blue cheese.

Serves 6

1–2	tablespoons olive oil
3	celery stalks, diced
1	large onion, diced
3–4	garlic cloves, minced
4½	cups chicken broth
1	large head cauliflower, cored and chopped
½	cup dry white wine
1	tablespoon fresh lemon juice
2	teaspoons Worcestershire sauce
2	teaspoons cracked anise seed
2	teaspoons dried thyme
2	teaspoons hot sauce
1	cup blue cheese, crumbled
2	cups heavy cream
	Bacon, cooked until crisp and crumbled, as optional garnish

1. Heat the oil in a large soup pot over medium-high heat. Add the celery and onion and sauté until slightly tender, about 5 minutes. Add the garlic and sauté for 1 minute longer. Stir in the broth, cauliflower, wine, lemon juice, Worcestershire, anise seed, thyme, and hot sauce. Bring to a boil, then reduce the heat and simmer until the cauliflower is tender, about 15 minutes.

2. Transfer about half of the soup to a blender (careful, it's hot) and purée until smooth, and return it to the pot. Or use an immersion blender and purée the soup right in the pot. Stir in the blue cheese and cream. Stir until the cheese is melted and the soup is slightly thickened.

3. Serve hot with a sprinkling of crisp bacon, if you like.

Make ahead? Yes, if you need to, but this comes together quite quickly.

For large crowds: You could easily double this recipe, but you might wish to increase the blue cheese only 1½ times. Some people find blue cheese too strong (foolish, I think, but there you go).

Slow-Cooker Chili

Recipe from Nicole Adrian and Nathan Huitt, Milwaukee, Wisconsin (profile, page 190)

Nicole says: Nathan and I like our chili spicy, so we often add more "fire" at several stages. When browning the meat, we might add a few extra shakes of chili powder, garlic powder, and crushed red pepper. And where many folks would discard the jalapeño seeds, we leave them in. Of course, you could use ground turkey or chicken in place of the ground beef, but I have to admit that it tastes best with beef.

Serves 12–14

1 pound ground beef or turkey

1 (28-ounce) can diced tomatoes

1 (10-ounce) can chopped tomatoes with green chiles

2 tablespoons chili powder, or more to taste

1 teaspoon ground cumin

1 teaspoon ground coriander

1 teaspoon dried oregano

3 garlic cloves, minced

1 medium onion, chopped

1 jalapeño chile, chopped (we leave the seeds in) (see page 186)

1 (15-ounce) can black beans, drained; or 2 cups cooked black beans (see page 27)

1 (15-ounce) can kidney beans, drained; or 2 cups cooked kidney beans (see page 27)

1 (16-ounce) can refried beans (I use the vegetarian kind)

1 (6-ounce) can tomato paste

Frank's Red Hot sauce

1 (12-ounce) bottle of beer, preferably some type of brown ale (we've used Newcastle in the past — delicious!)

Optional Additions

1 teaspoon garlic powder

1 teaspoon red pepper flakes

1. Brown the beef in a skillet. For more heat, add additional chili powder, garlic powder, and pepper flakes to the meat while it is cooking. Using a slotted spoon, remove the beef to a slow cooker.

2. Add to the cooker the tomatoes, chili powder, cumin, coriander, oregano, garlic, onion, jalapeño, beans, tomato paste, hot sauce to taste, and beer. It will be very, very full! Cook on low at least 8 hours, or all day.

Variation: Use ground turkey or ground chicken in place of the ground beef.

Make ahead? Yes, let the slow cooker do the work.

For large crowds: You'll be limited by the size of your slow cooker.

Tuna Chowder

Recipe from Lori Fredrich, Milwaukee, Wisconsin (profile, page 190)

Lori says: My mother was a miracle worker with a can of tuna. She made the best tuna salad sandwiches. The best casseroles. And, apparently, the very best soup.

There are some dishes that, once eaten, leave an indelible impression. For me, "tuna soup" was one of those dishes. Mom made it regularly. And she frequently brought it to potlucks and soup dinners. The flavors of the soup were so indelibly ingrained in my head by the time I went to college that I took after my mother, cooking up pot after pot of this fantastic soup. Of course, I had to give it my own special twist. So, I started calling it tuna "chowder" — after all, a chowder is much more sophisticated sounding than a soup. Right?

Like tuna casserole, this deliciously creamy soup pulls together the comforting flavors of tuna, dill, cream, and peas. But, rather than noodles, you'll find spoonful after spoonful of perfectly cooked potatoes that have been rendered deliciously tender by a gentle 20-minute milk bath.

Serves 6

2 tablespoons butter

1 medium onion, diced

2 celery stalks, diced

2 tablespoons dried dill weed

4 medium potatoes, diced

6 cups whole milk

2 teaspoons bouillon paste or powder

3 cans water-packed tuna, including juice

1 (10-ounce) package frozen peas

1 cup cream

Salt and freshly ground black pepper

Shredded mozzarella cheese, for garnish

1. Melt the butter in a large soup pot over medium heat. When the foam has subsided, add the onion and celery and sauté until the onion is translucent, 4 to 5 minutes. Stir in the dill and potatoes. Pour in the milk and bouillon paste or powder. Bring to a boil, then reduce the heat and simmer until the potatoes are tender, 15 to 20 minutes.

2. Using a fork to separate large chunks, add the tuna and its juice to the soup. Stir in the peas and cook just until warmed. Add the cream. Taste for seasoning, adding salt and pepper to taste.

3. Serve hot with a sprinkling of mozzarella cheese and plenty of crusty bread.

Crab-Apple Soup

No, not crab apples, those little bitty fruits no one knows what to do with, but crab and apple, plus velvety avocado.

Serves 6

2 cups crabmeat (2 7½-ounce cans, or equivalent fresh crabmeat)

2 tablespoons butter

2 large apples, cored, peeled, and chopped

2 celery stalks, diced

2 tablespoons all-purpose flour

4 cups chicken broth

2 avocados, peeled, pitted, and chopped

1 cup light cream or half-and-half
Salt and freshly ground black pepper
Fresh chives or chive blossoms, for garnish

Make ahead? Yes, through step 4.

For large crowds: Unless you live where people catch their own, crabmeat is a splurge. This soup is probably best for a small dinner party at home.

1. If using fresh crabmeat, sort through it carefully for bits of cartilage, and remove. If using canned crabmeat, drain well. Set aside.

2. Melt the butter in a large soup pot over medium heat, add the apples and celery, and sauté until soft, about 4 minutes. Sprinkle the flour over the apple mixture, stir well to coat everything, and sauté for 1 minute. Add the broth and simmer, stirring now and then, until mixture is thickened and bubbling.

3. Add the avocados, and stir well.

4. Working in batches, transfer the soup to a blender (careful, it's hot) and purée until smooth, then return it to the pot. Or use an immersion blender and purée the soup right in the pot.

5. Add the reserved crabmeat and cream, and simmer the soup until heated through. Top each serving with snipped chives. Or better yet, if you happen to have chives in your garden and they are blooming (usually early spring), separate the lovely purple flower heads into individual bits and sprinkle a few on each soup bowl.

Empty Bowls

LONG BEACH PENINSULA, WASHINGTON STATE

Empty Bowls is an international grass-roots effort with two goals: to fight hunger, and to advocate for arts education. There are events all over the United States and several other countries, but each one is run by local artists, who shape the event to the circumstances of their community.

The basic idea is this: local potters contribute handmade bowls, local cooks contribute soup and bread, and those who attend purchase an empty bowl for $5 and enjoy a simple meal of soup and bread. Each person goes home with a bowl, and the money is donated to a local hunger-relief agency.

The one I know best is located on the Long Beach Peninsula in Washington State, a tiny sliver of land in the bottommost corner of the state, where the Columbia River meets the Pacific Ocean. The peninsula itself is only 28 miles long and 1.5 miles wide, and while there are about half a dozen small towns and villages throughout those 28 miles, in truth, it's like one small town all stretched out. It is no surprise, then, that this Empty Bowls event pulls in people from the entire peninsula, all of whom seem to know each other.

The coordinator is Karen Brownlee, a local potter. The first year of the event, she was asked to contribute handmade bowls, and found the whole thing so touching that she volunteered to fill the coordinator shoes the next year. Because one of the goals is to expose young people to art, Karen brought her potter's wheel to every classroom on the peninsula to teach kids how to do it. It was a major commitment of her time: twelve classrooms, two trips each — to help students make the bowls, which she took back to her studio to fire, and back to the schools so students could paint their creations, then back to the studio for the second firing. But she knows it was well worth it, because that year they had more bowls, more soup, and raised more money.

> **Local potters contribute handmade bowls, local cooks contribute soup and bread, and those who attend purchase an empty bowl for $5 and enjoy a simple meal of soup and bread. Each person goes home with a bowl, and the money is donated to a local hunger-relief agency.**

The following year brought great drama. Exactly one day before the event, a major tsunami struck Japan, a disaster guaranteed to unnerve residents of the peninsula, which is a defined tsunami zone. Should we cancel, the organizers wondered? Will we all be underwater (a not unrealistic possibility)? But in the end, they decided to continue, and it was their best turnout ever. Everyone came because it gave them the opportunity to check on everyone else, to see that their neighbors were okay, and they raised a record $5,500 for local food banks.

I have had the pleasure of attending this event, and I can tell you it's a hoot. It's held in a local church, on a Saturday. They replace the pews with long tables, but leave the piano, and somebody always sits down to play. One long table along the side wall is filled with pots of soup donated by local restaurants, and baskets of homemade bread are set out on every table. Middle school students act as servers, replenishing breads and clearing tables, and they take their jobs very seriously.

As you first enter, tables in the vestibule area are filled with the bowls made by students. They are clearly kid-made and utterly charming. People admire all the bowls, choose their favorite, pay their

$5, and take a seat at one of the tables. The food was delicious, the conversation buzz was intense, and I met lots of new people.

I made an error that day, and learned something important in the process. I thought that all the soups were available for tasting, and so I asked for a new bowlful. It was gently explained to me that part of the concept of Empty Bowls is to educate people about hunger; one bowl of soup and a piece of bread is all some people have to eat in a day, and the intention was that we would have the chance to experience what that's like. It was a powerful, humbling lesson.

www.emptybowls.net

Albondigas (Mexican Meatball Soup with Rice)

Recipe from Suzy and Philip Poll, Houston, Texas (profile, page 61)

Suzy says: Our Soup Nights always have a theme, and this one is popular for our Southwestern night.

Serves 6

1	tablespoon olive oil
1½	cups chopped onion
3	garlic cloves, minced
4	cups reduced-sodium beef broth
2	cups reduced-sodium chicken broth
1	(28-ounce) can fire-roasted diced tomatoes
¾	cup medium-hot green salsa
1	teaspoon ground cumin
1	teaspoon dried oregano
½	cup chopped fresh cilantro
½	cup cornmeal
¼	cup milk
1	egg
½	teaspoon salt
½	teaspoon black pepper
1	pound lean ground beef
¼	pound spicy pork bulk sausage
⅓	cup uncooked long-grain rice

1. Heat the olive oil in a large soup pot over medium heat. Add the onion and sauté until softened, about 5 minutes. Add the garlic and sauté about 3 minutes longer. Add the broth, tomatoes with juice, salsa, and half of the cumin (½ teaspoon), oregano (½ teaspoon), and cilantro (¼ cup). Bring the soup to a boil, and then reduce the heat to a simmer.

2. Make the meatballs: Combine the cornmeal and milk, and let rest until the milk is absorbed. Add the egg, salt, pepper, and remaining cilantro, cumin, and oregano. Mix well. Add the ground beef and sausage and stir to combine thoroughly. Form 1-inch meatballs.

3. Drop the meatballs into the simmering soup. Stir occasionally.

4. Add the rice and allow the soup to simmer until the rice is tender, about 20 minutes.

5. Ladle the soup into bowls and serve hot.

Make ahead? Yes, but Suzy cautions that over time the rice will puff and the soup will thicken. Add water or additional broth to thin as needed. Or, complete steps 1 and 2, but refrigerate the meatballs uncooked.

For large crowds: Suzy's original recipe makes twice this amount; I'm sure you could do more if needed.

Cream of Sherried Mushroom Soup

Recipe from Channing Meyer, Loveland, Colorado (profile, page 204)

Channing says: This is a variation on a recipe from one of the best chefs I have worked with, Brent Beavers. It has been adjusted to give it more of a sherry flavor, and has the addition of nutmeg for more complexity. It really is love in a bowl.

Serves 6

1 tablespoon olive oil

1 cup mirepoix (1 stalk celery, 1 carrot, and about ¼ medium onion , finely chopped; see note)

2 garlic cloves, minced

1½ teaspoons dried basil

1 teaspoon dried oregano

1 pound mushrooms, sliced (I use white button)

½ cup cream sherry

3 cups vegetable broth

3 cups heavy whipping cream (do not skimp, heavy is the best)

¼ teaspoon ground nutmeg

¼ teaspoon ground coriander (optional; makes the soup a bit sweeter)

1 teaspoon black pepper
   Salt

Roux (optional)

1 tablespoon butter

1 tablespoon all-purpose flour

Note: Mirepoix, a blend of aromatics in equal measure, usually contains celery, onion, and carrots. I like to use red onions, but other types will work. Cut the vegetables into very fine dice.

1. Heat the oil in a large soup pot, add the mirepoix and garlic, and sauté over medium-high heat until the onion is translucent and the carrots slightly softened, 4 to 5 minutes. Add the basil, oregano, mushrooms, sherry, and ½ cup of the broth. Cook until the mushrooms are softened slightly, stirring occasionally; check to see that there is still liquid in the bottom.

2. Add the remaining 2½ cups vegetable broth, cover, and simmer for 10 minutes.

3. Add the cream, nutmeg, coriander, and pepper. Simmer until the soup is reduced and thickened, about 45 minutes.

4. Some folks prefer a cream soup that is a bit thicker, especially in winter. To thicken the soup a bit more, make a roux: Melt the butter in a small saucepan, then add the flour, constantly whisking over medium heat. The roux will become brown and have a nutty flavor. Make sure not to get it too "hard" or dry, or it will be a bit more difficult to dissolve in the soup. If you do, just add a bit more butter. While the soup is at a slight boil, add the roux a bit at a time, using a whisk to dissolve. Add and wait for a minute to see how thick the soup is becoming.

5. Season with salt to taste, but go carefully; you do not want to actually taste salt in the finished soup. If you like, add a little more sherry or more of the herbs. Feel free to adjust as you see fit.

Make ahead? Yes, through step 5. Wait until reheating to determine whether it needs additional thickener.

For large crowds: Channing's full recipe makes 8 quarts — 32 servings!

Souperhood Soup Night

LOVELAND, COLORADO

They call themselves the West Endies, the residents of this very active historic neighborhood on the west side of downtown Loveland. And they do a Soup Night with gusto.

As is often the case with long-standing traditions, it's not completely clear how this Soup Night got started.

Laurie Wells remembers it this way: "We moved into the neighborhood in 2006, and didn't know anyone. I had read a magazine article about a Soup Night in California, and I thought, 'We could do that. Let's start it at our house.' So that first year we were hosts. Other people contributed ideas. Flyers announced 'BYOBS' — bring your own bowl and spoon — so the host didn't have to do lots of dishwashing afterward. The very first night, we learned that we needed to set an ending time. People were having such a good time they didn't want to leave! Later we put out a sign-up sheet for hosts, and that's all it took."

Regina Roberts has a different picture in her mind: "At the end of one of our streets there's a guardrail and beyond it is a beautiful view of the Colorado Rockies. Some of our neighbors used to gather there on summer evenings with a glass of wine and watch the sunset. At one point someone said, 'What shall we do in the winter?' Then Channing [Meyer] came up with the idea of Soup Night in people's homes."

I like to think that both these neighbors are right, that both these things happened simultaneously — and besides, does it really matter? Of course not.

"The main idea was to make it completely inclusive," Laurie says. "We were really worried that people would hear about it and realize that they weren't invited. So we sent kids around the neighborhood with flyers: 'Everyone's invited — bring your friends too.' It also coincided with the start of the recession. People seemed to become more interactive then, sharing tools, things like that. Soup Night just seemed to fit with where people were at the time."

As the months passed, they fine-tuned the idea. Now Soup Night is every other week during the winter months, January through May. Somebody came up with the name West Endies, and **Channing Meyer**, who owns an advertising agency, created an e-mail newsletter and a website for the neighborhood, including a calendar that lists all the events.

The full e-mail list (neighbors plus friends) has more than 100 names, and somewhere between 25 and 40 people usually attend. There are always two soups, one of which is vegetarian. To handle that many people, cohosting is

common. Sometimes people bring wine and other dishes to share, but the only real requirement is that everyone bring their own bowl and spoon. The invites always remind folks: BYOBS.

"It's a really nice event for everyone," Laurie says. "We have drawn people of all ages, and I've seen really good connections develop. For example, two single women lived around the corner from each other but didn't know each other until they met at Soup Night. They ended up traveling to Mexico together. It's really sweet to watch those kinds of connections happen."

Channing Meyer, who created the website that keeps the neighbors informed, points out that the Soup Night spirit has spilled over into other neighborhood events. They have a block party, a neighborhood garage sale, "orphan Thanksgiving," and movie nights in the summertime. The movie nights include a potluck dinner, tied to the theme of the movie. To view *Like Water for Chocolate*, people were asked to bring something chocolate; and for *The Help*, a Southern dish. All these activities nourish the sense of community in this neighborhood.

"Sometimes," Channing says, "people don't realize that they want community, until they see it in action. It doesn't just happen, we have to take the time to make it happen. You can't just stand aside. So we do it — we just do."

Regina Roberts adds a poignant personal story: "My husband and I came from West Virginia 13 years ago. Back there we had a community of like-minded friends who met once a month for Sunday brunch. We really missed that when we came to Colorado. Then we started this Soup Night, which led to other types of neighborhood gatherings, and suddenly there was a community — just what we had been looking for, and it was right in front of us. Everyone needs support and friendship — everyone. I believe that if everyone had a Soup Night to go to, there would no more crime, no more war. I really do believe that."

FOR RECIPES FROM SOUPERHOOD SOUP NIGHT, SEE:

Cream of Sherried Mushroom Soup, page 202

Carrot-Orange-Ginger Soup, page 206

Cornbread Souffle, page 221

Carrot-Orange-Ginger Soup

Recipe from Regina Roberts, Loveland, Colorado (profile, page 204)

Regina says: Since one [carrot soup] recipe called for orange juice, and we eat a lot of organic oranges, we developed the habit of saving the zest of every orange through the season. I thought it would make the soup especially unique if I added a lot of zest. We also love nutmeg and ginger, of which I added plenty. And of course, maple syrup makes everything better! We often serve this with [husband] John's delicious Cornbread Soufflé (see page 221).

Serves 6

2	pounds carrots, preferably organic
3	cups water or vegetable broth
1	bay leaf
1½	teaspoons salt
2	oranges
1	lemon
6	tablespoons vegetable oil
1	large onion, diced
6	garlic cloves, minced (more if you really like garlic)
1	(2-inch) piece fresh ginger, peeled and grated (more if you really like ginger)
⅓	cup chopped almonds
1	tablespoon pure maple syrup
¼	teaspoon freshly ground nutmeg, or more to taste
	Freshly ground black pepper
½	cup finely chopped fresh flat-leaf parsley

1. Scrub the carrots but don't peel them, and slice thinly. Add the water or broth to a large soup pot along with the carrots, bay leaf, and salt. Bring to a boil, then simmer on medium heat until the carrots are tender, about 20 minutes. Remove and discard the bay leaf, and let the soup cool to room temperature.

2. While the carrots are cooking, prepare the oranges and lemon. From one orange, remove the zest in strips, then slice the strips into thin matchsticks; reserve, for garnish. Grate the zest from the other orange and the lemon. Then slice all three fruits in half and squeeze out the juices. Set aside all zest and juice.

3. Heat the oil in a medium skillet over medium-high heat. Add the onion, garlic, ginger, and almonds, and sauté until golden. Add the sautéed mixture to the soup pot.

Garnishes

> Sour cream or plain yogurt
>
> Sliced almonds, toasted (see note, page 155)
>
> Orange zest strips (see step 2 for preparation)
>
> Additional finely chopped fresh parsley

Make ahead? Sure, all the way up to the garnishing. Refrigerate until serving time; reheat gently.

For large crowds: A very good choice for large gatherings, since the ingredients are so economical and so healthy!

4. Using an immersion blender, begin puréeing the soup right in the pot. Meanwhile, gradually add the orange and lemon juices and the grated orange and lemon zest. Add enough juice to create a soup that is creamy, not too thin. Stir in the maple syrup and nutmeg. Taste and adjust the seasonings as needed.

5. Keep the soup warm over low heat, stirring frequently so that it doesn't stick to the bottom of the pot. Just before serving, stir the chopped parsley into the soup.

6. Garnish each soup bowl with a swirl of sour cream, a sprinkle of toasted almonds, the reserved orange zest, and additional parsley.

Stone Soup, Project MANA
(MAKING ADEQUATE NUTRITION ACCESSIBLE)
TRUCKEE, CALIFORNIA

In 2009, deep into the recession, two restaurant chefs decided to try to help feed people who were struggling financially. The result was Stone Soup, occurring every Sunday night from January through April, designed to "bring the community together in times of economic stress. If you're not in need, you can come eat soup and donate some money. Bring your own bowl and spoon."

The dinners are held in the local community arts center, with generally 40 to 50 guests. Each week a different local organization cooks and serves for that night. Local bands play music and local restaurants donate dessert.

"We take only donations," project director Stephanie Blume explains, "but in the end the donations are enough that we are able to hire an organizer, so now the event really runs itself. We have a broad range of ages and demographics, and together they create an overall atmosphere that is very welcoming and kind. The whole idea was to bring the entire community together for soup, and it's working."

www.projectmana.org

Darya Pino
SAN FRANCISCO, CALIFORNIA

Darya started her Soup Night when she was living in a house in the San Francisco area with three roommates. Darya and her roommates never felt really comfortable inviting strangers into their home (young women in a big city, very understandable), so rather than reaching out to unknown neighbors, they decided that each roommate would invite friends and encourage them to bring other friends. This produced a free-floating happy mix of folks who often found interesting connections. A typical gathering was 20 people.

The four roommates took turns cooking, two people per month, always one vegetarian soup and one not. When interviewing potential new roommates, along with all the usual conversation about smoking, friends staying over, and garbage detail, Darya always made it clear they would have to be willing to cook for a large group of people, many of whom they would not know, once a month.

Orange Chicken Soup

Unexpected flavors of orange and allspice take this chicken soup to a new level. For an even richer taste and extra protein, swirl in about ¼ cup peanut butter. You don't appreciably taste it as peanut butter, but it lends a deeper flavor to the broth.

Serves 6

1 tablespoon olive oil
1 whole boneless, skinless chicken breast, cut into bite-size chunks
1 medium onion, diced
1 garlic clove, minced
1 green pepper, cored, seeded, and chopped
2 carrots, scrubbed and chopped
2 tablespoons butter
2 tablespoons all-purpose flour
1 (8-ounce) can tomato sauce
¼ teaspoon orange zest
⅓ cup orange juice
½ teaspoon sugar
¼ teaspoon salt
⅛ teaspoon ground allspice
4 cups chicken broth

1. Heat the oil in a heavy skillet over medium-high heat. Add the chicken and cook until the meat loses its pink color. Reduce the heat to medium. Add the onion, garlic, pepper, and carrots to the same skillet and sauté until the carrots are beginning to soften, about 5 minutes.

2. Melt the butter in a large soup pot over low heat; whisk in the flour, and cook for 1 minute. Stir in the tomato sauce, orange zest and juice, sugar, salt, and allspice, and cook 2 to 3 minutes, stirring constantly.

3. Add the broth and the chicken mixture to the soup pot. Bring to a boil, reduce the heat, and simmer about 15 minutes. Serve hot.

Make ahead? Yes.

For large crowds: You could easily double or triple everything but the chicken, increase it fractionally, and still have wonderful soup.

Thai Ginger-Chicken Soup

Rich with the flavors of Thailand — coconut milk, ginger, and lime — this wonderful soup is comfort food at its most exotic.

Serves 6

1 (14-ounce) can unsweetened coconut milk

1 (14-ounce) can unsweetened light coconut milk

3 cups reduced-sodium chicken broth

1 (1-inch) knob fresh ginger, peeled and grated

2 tablespoons fish sauce

3 tablespoons fresh lime juice

1 tablespoon grated lime zest

1½ pounds boneless, skinless chicken thighs, cut into ½-inch chunks

1 cup sliced mushrooms

2 scallions, thinly sliced, including some tender green tops

1 tablespoon chopped fresh cilantro

1 cup thinly sliced sugar snap peas

1½ cups frozen corn kernels

Garnishes

Thai red curry paste

Lime wedges

Chopped fresh cilantro

1. Combine the coconut milks, broth, ginger, fish sauce, lime juice, and zest in a large soup pot, heat to medium-low, and add the chicken. Simmer until the chicken is cooked through and the flavors have melded.

2. Stir in the mushrooms, scallions, cilantro, snap peas, and corn. Bring the soup back to a simmer, and cook just until the snap peas are tender-crisp, about 3 minutes.

3. At the table, add curry paste to taste (start with ¼ teaspoon or less per serving) and garnish with lime wedges and cilantro.

Make ahead? Through step 1; refrigerate.

For large crowds: Multiply by as much as 4.

Community Soup Night, Logan Square Kitchen
CHICAGO, ILLINOIS

Noah Stein is a young man on a mission: getting families involved in projects that promote healthy living — in particular, urban farming.

In Chicago neighborhoods, as in much of the country, community gardens are a very popular way for people without traditional garden spaces to grow fresh produce. Noah, a Chicago native who returned home after living in California for several years, was struck by what he describes as the "territorial nature" of community gardens there.

To break through that, he hit upon the idea of a community soup night. The overall goal is to get people who are involved in community gardens and gardening in general to know each other, to share ideas and resources. "Sharing soup," he says, "is of course an age-old idea."

He found a perfect venue in the Logan Square Kitchen, a commercial kitchen and event space committed to sustainability. He recruited volunteers to help with cooking and cleanup, got local grocers to donate bread and crackers, and found a sponsor in a local food co-op that offered him wholesale prices.

Noah did all the organizing, but "people I had never met came to help wash dishes. Some people brought desserts; we didn't ask, they just showed up." Sitting together at long tables, people were meeting each other for the first time and making good connections.

Soup Night is held monthly, on Tuesday evenings. There is no specific charge, but donations are welcome. At the first event, February 2011, more than 50 people attended; the next month, 75; and the third month, 100. Noah is especially pleased that about 25 percent of those attending are children. Getting whole families involved was his main goal.

www.logansquarekitchen.com

Roasted Garlic and Onion Cream Soup

Dennis Battles has had the great joy of taking cooking classes at Le Cordon Bleu in France. Back home in Long Beach, Washington, he uses those skills to create his own specialties, including this soup that honors the one item he says he can't imagine cooking without — garlic.

Serves 6–8

6 large sweet onions (such as Walla Walla or Vidalia), cut into ½-inch slices

2 heads garlic, cloves separated and peeled

5 cups chicken broth

1½ teaspoons dried thyme

1 teaspoon coarsely ground black pepper

1 teaspoon coarse kosher salt

4 tablespoons unsalted butter

2 cups heavy cream

2 tablespoons chopped fresh flat-leaf parsley

1. Preheat the oven to 350°F.

2. Place the onions and garlic in a shallow roasting pan, and add 3 cups of the chicken broth. Sprinkle with the thyme, pepper, and salt. Dot with the butter. Cover the pan with aluminum foil and roast for 1½ hours. Stir once or twice while roasting.

3. Purée the onions and garlic with the liquid, in batches, in a blender or food processor until smooth. With the motor running, gradually add the 2 remaining cups chicken broth and the cream.

4. Pour the soup into a large saucepan. Taste and adjust the seasonings and slowly heat through. Do not allow the soup to boil. Sprinkle with the parsley and serve.

Make ahead? Yes. Or, depending on your schedule, through step 3.

For large crowds: If you have a big enough roasting pan, you could double or triple this recipe.

Carrot Vichyssoise

This simple carrot soup is delicious both hot and cold. In warm weather, consider serving it chilled, in tall drinking glasses.

Serves 6–8

4	cups peeled and diced russet potatoes
2½	cups sliced carrots
2	leeks, trimmed and sliced (see page 186), or 1 small red onion, diced
6	cups chicken broth
2	cups cream or half-and-half
1–2	teaspoons salt
	Pinch white pepper
	Shredded carrots, for garnish
	Chopped fresh parsley, for garnish

1. Combine the potatoes, carrots, and leeks with the chicken broth in a large soup pot. Bring to a boil, reduce the heat, and simmer until the vegetables are very tender, about 20 minutes. (The potatoes will be falling apart, which is good.)

2. Working in batches, transfer the soup to a blender (careful, it's hot) and purée until smooth, then return it to the pot. Or use an immersion blender and purée the soup right in the pot.

3. Gently mix in the cream, salt, and white pepper. Bring the soup to a simmer and heat through.

4. Garnish each serving with shredded carrots and parsley.

Make ahead? Through step 2.

For large crowds: It's perfect for a crowd. Just multiply by as much as you need for your party.

Soup Sunday, Unity Church

SALEM, OREGON

On the first Sunday in May, the youth group of this church puts on a soup luncheon in the downstairs meeting room. It's a fund-raiser for the youth programs.

Parents and other adults have volunteered to bring soup, bread, or dessert. For a while the large, bright room is mostly empty and quiet. Then, about the time church service begins upstairs, chaos slides in downstairs. Seven soups arrive in large slow cookers, and there is a mad scramble for more extension cords. There aren't enough ladles. One of the tent cards, displaying the soup name, has fallen in the soup kettle. Teenage boys stand around, willing to work but clueless. Teenage girls take over, directing the boys to set up tables and chairs. Over all, the calm guidance of **Ann Armstrong**, youth education coordinator, keeps everything moving smoothly. She ran a restaurant kitchen for many years; she knows what she's doing.

When the worship service ends, people start to filter downstairs, dropping donations into a beautiful woven bowl, and line up to be served their choice of soup. In what seems like no time, everyone is seated at one of the long tables, enjoying hot soup, and the noise level has ratcheted up significantly.

One of the parents (and soup contributors) explains why she loves this event: "We're a family, people in this church. So on this day, I get to sit down with all my friends in one place and enjoy this lovely lunch. What could be better?"

Marilee Corey and her daughter Allison came up with the idea of Soup Sunday, and still serve as sponsors. "It's our way of giving back to the congregation that has given us so much," Marilee says. "These Sunday Soup lunches give everyone a chance to support our kids and get a nice meal at the same time." Allison, herself not far from teenagerdom, adds, "And the kids helping here get the satisfaction of knowing they are doing a service to the church."

Unlike some of the neighborhood gatherings profiled, this soup event was not created as a way to bring people closer. Most church members already know one another, in varying degrees of closeness. But it has that effect nonetheless. Eating together means that acquaintances grow into friendships, friendships get deeper and richer.

FOR SOUP RECIPES FROM THIS YOUTH MINISTRY, SEE:

African Peanut Soup, page 217

Fruit Soup Fit for a Princess, page 269

African Peanut Soup

Recipe from Ann Armstrong, Unity Church, Salem, Oregon (profile, page 216)

The taste of the peanut butter is almost unrecognizable here, but it adds a depth of flavor that you don't want to miss. Don't skip the sesame oil; it provides a flavor note I can only describe as haunting and essential. And sesame oil also adds authenticity: along with peanuts, sesame seeds were introduced into the United States by slaves from Africa, who called them benne. The soup is equally good and equally nutritious with or without the chicken.

Serves 6–8

2	tablespoons salad oil
1	tablespoon sesame oil
1	large onion, chopped
1	large green bell pepper, seeded and chopped
3	garlic cloves, chopped
4	cups chicken or vegetable broth
2	cups water
2	(14- to 15-ounce) cans diced tomatoes
1	tablespoon curry powder
½	teaspoon black pepper
¼	teaspoon red pepper flakes
½	teaspoon salt
½	cup uncooked rice
½	cup peanut butter
2–3	cups diced cooked chicken (optional)

1. Heat the salad oil and sesame oil in a large soup pot over medium heat. Add the onions, bell peppers, and garlic, and sauté until translucent, about 4 minutes. Add the chicken broth, water, tomatoes with their juices, curry powder, black pepper, pepper flakes, and salt, and simmer uncovered for 35 to 40 minutes.

2. Add the rice, and cook, covered, over low heat for about 20 minutes, or until the rice is tender.

3. Add the peanut butter, whisking until dissolved. Taste and add seasonings, if needed.

4. Add the diced chicken, if you wish, and bring the soup back to a simmer before serving.

Make ahead? Sure. But hold off on adding the chicken until dinnertime, so it doesn't get rubbery.

For large crowds: This is very easy, and very economical, to expand, especially if you opt for the vegetarian version.

For vegetarians: Use vegetable broth, and skip the chicken.

Skillet Flatbread

Recipe from Rebecca Gagnon, Milwaukee, Wisconsin (profile, page 191)

Rebecca says: The original recipe, which I have adapted for our family, was made in a food processor. That's quicker, but I usually make it by hand, because the truth is, I absolutely hate washing the food processor. A cast-iron skillet is essential here. I don't usually need to add any grease to the skillet since my pans are very well seasoned, but if the breads seem to stick, add a little oil to the pan. I use my homemade yogurt, which is the consistency of buttermilk, but I also like this recipe made with sour cream if I have it on hand, or I mix my runny yogurt with sour cream to equal ¼ cup. For the wheat flour, I use a high-protein whole wheat, or "white wheat" that is milled in Wisconsin and doesn't have a lot of wheat bran particles, but plain whole-wheat flour works well too.

Makes 8 breads

2¼	teaspoons instant yeast
1	cup warm water (110°F)
1	tablespoon olive oil or grapeseed oil
2	teaspoons honey
¼	cup sour cream or plain yogurt
½	cup whole-wheat flour
1½	teaspoons kosher salt
2	cups bread flour, plus additional as needed

1. In a medium bowl, sprinkle the yeast over the warm water. (If you are using regular yeast rather than quick-rise, add a bit of the honey at this point and wait for the yeast-water to "proof" — i.e., start bubbling.)

2. Add the oil, honey, and sour cream or yogurt, and mix with a sturdy spatula or wooden spoon until well combined. Add the whole-wheat flour and salt, and continue mixing until the batter is smooth. Add the bread flour, and continue mixing with a spoon or spatula until all the flour is incorporated, about 3 minutes.

Variations: Rebecca says, "You can also make pita-type breads with a pocket using this same dough. Roll the dough to the thickness of an earlobe, and bake them on a preheated pizza stone (500°F) for 5 to 6 minutes. You can usually fit 3 to 4 pitas on the stone at one time. I put the stone in the center rack position and watch to be sure they don't get too dark on the bottom. I have also made 16 smaller pitas rather than 8 rather large ones. It's really a good, versatile dough!"

Make ahead? Rebecca says, "I have had good luck making them earlier in the day, cooling them completely and wrapping them in foil, and then reheating in a medium oven or toaster oven."

For large crowds: An excellent choice for a Soup Night, since these breads appeal to both adults and kids.

3. Turn out the dough onto a lightly floured surface, and knead until smooth and elastic, 12 to 15 minutes, adding flour as necessary to aid in kneading. (Depending on the weather, the additional flour added can be substantial, more than 1 cup.) Squeeze the dough gently; if it is sticky, sprinkle with flour and knead briefly, just enough to combine.

4. Place the dough in a lightly oiled bowl, cover with plastic wrap, and let rise in a warm place for 30 to 45 minutes, or until the dough doubles in size.

5. Turn the dough out onto a lightly floured surface, and cut it into 8 equal pieces. Roll each piece into a tight ball (similar to forming a pizza dough ball), and cover with a clean towel.

6. Heat a cast-iron skillet (one with at least an 8-inch bottom surface) over medium heat until very hot. Throw in a drop of water; if it sizzles, your pan is hot.

7. One at a time, roll a ball of dough into a 4-inch round, let it rest for a few minutes, then roll it (or stretch it) until it is 6 to 7 inches round. Transfer the dough to the skillet, and bake on the first side until tiny bubbles appear, about 1 minute. Flip the bread, bake for 2 minutes, then flip again and continue baking for 1 to 2 minutes. Finished flatbread should be speckled with deep brown spots, but you should keep close attention on the heat, since cast iron tends to get hotter as it is heated.

8. When the breads come off the skillet, hold them in a stack of clean dishtowels to keep warm until serving.

Basic Batter Bread

Batter breads, by definition, are quick and easy — no kneading, no rising. This basic version is delicious all by itself (the sweetness of the molasses contrasts nicely with the tang of the buttermilk), but offers endless possibilities for improvisation. See suggestions below.

Makes 1 loaf

2½	cups all-purpose flour
1	teaspoon baking soda
1	teaspoon baking powder
1	teaspoon salt
4	tablespoons butter, melted
1½	cups buttermilk
½	cup molasses

1. Preheat the oven to 350°F. Butter an 8- by 4-inch loaf pan.

2. Combine the flour, baking soda, baking powder, and salt in a large mixing bowl. Stir in the butter, buttermilk, and molasses, mixing well.

3. Pour the batter into the loaf pan and bake for about 1½ hours, or until the top and sides of the loaf are golden brown and a toothpick inserted in the center tests clean. Cool the bread on a baking rack.

Variations: Use different flours, or a combination. Add a pinch of your favorite dried herb. Add raisins, nuts, or both. Add an egg for a richer batter.

Make ahead? You pretty much have to, but if you're smart you'll time it so the bread is coming out of the oven when your guests arrive.

For large crowds: Double the ingredients for two loaves. You may well want to make more than two, since the loaves freeze well, but you might find it easier to make the recipe multiple times, rather than tripling or quadrupling the ingredients.

Cornbread Soufflé

Recipe from John Roberts, West Endies, Loveland, Colorado (profile, page 204)

John says: I first tasted spoon bread when I was a college student in West Virginia 38 years ago. In the past 5 to 10 years, Regina and I have tried to create gluten-free versions of favorite recipes. This is one of the regular offerings from our oven.

Serves 6–8

2½	cups milk
1	cup cornmeal
2	tablespoons butter
4	eggs, separated
1	teaspoon salt
1	teaspoon baking powder

1. Put an 8-inch cast-iron skillet in the oven and preheat to 375°F.

2. Scald the milk in a large saucepan over medium-high heat. Reduce the heat and slowly add the cornmeal to the milk, whisking constantly until the mixture is quite thick. Remove from the heat.

3. Add the butter, then whisk in the egg yolks. Add the salt and baking powder.

4. In a separate bowl, beat the egg whites until stiff and fold into the cornmeal mixture.

5. Liberally oil the hot skillet and pour in the batter (listen to it sizzle!). Bake 45 minutes. Cut into individual portions and serve immediately.

Make ahead? Afraid not.

For large crowds? Yes, if you have a large enough skillet.

Claudia and Dave Darmofal
MEDFIELD, MASSACHUSETTS

In 1998, Claudia and Dave moved from Texas to Massachusetts, with two kids, a dog, and no family anywhere nearby. But they had known Suzy and Philip Poll in Houston, and knew all about their Soup Night (see page 61), so they decided to start one in their new Boston-area neighborhood. "It seemed a good way to get to know others in a concentrated way," Claudia says, "so we stole the Poll model. We love cooking, and we had seen how wonderful their Soup Night was, so it seemed a natural thing to try."

They began in 2000 with four other couples, all with small children. Those same couples are the core of the group to this day, even though some have moved away and others have been included. Visiting relatives are welcome; everyone's parents are honorary members.

"The adults are all pretty different," Claudia says, "but our kids are the common denominator. Somehow it just worked. You get a bunch of people sitting around a table sharing food, and good things will happen. We are closer to those people than to almost anybody else. We had no idea it would turn out this way."

Their standard format is a monthly Soup Night, on a Saturday. "When the kids were young, we started early, so it went from 4 to 8 PM. Then people started bringing pj's for the kids so they could stay later. Then as kids got older we gradually made it later; now it's 5 or 6 to 11.

When the kids were younger, we served them a full meal first, then they would go downstairs and watch a movie or something while the adults ate. Now sometimes they join us."

For the first seven or eight years Soup Night was always at the Darmofal home, but in recent years others have hosted. In any case, there's a community approach to the dinner, which always features two soups, one vegetarian and one meat, along with appetizers and dessert. "We have a good-sized kitchen," Claudia says, "and a stove with six burners. When we host we make the soups the night before, since they're better the next day anyway. Now people know where the

> We hear from all the kids how much they look forward to it. They've grown up together, these past 12 years, and they're really close. That's one of the best things for us, to see how the kids interact.

cutting boards are, and they just jump in and do what needs doing. Something about making and sharing food just brings people together."

The Darmofals plan out a full year's Soup Night calendar — October to May — and e-mail it to everyone all at once, with dates. "We never cancel; even if just one family can make it, we still do it. But now that other people are doing the hosting, they can change the dates if they need to for some reason."

One of the aspects of Soup Nights that I find spectacularly touching is how much the tradition means to the children; it's a theme that comes up over and over, and the Darmofals are no exception. Claudia explains: "We have two teenage girls, Madison and Abigail, and they LOVE it. We hear from all the kids how much they look forward to it. They've grown up together, these past 12 years, and they're really close. That's one of the best things for us, to see how the kids

interact. Most of them are now 16 or 17, in that range, both boys and girls. One thing I really appreciate is that our girls know these boys in a healthy way, and so some of that awkward boy-girl stuff goes away. All these kids look forward to coming. We know that the parents juggle schedules so that even if there's something like a soccer practice, one parent comes for a while and then the other so that everyone can be here at least part of the time. They don't want to miss it."

Anna Bueno echoes this idea. "Our children are linked to each other by Soup Night. As they've gotten older, of course they're busier with their activities, and so they don't always make it. But our three boys love it, and they would never miss two in particular — Halloween and Cinco de Mayo. One year on Cinco de Mayo night my husband and I had a conflict and told the kids we couldn't go. We had a mutiny on our hands: 'No way are we going to miss that,' they said. So we had

to drive them over, go to our own commitment, and come back to pick them up. We didn't even get to go!"

Dave describes the personality of the event. "Our Soup Nights have themes, and we do it top to bottom; every part of the evening reflects that theme. The first and the last Soup Night (October, May) coincide with our daughters' birthdays, so we make them extra-special. For the October birthday, we set up a haunted house in our basement for the kids. One year my mother and her sister surprised the kids by showing up in costume in the haunted house. In May, we always have Cinco de Mayo for the May 11 birthday. We make it a big party, with piñatas for the kids and margaritas for the adults; one year we even had a small mariachi band."

The soup themes match the calendar pretty closely. October, Halloween month, there is always one black soup and one orange soup. In December, one red soup and one green. January is a Chinese soup, in honor of Chinese New Year, and March celebrates Mardi Gras with some New Orleans specialty. The other, non-holiday months are opportunities for other themes. "Once our theme was 'Going Green,'" Dave says. "We had green soups, and we recycled

everything. We turned off all the electricity and so there was no TV for the kids. Instead we asked them to do a talent show for us, and it was fantastic, one of the best Soup Nights ever."

Before my scheduled telephone visit with them, Claudia and Dave had contacted all their friends and asked if there was anything they wanted to pass on to me. Almost everyone said versions of the same sentiment: Be sure to tell her it's not just about the soup. It's about spending time together. "And really you can see it when people walk in the door," Dave adds. "It's something like a sigh of relief, knowing it will be an easy, warm, comfortable evening. Just good friends getting together, no pressure. We all look forward to it. No one wants to miss it. In fact, on one recent Soup Night one of our families was in Singapore; the husband was on sabbatical and the whole family went. We decided to Skype them in that evening, even though it was breakfast time for them. So we all still ate together — they were eating breakfast and we were having soup. It was great."

You get a bunch of people sitting around a table sharing food, and good things will happen.

FOR A RECIPE FROM THIS GROUP, SEE:
Strawberry Gazpacho, page 240

Yummy Coleslaw

Recipe from Elizabeth Newland, Civano Soup Supper, Tucson, Arizona (profile, page 46)

Elizabeth says: I serve this to houseguests in Arizona with cornbread and my no-pepper chili (see page 50). It is even better on Day 2! I make it and the cornbread a day ahead, and leave the chili simmering in the slow cooker while we all go out for a day of sightseeing. When we get back, all we need to make are the margaritas and dinner is ready!

Serves 6

4   cups cabbage (a mixture of red and green is pretty)

6   scallions, chopped

2   carrots, grated

1   cup golden raisins

Dressing

¾   cup good-quality mayonnaise

2   tablespoon red or white wine vinegar

1   teaspoon caraway seeds

½   teaspoon salt

¼   teaspoon freshly ground black pepper

1. Thinly slice the cabbage; a mandoline is a great tool for this. Put the cabbage in a bowl and add the scallions, carrots, and raisins; mix well.

2. Make the dressing: Combine the mayonnaise, vinegar, caraway seeds, salt, and pepper in a small bowl or jar; mix well.

3. Fold the dressing into the salad and chill in the refrigerator for at least 1 hour.

Make ahead? It's recommended — see Liz's comments above.

For large crowds: Easily multiplied.

Not Your Grandmother's Green Pea Salad

Virginia Tackett of Hillboro, Oregon, created this salad after a friend complained, "I like all the individual ingredients in pea salad, but it always lacks something — and I really don't like mayonnaise!" Well, Virginia said, I can fix that. And this recipe is the result. It was such a hit that she has been asked to make it again and again. It's wonderful as is, but Virginia notes that it's also easy to "fancy up" for parties.

Serves 6

1   (16-ounce) package frozen petit pois (tender young peas), thawed and drained

2   celery stalks, thinly sliced

1   bunch small scallions, thinly sliced, including some of the green tops

1   (6-ounce) can sliced water chestnuts, drained

3   ounces blue or Gorgonzola cheese, crumbled

½   cup slivered almonds

¾–1   cup good-quality thick blue cheese dressing

1. Layer the peas, celery, scallions, water chestnuts, blue cheese, and almonds in a medium salad bowl and stir gently to combine. Add the dressing gradually; the salad should be moist, but not runny.

2. Chill for an hour or so, longer doesn't hurt. Serve cold.

Variations: Add one or more of the following: ¼ cup green bell pepper, seeded and finely chopped; ½ cup extra-sharp white cheddar, cut into small cubes; ½ cup thinly sliced red or white radishes. For Christmas, Virginia also adds ¼ cup sweet red pepper, finely chopped, to the green pepper.

Make ahead? Yes.

For large crowds: Virginia is often asked to bring this salad to potlucks, and she makes double or triple, depending on the number of guests she anticipates.

Country Cooks

Virginia Tackett is one of those wonderful "country" cooks that the world needs more of. She was raised on an Iowa farm, with grandparents a mile away and lots of aunts, uncles, and cousins nearby.

At harvest time, all the men and boys from nearby farms would form themselves into a giant threshing crew and move from farm to farm. Each family was expected to feed the whole crew when it came, and at the end of the season there was a huge community-wide feast.

It's no surprise, growing up in that environment, that Virginia started cooking seriously when she was five, so small she needed a stool to reach the stovetop. And it's also no surprise that she has continued a lifelong love of cooking and feeding people.

Spinach-Almond Salad *(photo, page 181)*

Recipe from Albertina's Restaurant, Portland, Oregon (profile, page 55)

This salad, made with rice, bacon, and fresh spinach, comes close to being a main dish. Together with a vegetarian soup (maybe Carrot Vichyssoise, page 214), it makes a lovely luncheon.

Serves 6–8

Almond Dressing

- ⅓ cup canola oil
- ¼ cup red wine vinegar
- 1 tablespoon sugar
- 1 teaspoon dry mustard powder
- ¼ teaspoon almond extract

Salad

- 3 cups cooked long-grain rice, chilled
- ½ cup thinly sliced red onion, plus extra for garnish
- 8 bacon strips, crisply fried and crumbled

  Freshly ground black pepper
- ¼ cup sliced almonds, toasted (see page 155)
- 6 cups spinach leaves, washed and torn

1. Make the dressing: Whisk the oil, vinegar, sugar, mustard, and almond extract together in a small bowl.

2. Combine the rice, red onion, and dressing in a bowl. Refrigerate.

3. At serving time, mix in the bacon, pepper to taste, and almonds. Toss the rice mixture with the spinach in a serving bowl. Garnish each serving with a few red onion rings.

Make ahead? Yes, up through step 2.

For large crowds: This salad is quite easy to expand, either double or triple.

Apple Cider Vinaigrette

Recipe from Albertina's Restaurant, Portland, Oregon (profile, page 55)

This is a very light, fresh-tasting dressing that goes well with all types of green salads. It's low in calories, too, thanks to the lower-than-usual ratio of oil to vinegar.

Makes 4 cups

1   (12-ounce) can apple juice concentrate, thawed but *not* diluted

1½   cups cider vinegar

½   cup Dijon mustard

1¾   cups olive oil

1. Combine the apple juice concentrate, vinegar, and mustard in a blender.

2. Add the olive oil in a slow stream and blend until combined.

Variation: Substitute orange juice concentrate for the apple, for a citrus version that is equally delicious.

Make ahead? I recommend it; the flavors will meld better.

For large crowds: Of course. One year I made a huge batch and gave away pretty bottles of it as Christmas gifts; now my friends nag me for more.

Wonder Bars *(photo, page 181)*

Another wonderful recipe from David Kenworthy (see page 179). These can be made with lemon, lime, key lime, or Meyer lemon juice. They're so low-calorie (relatively speaking, of course), David thought they should be promoted by Weight Watchers!

Makes 9 bars

Crust

5	tablespoons butter, softened
¼	cup packed brown sugar
	Pinch salt
¼	teaspoon freshly grated nutmeg
1	cup all-purpose flour
	Cooking spray

Filling

1	cup lowfat (1%) cottage cheese
1	cup granulated sugar
2	tablespoons all-purpose flour
1	tablespoon lemon or lime zest
3½	tablespoons freshly squeezed lemon or lime juice
1	large egg
1	large egg white

Make ahead? It's necessary (see step 6).

For large crowds: I would make this recipe multiple times, rather than trying to multiply the ingredients.

1. Preheat the oven to 350°F.

2. Make the crust: Place the butter, brown sugar, salt, and nutmeg in a mixing bowl and beat with a mixer at medium speed until smooth. Add the flour to the butter mixture and beat at low speed until well blended.

3. Lightly press the crust with a spatula into an 8-inch square baking pan coated with cooking spray. Bake for 20 minutes, until browned.

4. While the crust is baking, make the filling: Place the cottage cheese in a food processor and process 2 minutes or until smooth, scraping the sides of the bowl once. Add the sugar, flour, zest, juice, whole egg, and egg white, and process until well blended.

5. Pour the filling over the hot crust. Bake for 25 minutes or until set (the edges might get lightly browned), then cool on a wire rack.

6. Cover the bars and place in the fridge overnight. Cut into 9 bars and devour.

Cuban Flan

My good friend Mary Knight, of Spokane, Washington, says she has been making this dessert for 15 years, and it gets raves every time. Flan, something like a Latin American cheesecake, is a wonderful dessert to include in a Cinco de Mayo celebration or accompany Albondigas soup (see page 200).

Makes 6–8 servings

½ cup sliced almonds
Cooking spray
½ cup sugar
1 (13-ounce) can evaporated milk
1 (14-ounce) can sweetened condensed milk
1 (8-ounce) package cream cheese
3 eggs
1 teaspoon vanilla extract

Make ahead? It's necessary.

For large crowds: If I were doing this, I would make the recipe twice, rather than doubling ingredients.

1. Toast the almonds (see note on page 155).Set aside, and increase the oven temperature to 350°F.

2. Fill a large roasting pan with water to a level of 1 inch. Lightly grease a 9-inch cake pan with nonstick spray.

3. Caramelize the sugar in a saucepan over low heat; this requires stirring constantly to prevent the foaming syrup from scorching. When the sugar is a thick, brown liquid, pour it into the prepared cake pan, spreading evenly. (Be careful; melted sugar is extremely hot.) Set the cake pan into the water bath in the roasting pan.

4. In a blender or food processor, combine the milks, cream cheese, eggs, and vanilla; blend thoroughly. Carefully pour the mixture over the sugar in the cake pan.

5. Bake for 55 to 60 minutes, until the custard is completely set; a toothpick inserted into the center should come out clean. Cool on a wire rack, and then chill the flan thoroughly in the refrigerator.

6. Invert the flan on a serving plate. Sprinkle with the toasted almonds.

CHAPTER FIVE

Summer

Summer — is there anything better? Fireflies and crickets, long hours of sunlight, spur-of-the-moment barbecues, and air so soft and sweet you wish you could bottle it. People who love to cook are downright giddy over the bounty of fresh vegetables and fruits in farmers' markets and home gardens, and eager to experiment.

Soup lovers turn their attention to recipes that feature the fresh vegetables of the season — tomatoes, peppers, eggplants, summer squash. This is also the season for fruit soups, using the bounty of fresh-as-can-be berries and peaches; they sparkle as either dessert or a first course. And now good cooks look for inventive ideas for cold soups, including the all-time summer classic: gazpacho, presented here in three versions.

Soup Night on Stanton Street: May

The last Soup Night of the season brings nice weather. In Oregon's fickle climate, late spring comes with no guarantee, but tonight is pleasantly warm — not soft like the evening air in August, but sweet with the promise of summer. Many folks take their soup bowls and wineglasses out to the front steps. It gives them a good view of the brand-new treehouse, now being christened by all the kids. It's the latest Stanton Street adventure, and a tangible demonstration of what happens when people come together in joyful cooperation, creating something for all.

It started with a sidewalk encounter. A teacher at the local elementary school, who lives a few blocks south but walks down Stanton Street on his way to work, stopped to chat with Becky and her young son Sam.

Chilled Cucumber Soup with Shrimp (page 267), Raspberry-Lemon Pie (page 284), and Ariana's Pink Potato Salad (page 276).

"I have an idea," he said. "We have this wooden play structure in our backyard that our kids have outgrown. Your boy is about the right size, and I'd like to give it to you."

Next thing Becky knew, a pile of used lumber and rusty bolts appeared by her front porch. Becky, who is codirector of an alternative school, firmly believes that children need adventures. So she said, "To heck with a play structure, let's build a treehouse."

Her first step was to find a library book on treehouses, and her second was to enlist Chuck, a retired attorney with lots of construction skills. Chuck in turn recruited his son Sam, a third-year architecture student.

It's hard to overstate how great it is, how much the neighborhood means in my life. I believe that our lives are what we make them. We could choose to stay in and be lonely, or choose to find a way to bring people together. We're making the neighborhood what we want it to be, in a positive way. And besides, it's just so much fun.

— *Alex*

Some parameters became clear immediately.

The tree needed to be in someone's front yard, because all the life of the block happens out front, and it needed to be tall enough, strong enough, and with a branch structure open enough to accommodate the treehouse. Only one tree fit that bill, a cherry tree growing in the parking strip at Becky and Lisa's. A perfect location, since that house is already central for all the kid activities.

All the pieces of donated lumber were 4 feet long, so the construction plan had to start with that common denominator. Safety was paramount. And the goal was to make the treehouse look like kids built it.

When all this was agreed on, the father-and-son team started work. There was always a gaggle of kids bouncing around, wanting to help, offering suggestions (Reuben wants a crow's nest; sorry, Reuben), asking when will it be finished. Four-year-old Sam (known on the block, inevitably, as Little Sam) spent most of his time trying to figure out how to keep a carpenter's pencil behind his ear, so he could look just like Chuck.

The safety mechanism is brilliantly simple. About two-thirds of the way up from the ground, wooden rungs are bolted to the tree trunk. If kids are tall enough and strong enough to get to them on their own, then they are free to do

so. The smaller kids have to use a ladder built especially for the purpose, and it is kept in the backyard under adult supervision — the little kids have to ask for it, and they can't climb the tree without it.

Construction was halted at one point when Alex wandered over and expressed some concern that the side walls made of threaded ropes left large enough openings for little kids to fall through. And since Alex the MD is the one who would get called on in the event of bloodshed, he asked the designers to reconfigure the ropes. So extra cross-members of wood were added and the ropes rethreaded.

The finished treehouse is seldom unoccupied. On any given day, several kids are up there, giggling and making up pirate games. It was meant to be a platform for creativity, and I have no doubt it has succeeded magnificently. But I can't tell you what goes on up there because grown-ups are not allowed.

And it definitely looks kid-made. The flat surfaces aren't quite even, and the corners aren't exactly square. This is deliberate, and it only adds to the charm. Reuben the Fearless has a suggestion for the next step: add a zipline from the roof of his house across the street to the top of the treehouse. Sorry, Reuben.

This night, watching the kids enjoy the treehouse, the adults turn their conversation to plans for the summer. Several offer suggestions for upcoming movie nights, a favorite summertime activity on the block. They spread out blankets on two adjoining lawns for picnic suppers, and screen movies using equipment borrowed from the teacher's school.

It's also not too early to start thinking about the block party. Soup Night is on hiatus in the summer, and the block party in September, the first "official" get-together for the whole block, takes the place of Soup Night for that month. It is at the block party that the sign-up sheet for the coming year's Soup Nights is posted. Discounting the three summer months, and September, that leaves only eight slots to be filled in. There's no difficulty getting hosts, in fact there's some fairly serious competition for the privilege. In a matter of minutes, the whole Soup Night calendar for the coming year is filled.

And so it continues.

Macho Gazpacho

Recipe from Eric and Kat Meyer, Cleveland, Ohio (profile, page 132)

Like a great many peasant dishes, gazpacho allows for unlimited variations. The idea is to take advantage of the season's vegetable bounty, using whatever is perfectly ripe and ready.

Serves 6

4	large tomatoes, diced
2	medium cucumbers, seeded and diced
5	cups V-8 juice (the spicy variety if you're a glutton for punishment)
1	onion, chopped
	Juice of ½ medium lemon (about 1½ tablespoons)
	Juice of ½ medium lime (about 1 tablespoon)
2	tablespoons vinegar
2	tablespoons olive oil
2	teaspoons honey
1	tablespoon chopped fresh basil
¼–1	teaspoon red curry paste (yellow curry is slightly less hot; we like Thai Kitchen brand)
	Crème fraîche (facing page), sour cream, or plain yogurt, for garnish

1. Set aside about one-third of the diced tomatoes and cucumber.

2. Put the remaining tomatoes and cucumber in the blender, along with the V-8 juice, onion, lemon and lime juices, vinegar, oil, honey, and basil. Add curry paste to taste, and purée.

3. Place the soup in a large serving bowl; stir in the reserved tomatoes and cucumbers.

4. Garnish each serving with crème fraîche, sour cream, or yogurt; serve with warm French bread.

Make ahead? It only gets better. It's best very cold, so the time in the refrigerator is a good thing.

For large crowds: Easy to multiply, although you'll probably have to do the blending in batches.

MAKING CRÈME FRAÎCHE

You can buy crème fraîche already made, but why would you, when it's so very easy to make at home? In a glass jar with a lid that really fits, combine 2 cups heavy cream with 2 tablespoons buttermilk. Shake hard for a minute or two, and leave the jar on your counter for a day, or overnight. Stir, and then refrigerate 24 hours before serving. No buttermilk on hand? You can use plain yogurt or sour cream instead.

Garden Gazpacho

Pure summer, in a bowl. Refreshing, healthy, and beautiful to look at. In a perfect world, I would make gazpacho from vine-ripened tomatoes that I picked that very morning from my own garden and puréed with a little lemon juice or red wine vinegar. But I live in rainy Oregon, where we have all too many "green tomato summers" (not enough warm days to ripen anything), and so I have relied on commercial tomato juice instead. And it works just fine. If I happen to have a can of tomato paste open, I might add a tablespoon of that as well.

Serves 6–8

1   cup cherry tomatoes, frozen (facing page)
1   (46-ounce) can tomato juice or tomato cocktail
1   cup peeled, seeded, and chopped cucumber
½   cup finely chopped onion
½   cup diced green or red bell pepper
3   tablespoons olive oil
2   tablespoons lemon juice or red wine vinegar
1   teaspoon garlic powder
1   teaspoon hot sauce (optional)
    Salt and freshly ground black pepper

Garnishes

Prepare about 2 cups each of your choices from the following:

Red, yellow, orange, or purple bell pepper, diced

Red onion, finely diced

Green or yellow zucchini, sliced thin and cut into half-rounds

Avocado, peeled, pitted, and diced

Scallions, diced

Cucumber, diced

Yellow tomatoes, diced

Fresh cilantro, finely chopped

Fresh-made croutons (see page 248)

1. At least a day ahead (or whenever you have them on hand), freeze the cherry tomatoes.

2. Using a blender or food processor, blend the tomato juice with the cucumber, onion, bell pepper, olive oil, lemon juice, and the seasonings. Chill the soup for at least 1 hour.

Variation: To make the soup spicier, you can either add hot sauce or substitute tomato cocktail (such as V-8) or Bloody Mary mix for the plain tomato juice.

Make ahead? You'd be silly not to — the longer it waits in the refrigerator, the better.

For large crowds: You can make a train-car full if you have enough veggies. This is a perfect thing to do in late summer when your garden is going crazy.

3. Prepare the garnishes, choosing with an eye to color as well as taste. You have already put cucumber, onion, and bell pepper in the soup itself, because those flavors are traditional, but it's nice to serve extra, along with other fresh ingredients from the list.

4. To serve, place all the garnishes in your prettiest bowls or clear glass tumblers, to show off the luscious colors. Return the soup to the blender, add in the frozen tomatoes, and blend. Serve immediately with warm bread.

TOMATO ICE CUBES

Some gazpacho recipes call for adding chunks of bread, soaked in water and then squeezed. I tried it, but never liked it much. Its purpose is to add body, and it does, but I never could get away from knowing I was eating mushy bread.

Then I came up with another idea.

Here's my trick: Freeze a handful of cherry or grape tomatoes, and add them to the blender at the last minute. These "tomato ice cubes" make the soup thick, in exactly the same way that ice cubes do for frozen daiquiris or frozen fruit does for your breakfast smoothie. And you're eating pure tomato goodness, not bread.

Strawberry Gazpacho

Recipe from Anna Bueno, Bedford, Massachusetts (profile, page 223)

Anna says: I learned to cook from my mother. When I was growing up in Barcelona, we all went home for lunch from school, and I would watch her cook and she would teach me things. Just little things about whatever she was making at the time. No recipe, just talking.

One of the things we often had on hot summer days was a bowl of cold gazpacho. But sometimes, the strong aroma of the garlic and the onion was too much. A couple of years ago, while having a lovely dinner at home with some friends, one of the guests suggested adding some strawberries to the traditional gazpacho and using less garlic. I decided to try it, and I also reduced the usual amount of sweet red pepper and cucumber. The result was an incredibly refreshing, fruity gazpacho. Make sure you only use the freshest, highest-quality ingredients for this soup.

Serves 6

6   ripe tomatoes, seeded and chopped (about 4 cups)

4   cups hulled and sliced fresh strawberries

¼   onion, finely chopped

¼   English cucumber, peeled, seeded, and chopped

¼   bell pepper, red or green, seeded and chopped

¼   garlic clove, minced

⅓   cup olive oil

¼   cup sherry wine vinegar
     Salt and freshly ground black pepper

1. Measure the chopped tomatoes. If you have more than 4 cups, slice additional strawberries to equal the volume of the tomatoes.

2. Combine the tomatoes and strawberries in a blender, and add the onion, cucumber, bell pepper, garlic, oil, vinegar, and salt and pepper to taste. Blend to a smooth consistency.

3. Place the soup in a container, cover tightly, and refrigerate overnight, allowing the flavors to blend. Serve very cold.

Make ahead? It's necessary; see step 3.

For large crowds: This is a fine choice for large groups when gardens are overflowing with tomatoes.

Cold Tomato-Yogurt Soup

The yogurt adds a pleasant tang — and protein — to this simple, refreshing summer soup.

Serves 6

4 cups chopped tomatoes, or tomato juice

2 cups plain yogurt

½ cup finely chopped celery

2 tablespoons lemon juice

  Salt and pepper

  Chopped parsley or chives, for garnish

1. Purée the tomatoes in a blender; strain. In a pinch (or in a different season), you can use canned tomato juice.

2. Combine the tomato purée, yogurt, celery, and lemon juice. Taste the soup, and season with salt and pepper.

3. Chill the soup for at least 1 hour; even overnight is fine. Serve very cold, garnished with parsley or chives.

Make ahead? Yes; see step 3.

For large crowds: As many multiples as you have fresh tomatoes; this is another good use for your rambunctious garden.

MAKE YOUR YOGURT GREEK

Greek-style yogurt, suddenly so popular and omnipresent in America, is nothing more than regular yogurt from which the excess water has been removed. Straining yogurt is easy to do yourself: Place a very fine sieve (or regular sieve lined with cheesecloth) over a bowl, pour in yogurt, and let it drain. When all the water that is going to drain away has done so, you'll have about half the volume of yogurt you started with. And if you enjoy baking, save the whey; this nutritious yellowish liquid adds a tang to homemade bread and rolls that will remind you of sourdough.

Red Pepper–Tomato Bisque

On an unexpectedly chilly summer night, serve this delicious soup hot; otherwise, it's splendid served cold.

Serves 6

4 red bell peppers
1 yellow bell pepper
1 tablespoon olive oil
½ cup diced onion
1 garlic clove, minced
1 potato, diced
⅔ cup tomato juice
3 cups water
1 tablespoon balsamic vinegar

Garnishes

Parsley, scallions, chives, or cilantro, finely chopped

Parmesan Lace (page 37), (2–3 pieces per serving)

1. Roast 3 of the red bell peppers on your outdoor grill, stovetop burner, or under the broiler until the skin starts to bubble and blacken. Place the roasted peppers in a plastic bag for 5 to 10 minutes. When cool enough to handle, remove the skin and seeds, and roughly chop the flesh.

2. Remove the seeds from the remaining red bell pepper and the yellow bell pepper; dice and set aside for garnish.

3. Heat the oil in a large soup pot over medium heat and sauté the onion, garlic, and potato for 1 minute. Add the tomato juice and water and bring to a boil, then reduce the heat, cover, and simmer until the potato is tender, 15 to 20 minutes.

4. Place the tomato mixture, vinegar, and roasted red peppers in a blender and purée until smooth.

5. Serve the soup hot or cold, depending on the weather and your whim. Garnish with the reserved bell peppers.

Shortcut: Red peppers in a jar, already roasted and peeled, are available in most supermarkets — and are a whole lot easier to use.

Make ahead? You bet.

For large crowds: With its inexpensive and nutritious ingredients, this is an ideal choice for a summertime patio party.

Portland Stock,
a Sunday Soup initiated by InCUBATE
PORTLAND, OREGON

InCUBATE (Institute for Community Understanding Between Art and the Everyday) is a national, and now international, nonprofit that focuses on finding alternative ways to support the arts. One of their most popular programs is called Sunday Soup, in which individual communities provide micro-grants to local artists by hosting affordable suppers. As of 2012, there were 71 different Soup Supper groups around the world, most in the U.S. but also in Ukraine, South Africa, Spain, Egypt, the United Kingdom, Australia, and Canada.

Each city decides for itself how to orchestrate the soup supper, but certain basics are the same: Everyone who attends buys a $10 meal ticket, local artists describe a project they would like to do, and the diners vote on their favorite. At the end of the evening, the winner is awarded the net proceeds from the dinner sales. Here are some numbers from 2012: The 71 groups around the world have awarded a total of $64,480 in micro-grants to local artists.

The Sunday Soup event in Portland, Oregon, is called Portland Stock. It's a nice play on words: *stock* as in soup broth, *stock* as in an equity investment vehicle, *stock* as in "we who came tonight have a stake in this thing." Portland Stock was started in 2009 by three women artists, all graduate students interested in what they term "socially engaged art." They were also intrigued with the idea of using food and cooking as a way to create community, and decided a Portland version of Soup Supper could accomplish both.

The first diners sat on borrowed chairs and ate homemade soups out of flea-market bowls. Then the curator of the gallery at the local arts college offered his space — big tables, lots of chairs, and a real kitchen — and the event really took off. Now they attract about 100 people to the dinners, and have created a format that encourages — almost

Everyone who attends buys a $10 meal ticket, local artists describe a project they would like to do, and the diners vote on their favorite. At the end of the evening, the winner is awarded the net proceeds from the dinner sales.

demands — conversation among the guests.

Here's how it works: The candidate projects (always limited to 10) are described on large posters on the gallery walls. The guests study the posters, then take their place in the food lines and find a seat at one of the long tables. Because the tables are set for 10, it is almost inevitable that people end up sitting with folks they don't know. During dinner, they discuss the 10 projects (a reminder sheet on each table summarizes the 10 proposals), and then vote for their favorite. The top three are announced, and the diners start another round of discussion.

The most recent past winner makes a brief presentation about her or his project, and often other prior winners circulate among the tables, talking about how much the grant meant to them and facilitating discussion of the final three. After a second vote, one person is named the winner and leaves with a bundle of cash. After expenses are recovered, the award is usually in the range of $500 to $600.

It's not a huge amount of money, but it definitely helps. And the nonmonetary benefits are equally important. The organizers particularly note how valuable it is for the artists to learn to discuss their ideas with strangers, even if they don't win. The benefit to the audience may be even greater. While many of them originally came to support a friend's proposal, they usually end up experiencing something bigger: a roomful of interesting, engaged people who want to be part of supporting original art in all its shapes and forms.

To manage the meals, the planning team relies on a volunteer chef to create the menu and then they jump in as volunteer sous-chefs. The dinners, laid out buffet style, usually comprise two soups, several salads, breads, and desserts. In their first three years, they held a dozen dinners and awarded more than $6,500 in grants.

Portlandstock.blogspot.com

FOR RECIPES FROM PORTLAND STOCK, SEE:

Cardamom Pavlova, page 98

Ariana's Pink Potato Salad, page 276

Mock Cream of Tomato Soup

Patty and Bruce Wood's deli on Washington's Long Beach Peninsula (see page 198) was as popular with full-time peninsula residents as with the beach-loving vacationers. They came up with this soup out of a desire to create something creamy without actual cream. Potatoes to the rescue. And by the way, it works just as well with broccoli as with tomatoes. We're all accustomed to the idea that cream of tomato soup is hot, but this is also good cold.

Serves 6

2   tablespoons olive oil or butter

6   medium russet potatoes, peeled and thinly sliced

2   large onions, thinly sliced

9   Roma tomatoes, chopped

2   tablespoons tomato paste

6   cups chicken or vegetable broth

1   teaspoon sugar
    Pinch of cayenne pepper
    Salt
    Chopped chives or parsley; or homemade croutons (page 248), for garnish

1. Heat the oil in a large soup pot, add the potatoes and onions, and sauté until tender, about 10 minutes.

2. Add the tomatoes, tomato paste, broth, sugar, and cayenne, and simmer until everything is tender.

3. Transfer the soup to a blender (careful, it's hot) and purée until smooth, and then return it to the pot. Or use an immersion blender and purée the soup right in the pot. Taste, and add salt as needed. Serve hot or cold with your choice of garnishes.

Variation: To make a broccoli variation of this soup, cut broccoli florets small, remove the tough peel from the stem, and chop the stalks into small pieces. You want to end up with about 2 cups. Add the broccoli at the end of step 2, when the sautéed onion and potato are tender. Omit the tomatoes and tomato paste.

Make ahead? Certainly. Time in the refrigerator chills this soup nicely, for serving cold. For hot soup, reheat slowly.

For large crowds: A very economical and nourishing choice for a party. Add the extra cayenne slowly, tasting as you go.

HOW TO MAKE CROUTONS

All the recipes I have ever seen tell you to spread the cut-up bread on a sheet pan or jelly-roll pan (which is nothing more than a cookie sheet with rims), sprinkle with olive oil, and toss the bread to coat with oil. When I try to do it that way, those little bread pieces want to jump all over the counter. It's so much easier to use a bowl.

Put a thin layer of olive oil in the bottom of a mixing bowl, sprinkle in any herbs or spices that you like, dump in the bread cubes, and quickly toss them around. If you're making a large amount, say more than 2 cups, I've found that it works better to do two small batches in the bowl, otherwise the bread that lands on the bottom absorbs all the oil before you can finish tossing.

Croutons from Scratch

1. Preheat the oven to 375°F.

2. Start with sliced bread of your choice: white, whole wheat, rye, sourdough, whatever you have on hand. If it is a few days old, so much the better. Cut the bread into cubes somewhere between ½ and 1 inch square, whatever looks right to you.

3. For each cup of bread cubes, add 1 tablespoon olive oil to a mixing bowl. For optional flavoring, add ½ teaspoon or so of herbs or spices of your choice, such as garlic powder, basil, smoked paprika, or spice blends like Italian or Mexican seasoning — whatever complements the flavor of the dish they will be used with.

4. Add the bread cubes to the oil and stir them around quickly, to coat.

5. Spread the bread cubes in a single layer on a baking sheet and place in the oven, shaking the pan once or twice for even toasting. The croutons are ready when they are lightly browned and start to smell like toast, 4 to 5 minutes. The croutons will be soft when they first come out of the oven, but will get crisper as they cool. If you leave them in the oven long enough to get crisp while they are still hot, they will be hard as rocks when they cool, and probably burned to boot.

Robin Simpson

MENLO PARK, CALIFORNIA

Robin's story is familiar: wanting to foster a sense of community in her neighborhood, she decided to start a Soup Night after reading a magazine article some years ago. For her first Soup Night, she prepared flyers that she and her children then hand-delivered through the neighborhood. "People were so gracious," she remembers, "so appreciative of the opportunity. And it was so much fun to see my sweet neighbors meeting each other. I think we all need community."

A busy mom who home-schools her two children, Robin soon realized she had to find ways to do Soup Night that didn't wear her out. Switching to e-mail invitations saved a lot of time. But the biggest change came when she realized she didn't need to spend a lot of energy cleaning up beforehand. "That just destroys the intent. And I don't fuss at the kids to clean up their room either. Who cares about that? That's not the point of Soup Night."

Smoked Salmon Corn Chowder

Recipe from Katie Pool, Stanton Street, Portland, Oregon

Katie says: This recipe is adapted from a fabulous cookbook called *The New Basics,* from the Silver Palate ladies. I love everything I've ever made from that book, but this time I needed something for pescatarians, so I started with their Corn Chowder and made a few changes. They called for bacon and chicken broth; I substituted smoked salmon and vegetable broth. It was so good, I never went back to the original recipe. It is best when I use fresh corn in the dead of summer; second best is corn I froze myself, but any other frozen corn is okay. It's very rich, so sometimes I reduce the half-and-half and add regular milk.

Serves 6

2	tablespoons butter or 1 tablespoon each butter and vegetable oil
2	cups chopped onions
8–12	ounces smoked salmon
2	tablespoons all-purpose flour
4	cups vegetable broth
2	large potatoes, peeled and cut into ¼-inch dice
1	cup half-and-half
4	cups corn kernels, fresh or frozen
¾	teaspoon freshly ground black pepper
	Salt
1	large red bell pepper, seeded and cut into ¼-inch dice
3	scallions (use white bulb and about half of the green tops), cut into ¼-inch slices
	Chopped fresh cilantro

1. Melt the butter in a large soup pot. Add the onions and cook over low heat until wilted, about 10 minutes.

2. Crumble the salmon into small pieces and add to the onions, along with any juices that have collected in the package. Add the flour and cook, stirring, for another 5 minutes.

3. Add the broth and potatoes. Continue cooking over medium-low heat until potatoes are just tender, 12 to 15 minutes.

4. Add the half-and-half, corn, black pepper, and salt to taste. Cook for 5 to 7 minutes, stirring occasionally.

5. Add the bell pepper and scallions. Adjust the seasonings and cook for 5 minutes longer.

6. Garnish with cilantro and serve.

Make ahead? Yes, up through step 4. But it's best if you make this the same day you plan to serve it.

For large crowds: Smoked salmon is spendy, but a little bit goes a long way, so if you need to cut back on this ingredient when multiplying, it'll still be fine.

Zucchini-Tortellini Soup

If you've ever grown zucchini, you know the danger — in the dead of summer, this incredibly prolific plant seems to go from blossom to squash overnight, and then to HUGE in another day. People have been known to sneak onto neighbors' porches in the middle of the night, leaving a pile of squashes anonymously. For all I know, there are 12-step programs to help gardeners and their friends cope with the overflow. Here's one solution: a delicious vegetable soup that also features some of your late-season fresh tomatoes and basil, made hearty with the addition of cheese tortellini pasta bundles.

Serves 6

1   tablespoon olive oil

1   medium onion, diced

2   carrots, diced

1   celery stalk, diced

1   leek, white part plus a little of the green, trimmed and diced (see page 186)

2   thin-skinned potatoes, diced

2   large tomatoes, peeled and chopped

8   cups vegetable broth

12 ounces fresh or frozen cheese tortellini

2–3 small zucchini squash, sliced into half-rounds

1   tablespoon minced fresh basil, or basil pesto

    Parmesan cheese for garnish

1. Heat the olive oil in a large soup pot over medium heat. Add the onion, carrot, celery, leek, and potatoes, and sauté just until the vegetables begin to soften, about 5 minutes.

2. Add the tomatoes and the broth, and simmer until the potatoes and carrots are tender, 10 to 15 minutes.

3. Bring a large pot of salted water to a boil and cook the tortellini for about 5 minutes, or according to the package instructions. Remove when still al dente; don't overcook. Drain and set aside.

4. Add the zucchini to the soup and simmer just until crisp-tender. Stir in the reserved tortellini.

5. Stir in the basil (or pesto) and serve each bowl sprinkled with grated Parmesan.

Make ahead? Through step 3 if you have to, but remove the soup from the heat before the vegetables are fully done, so that they don't become mushy during reheating.

For large crowds: How else are you going to get rid of all that zucchini?

Brunswick Stew

Like most "country" dishes, Brunswick Stew was originally made from whatever was on hand, so over time many versions have developed, along with fierce rivalry over which is authentic. But the one from my grandmother's South Carolina kitchen always had chicken, corn, tomatoes, okra, and lima beans (which Southerners call butterbeans), and so that's what I consider the real thing. Common additions are ketchup, Worcestershire sauce, Tabasco, brown sugar, vinegar. You may think you don't like okra, but if you leave it out you'll have to call this dish something else — Yankee Stew, maybe.

Serves 6–8

1–2 cups all-purpose flour
1 teaspoon salt
½ teaspoon black pepper
2 pounds boneless skinless chicken breasts and thighs, cut into bite-size chunks
3 tablespoons vegetable oil, or half oil and half bacon drippings
2 medium onions, chopped
1 hot red pepper, deseeded and minced
1 pound butterbeans (baby lima beans)
1 pound okra, trimmed and sliced
6 ears of corn, kernels cut from the cobs
2 pounds tomatoes, peeled and chopped
2 teaspoons sugar
1 teaspoon Worcestershire sauce
Salt and freshly ground black pepper

1. Mix the flour, salt, and pepper in a large ziplock bag; add the chicken and shake like mad so the chicken pieces are well coated. Remove the chicken pieces, shaking off excess flour, and discard the flour mixture. Heat the oil in a large soup pot.

2. Brown the chicken thoroughly, over medium-high heat, until no pink shows. Don't crowd the chicken pieces in the pan; they'll steam rather than brown. If you need to do several batches, set the first batch of browned chicken on a plate and cover lightly with aluminum foil while you do the rest.

3. Add the onions, peppers, butterbeans (baby limas), okra, corn kernels, tomatoes, sugar, and Worcestershire, plus the reserved chicken and any juices that collected on the plate. Cover the pot and reduce the heat to low.

4. Simmer until the chicken is thoroughly done and the vegetables are tender, about 15 minutes.

5. Taste and adjust for salt and pepper, if needed. Serve hot.

Make ahead? You bet. Like all stews, this improves with age.

For large crowds: Well, my grandmother used to feed about 30 when the whole family was together, so it's safe to say this recipe can be expanded.

A Southern Childhood

I am a child of the South. And even though I have now lived in the Pacific Northwest much longer than the 21 early years I spent in the Carolinas, some bits of the South are still deep in the marrow of my bones. Food, in particular. And memories.

I especially remember my grandmother's house, a wonderful old farmhouse with a wide front porch, a long lane lined with pecan trees and daffodils, and a huge vegetable garden out back. I spent many happy weeks there each summer, and it was here that I learned about growing good things to eat. Of course in that place and time, big vegetable gardens were the norm, not worth commenting on, but I know for a fact that my passion for fresh vegetables, and my love of vegetable gardening, started in my grandmother's garden on this old cotton farm outside Bishopville, South Carolina.

Sundays after church there was always a mammoth dinner (the meal in the middle of the day) with some constants: fried chicken and maybe country ham, rice, green beans, butterbeans, corn, okra, maybe sweet potatoes, sliced tomatoes, green onions standing upright in a mason jar of vinegar, biscuits, some kind of pie. After everyone was stuffed, the edges of the tablecloth were pulled up over the bowls and platters on the table to keep the flies off, and then people would wander in during the afternoon, nibbling or making a small snack plate. Why we didn't all die of food poisoning, I don't know.

Other days, we might have a nice supper of Brunswick Stew. A quintessentially Southern summertime dish that I love to this day, it was made from all those garden vegetables, plus a freshly killed chicken and maybe a piece of pork from the smokehouse. It could be left simmering on the iron cookstove as long as needed while everybody finished other chores. Nowadays, of course, the chicken comes from the supermarket, but in every other way I do my best to make my grandmother proud.

Pistachio-Chicken Minestrone

A great way to use two summertime treasures: fresh zucchini and basil.

Serves 6

1½ tablespoons olive oil

1 pound boneless skinless chicken breast, cut into bite-size pieces

1 medium onion, chopped

1 celery stalk, sliced

1 carrot, sliced

3–4 red potatoes, thinly sliced

1–2 small zucchini, thinly sliced

2 tomatoes, peeled, seeded, and diced

6 cups reduced-sodium chicken broth

Salt and freshly ground black pepper

1 cup acini di pepe pasta (see note)

2 cups packed fresh spinach

½ cup chopped fresh basil

Freshly grated Parmesan, for garnish

¼ cup coarsely chopped salted pistachio nuts, for garnish

Make ahead? Yes, through step 2. You can also cook the pasta ahead.

For large crowds: A good one to make in large batches, double or triple.

1. Heat 1 tablespoon of the oil in a large saucepan on medium-high heat. Sauté the chicken until browned on all sides and no pink is showing. Remove the chicken with a slotted spoon and set aside.

2. Add the remaining ½ tablespoon oil to pan, heat to medium-high, and sauté the onion, celery, carrot, potatoes, and zucchini for about 5 minutes. Stir the vegetables gently, being careful not to break them up. Add the tomato, the reserved chicken, and broth. The broth should cover the vegetables; add more if needed. Simmer until the chicken is thoroughly cooked, about 10 minutes. Add salt and pepper to taste.

3. Bring a large pot filled with 3 to 4 quarts salted water to a boil. Add the acini di pepe pasta and boil 8 minutes or until the pasta is cooked and tender but firm to the bite. Drain.

4. Remove the soup from the heat and stir in the spinach and basil; let stand 1 minute.

5. Spoon the pasta into bowls and ladle the soup on top. Sprinkle each bowl with Parmesan and pistachios.

Note: Acini di pepe is pasta shaped in tiny beads. If you can't find it, orzo is a good substitute; it will need longer cooking, 10 minutes or so.

Lemon Chicken Soup

When a soup has so few ingredients, a quality broth is critical, and that's why I strongly recommend homemade chicken broth here. Lemon thyme is an amazing herb — both lemony and thymey, in equal measure. But if you can't find it, regular thyme will do.

Serves 6

2 lemons

2 boneless, skinless chicken breasts

6 cups homemade chicken broth

3 sprigs lemon thyme, more for garnish

Make ahead? Yes.

For large crowds: Works just fine to increase proportions, but I would go easy with the thyme, and increase it only fractionally.

1. Remove the zest from one lemon in thin strips, and then juice that lemon. Cut the other lemon into paper-thin slices; remove the seeds, and set the slices aside. Trim any excess fat from the chicken, and cut the chicken into thin strips about 1½ inches long.

2. Bring the broth to a simmer in a soup pot. Add the chicken strips and simmer until done, about 10 minutes. Remove the chicken with a slotted spoon and set aside. Add the reserved lemon zest and lemon thyme to the broth. Simmer for 10 minutes.

3. Strain the broth through cheesecloth or a fine sieve; discard the solids. Return the strained broth to the pan and add the chicken and the reserved lemon juice. Bring to a simmer and heat through.

4. Float a lemon slice and fresh thyme leaves on each serving.

Mark Patterson

ORO VALLEY, ARIZONA

Through most of this book, you will meet people who love to cook soup and love to feed people in their homes. Mark's story is a little different — he did it at work.

His job was stressful and too demanding and dangerously close to damaging family life, so he switched to a different role within the company, only to find he missed the satisfaction of meeting impossible deadlines. Maybe, he thought, I could find satisfaction some other way. So Mark turned to his main hobby — cooking — for the calm pleasure it had always brought to his life, and hit upon a brilliant idea: make a big pot of soup and bring it to work, anonymously.

The first Wednesday of 2010 was a test run. Mark made the soup the night before, brought it to the kitchen area in a slow cooker, set out bowls and spoons and a small sign describing the soup. By the third week, he added his name to the sign. And that's when things began to change for him.

"I got e-mails, texts, and visits from people I had never met before," he says. "Some people contacted me just to discuss cooking. It was great!" Keeping up with coworkers' expectations meant many happy hours studying recipes and thinking about new soups to try. For someone who loves cooking, this is a very happy way to spend time.

But for Mark the real payoff was a change in his feelings about the job. "The soup has opened up new relationships with coworkers. I've interacted with many new people, and their positive feedback means a lot. The soup tradition has brought our whole team together. People call me the Soup Guy, and it's a good feeling to know that they count on me to bring the soup."

In fact, one of those new relationships that began with a chat about soup eventually led Mark to a new position within the company, one that gives him great satisfaction. He still takes soup to work once a week, and has no plans to stop. "I can't believe how much my life has changed," Mark says, "just from taking soup to work once a week."

Vegetarian Eggplant Chili

Recipe from Heather Vogel Frederick, Soup and Solidarity, Portland, Oregon
(profile, page 84)

This richly flavored vegetarian chili takes advantage of eggplant's propensity for soaking up flavors. Because eggplant is generally only available in summer, this is a summertime chili. And thus we have a chili for every season (see pages 50, 148, and 194).

Serves 6

2	tablespoons olive oil
1	large onion, chopped
1	large eggplant, cut into 1-inch chunks
2	16-ounce cans diced tomatoes
1	(6-ounce) tomato paste
1	(15-ounce) can kidney beans, drained; or 2 cups cooked kidney beans (see page 27)
1	(15-ounce) can black beans, drained; or 2 cups cooked black beans (see page 27)
½	teaspoon chili powder, more to taste
¼	teaspoon cayenne pepper
½	teaspoon basil
1	bay leaf
1	teaspoon salt
¼	teaspoon ground cumin
¼	teaspoon black pepper
1½	tablespoons apple cider vinegar

Garnishes

Sour cream or plain Greek-style yogurt (see page 242)

Shredded cheese (I like sharp cheddar)

Chopped fresh cilantro

1. Heat the oil in a large soup pot over medium heat. Add the onions and sauté until soft and transparent, 4 to 5 minutes. Add the eggplant and sauté briefly.

2. Add the remaining ingredients. Bring to a boil, then reduce the heat and simmer for several hours (or all day or overnight in a slow cooker). Remove the bay leaf.

3. Serve with a dollop of sour cream (or plain Greek-style yogurt), shredded cheese, and chopped fresh cilantro.

Make ahead? Of course. See Heather's comment in step 2. Besides, do you know any chili that isn't better the second day?

For large crowds: If you want chili for a crowd, this is an ideal choice since it does not contain any meat, the one ingredient that ups the cost when multiplied. I would double or triple the vegetables and beans, and gradually increase all the spices, tasting as you go.

Lewinna Solwing

BELLINGHAM, WASHINGTON

Sometimes community-minded folks start a Soup Night; sometimes they inherit them. That's what happened with Lewinna. She moved into a house in this city north of Seattle where a Soup Night was already happening.

The home was originally conceived as an intentional Christian community, and the Soup Night was part of that vision. It was a kind of ministry — anyone was welcome, including homeless people off the street. As far as Lewinna knows, none of them ever took advantage, but the idea did spread by word of mouth through ripples of acquaintanceship.

Once a month, Lewinna cooked a huge pot of soup (usually vegetarian); others often brought other food contributions, but that wasn't expected. The soup, Lewinna says, "is my gift."

All tech-savvy readers, take note. Lewinna gives us a good example of using technology to good advantage. She has created a social media group called A Moveable Feast, and uses that exclusively to contact her Soup Night list.

Kawandeep Virdee

BOSTON, MASSACHUSETTS

What does a young man do when he arrives in a strange city in the middle of a very cold winter, knowing only a few people? If it's a clever young man named Kawandeep, he initiates a Soup Night. "It helped me quickly grow my social circle," he says. "I think it's a very warm way to meet people. Whenever I run into someone I'd like to get to know better, I invite them to a Soup Night, and they always seem to like the sound of that. I have a much larger role in the creative community now, and to a large extent I owe it to having the Soup Nights, and encouraging them to be spaces to share ideas and connect with others through conversation. That's the underlying intention of many social gatherings, of course, but I spelled it out on the invitation, and I believe that helped."

Vegetable Soup with Andouille Sausage

Andouille sausage is a smoked, highly seasoned pork and beef sausage that is especially popular in the South. It adds a great spicy flavor to this soup. And here is another opportunity to use up some of your zucchini!

Serves 6

3½ cups water

2 cups reduced-sodium chicken broth

1 cup dried brown lentils, picked over and rinsed

1 medium onion, chopped

1 celery stalk, sliced

2 carrots, sliced

1 tablespoon chopped fresh parsley

1 teaspoon salt

1 medium zucchini, cut in half lengthwise, then sliced into ⅓-inch pieces

6 ounces andouille sausage, halved lengthwise and cut into ½-inch pieces

Lemon wedges, for garnish (optional)

1. In a large soup pot over high heat, bring the water, broth, lentils, onion, celery, carrots, parsley, and salt to a boil. Reduce the heat to medium-low and simmer, covered, for 45 minutes, stirring occasionally.

2. Add the zucchini and sausage and simmer, covered, until the vegetables are tender and flavors are blended, about 10 minutes longer.

3. Serve with a squeeze of lemon on top, if desired. Or set out bowls of lemon wedges so people can add their own. Or both.

Make ahead? Yes, up through end of step 1.

For large crowds: This soup lends itself well to being expanded. For economy, you might want to keep the amount of sausage proportionally lower, but its flavor will still come through.

Bread and Soup Suppers, Hiram College

HIRAM, OHIO

Thirty-some years ago, the chaplain at this liberal arts college not far from Cleveland, greatly distressed at the level of hunger in the small village of Hiram, proposed an idea: Rather than the regular dinner in the college dining hall, once a month students could choose a much simpler meal of bread and soup. The cost to the students would be the same, but because the cost to prepare the soup supper was less, $1 per meal would be donated to a local nonprofit.

The tradition continues, with some tweaking. Every Thursday of the spring quarter (January, February, March), Bread and Soup Suppers are held in the college's older, smaller dining hall. The students no longer choose between soup and the regular dinner — soup *is* the meal. Faculty, staff, and townspeople are invited, in addition to students. The supper costs $5 cash or student swipe, and $1 of each purchase is donated to local nonprofits that address hunger relief.

Jason Bricker-Thompson, director of the Office of Civic Engagement, reports that some of the faculty members have children, now adults, who have "grown up on our soup. Some people have been coming since the beginning, for 30 years. We sit at round tables, which promotes conversation. We so seldom have time to just sit and talk. But it's more than that. Most people see it as an opportunity to contribute to people in need, to demonstrate solidarity with the less fortunate."

Others agree. When the student newspaper in 2012 carried a story about the event on its 30-year anniversary, several alumni reminisced about their own experiences. One woman told about her freshman-year boyfriend who went to Bread and Soup only to please her, and eventually admitted he didn't really like soup all that much; she married him all the same. Several mentioned that they still make soup suppers in the winter months, and think of their college friends when they do. I can summarize a common refrain among all the comments this way: "It felt really good to know we were helping people, but that was only part of it. The soup was always great!"

www.hiram.edu

Roasted Red Pepper Soup with Shrimp

Recipe from Philip and Suzy Poll, Houston, Texas (profile, page 61)

These days most supermarkets carry roasted peppers in a jar. They are a wonderful convenience, but if you aren't pressed for time, roasting raw peppers yourself adds a hint of smokiness that's missing from bottled peppers.

Serves 6

7–8	large red bell peppers
2	tablespoons olive oil
½	cup chopped onion
½	tablespoon minced garlic
5	cups chicken broth
½	teaspoon paprika
1	tablespoon tomato paste
1½	teaspoons brown sugar
1	cup half-and-half
¾	cup grated Parmesan cheese
¼	teaspoon cayenne pepper
	Salt and freshly ground black pepper
24	large uncooked shrimp, peeled, deveined, coarsely chopped
½	teaspoon Creole seasoning
	Minced parsley, for garnish

1. Roast the peppers: Preheat the broiler, and broil the bell peppers, turning until the skin is blistered and blackened on all sides. Place them in a paper bag and let stand for 10 minutes. Peel and seed the peppers. Cut 2 peppers into matchstick-size strips and set aside. Coarsely chop the remaining peppers and set aside.

2. Heat 1 tablespoon of the oil in a large soup pot. Add the onion and garlic and sauté over medium-low heat until translucent, about 8 minutes. Add the chopped peppers and broth and bring to a boil. Reduce the heat and simmer until the peppers are very tender, about 15 minutes.

3. Using an immersion blender, purée the soup until smooth. Mix in the paprika, tomato paste, and brown sugar. Simmer for 5 minutes to blend the flavors.

4. Add the half-and-half and the Parmesan. Add the cayenne, and season to taste with salt and pepper. Keep the soup warm, but do not allow it to boil.

5. Heat the remaining 1 tablespoon oil in a medium skillet over medium-high heat. Add the shrimp and sauté until cooked through, about 3 minutes. Stir in the Creole seasoning and reserved red pepper strips, and heat through.

6. Ladle the soup into bowls and top with the shrimp mixture. Sprinkle lightly with parsley and serve.

ROASTING PEPPERS

The skins of bell peppers don't disintegrate during cooking, and many people (me, for instance) consider those tough little bits less than tasty. It's not feasible to peel peppers in the usual sense of that word, but the skins are easily removed after the peppers are roasted. Plus, roasting adds wonderfully to the flavor.

To roast peppers, fire up your outdoor grill, broiler, or even a burner on the gas stove, and place a pepper directly on the flame. Use tongs to turn it so all sides are exposed, roasting until the skin starts to bubble and turn black. Pop the roasted pepper into a plastic or paper bag, shut it tightly, and set on the counter for a few minutes. When the pepper has cooled enough to handle, it's easy to scrape off the peel. Then remove the seeds and membranes, and chop or dice as needed. And make it easier on yourself by paying attention when you select the fresh peppers in the market. Those with deepest channels between the lobes will be harder to peel.

Julaine Kammrath
AURORA, ILLINOIS

Julaine is another person who was inspired by the great success of Soup Night at a friend's house to start one in her own neighborhood. She candidly admits it was only partially successful.

It's important, I think, to realize that as wonderful as Soup Nights can be, success is not automatic. You might remember that Julie Dahlberg (page 58) stopped doing Soup Night when it got too big and too boisterous. Julaine, to her very great credit, is honest about her experience. Also to her credit, she isn't giving up!

"I got the inspiration from a woman I know, a single gal who invited all her neighbors over for a soup supper." (She's speaking of Kate Allen, whose story is on page 107.) "They were strangers to her and to each other, and I thought that was very impressive. I decided to try it, because it fit right in with what I had in mind when we were house hunting. I was more interested in good neighbors than in a wonderful house, because I've moved a lot in my life and realize that neighborhood matters much more than the appearance of the house.

"So I decided to try a Soup Night too. I invited half friends and half people I didn't know. I got their names from friends, and included that on their invitations, which I put in people's mailboxes. To my great disappointment, the new people didn't come. The people who already knew us did come, and we had a lovely evening, but still . . ."

Julaine believes she learned some good lessons, and she's determined to try again. In particular, she will make a point to speak to all the folks she doesn't know and invite them in person, rather than leaving an invitation in the mailbox.

Chilled Cucumber Soup with Shrimp *(photo, page 233)*

This lovely soup features the freshness of cucumbers, the light zing of buttermilk, and the subtle punch of horseradish — refreshing, unusual, and delicious.

Serves 6

3	English cucumbers, peeled and chopped
3	tablespoons Dijon mustard
2	teaspoons sugar
1½	teaspoons prepared horseradish
1½	teaspoons salt
1	teaspoon white pepper
3	tablespoons fresh lemon juice
6	cups buttermilk
3	cups cooked shrimp, shelled and deveined, with 6 for garnish
2	tablespoons chopped chives, for garnish

1. Combine the cucumbers, mustard, sugar, horseradish, salt, pepper, lemon juice, and buttermilk in a blender or food processor and purée until smooth.

2. If the shrimp are large, chop them into bite-size pieces. Reserve 6 whole shrimp for a garnish.

3. Combine the chopped shrimp and the cucumber mixture, cover, and chill at least 1 hour; more is better.

4. Serve the soup very cold, each bowl garnished with chopped chives and 1 whole shrimp.

Variation: If you have access to garlic chives and they happen to be blooming, sprinkle some of the dainty white flowerets onto each serving.

Make ahead? It's necessary — see step 3.

For large crowds: Certainly, although you might want proportionally lesser increments of shrimp, to ease your budget.

"Stone Soup Fellowship," Dr. Bruce Epperly

Theologian, pastor, teacher, and author, Bruce Epperly spent most of his working career in academic settings. With his wife, also an academic minister, he began monthly Soup Nights some 30 years ago, bringing together students, other faculty, relatives, and assorted friends for an evening of warm soup and cool conversations about hot ideas.

"We saw it as an occasion for not just eating, but talking and sharing ideas about common interests. Our students especially enjoyed it because they seldom had a chance to have a meal in someone's home. Here it is 30 years later, and I still hear from some of them. They all remark about our Soup Night and what it meant to them." The Epperlys served at several universities during their career, and Soup Night was an important part of their lives in each place.

In an article for the online community Jesus, Jazz, and Buddhism, which he has graciously allowed me to share with you, Bruce speaks eloquently about the intangibles of Soup Night:

"It's about sharing [a meal] . . . , but it's also about something more — casual, unpretentious, joyful gatherings with friends and loved ones. And that's what makes Soup Night special.

"Soup Night isn't fancy, but it is celebrative. It brings people together simply to share food, drink, and friendship. We aren't trying to accomplish anything and we have no agenda. We gather for the joy of it. Soup Night, like other intimate meals, is a celebration of life and a recognition of our gratitude for Earth's bounty and our friendships and one another. Soup Night, for us, is like church — we give thanks, we honor important events in our lives, we honor achievement, and we share pain. There are tears, but more often there is laughter."

Fruit Soup Fit for a Princess

Recipe from Marilee Corey, Unity Church, Salem, Oregon (profile, page 216)

Marilee says: Last year I went on a cruise for the first time in my life, one of the beautiful Princess ships — what a treat! It was fantastic in every way, including the wonderful food. I really loved this fruit soup, but adapted it so it fits our family better (left out the wine, used half-and-half rather than cream, and added a different garnish).

Serves 6–8

2 cups peeled and cored apple chunks	**1.** Purée the apples with the apple juice in a blender or food processor; pour into a large bowl.
1 cup apple juice	
2 cups peeled and pitted peach chunks	**2.** Purée the peaches with the orange juice in the same blender or food processor; pour into the bowl with the apple purée. Add the half-and-half, yogurt, honey, vanilla, cinnamon, and nutmeg; stir until thoroughly blended.
½ cup orange juice	
2 cups half-and-half	
1 cup low-fat plain yogurt	
1 tablespoon honey	
½ teaspoon vanilla extract	**3.** Cover the bowl and refrigerate for 1 hour or more.
½ teaspoon ground cinnamon	
½ teaspoon ground nutmeg	**4.** Serve the soup well chilled. Place the peach nectar into a small pitcher, and dribble a little into each individual bowl; it beads up and floats on top. Very pretty.
1 cup peach nectar	

Variations: Use low-fat vanilla yogurt and skip the honey and vanilla. Slice fresh mint leaves into ribbons and use as garnish. For a very elegant garnish, float one edible flower (rose petals, maybe) on each serving.

Make ahead? It's necessary — see step 3.

For large crowds: When I first tasted this delicate soup, there were about 80 people in attendance, so it's safe to say this recipe can be expanded.

Strawberry-Rhubarb Soup

The familiar flavors of a classic dessert, in a soup bowl.

Serves 6

4 cups strawberries, hulled and sliced

1½ pounds rhubarb, cut into 1-inch chunks (about 5 cups)

2 cups orange juice

¾ cup sugar, more or less

¾ cup peeled and chopped orange sections

1. Set aside 6 perfect strawberry slices for garnishes.

2. Combine the remaining strawberry slices, rhubarb, and orange juice in a large soup pot over medium-high heat. Bring to a boil, then reduce the heat and simmer, uncovered, until the rhubarb has softened, about 10 minutes. Remove from the heat, and stir in sugar to taste. Chill until cool enough to handle.

3. Purée the mixture in a blender or food processor until velvety smooth. Pour the mixture into a bowl and add the orange sections. Cover and refrigerate until well chilled.

4. Garnish each serving with a strawberry slice.

Variations: This is wonderful as is, but you could also add a hint of spice, such as ground cardamom, nutmeg, or allspice. Just a pinch, please; leave your guests guessing.

Make ahead? Yes; see step 3.

For large crowds: When strawberries are at their peak, and you have access to a bumper crop of rhubarb, you could easily make a gallon or two.

Cold Strawberry Soup

Recipe from Eric and Kat Meyer, Cleveland, Ohio (profile, page 132)

Here's another version of strawberry soup, this one creamy with yogurt and sour cream. One big advantage: it's made with frozen berries, so it can be enjoyed even when strawberry season is past.

Serves 6

2 pounds frozen strawberries, thawed, with juice

½ cup sour cream

1 cup plain or vanilla yogurt

1 cup whole milk, more or less

¼ cup sugar (optional)

Fresh strawberries, for garnish

Chopped mint leaves, for garnish

Make ahead? It's necessary; see step 2.

For large crowds: Easily doubled, or more.

1. Purée the strawberries, sour cream, and yogurt in a blender until smooth. Add enough milk for the desired consistency. Add sugar, if desired. (In our house there's always a battle between the sweet-tooths and non-sweet-tooths.)

2. Pour the soup into a bowl, cover, and chill for 4 to 8 hours. Stir well before serving (add more milk if needed). Garnish with fresh strawberries, if available; mint leaves if not.

Fresh Fruit Gazpacho

Elsewhere you will find recipes for traditional gazpacho, featuring summer-fresh vegetables, and Anna Bueno's fabulous strawberry-tomato creation (page 240). This one is almost all fruit, balanced with a base of tomatoes so it doesn't taste like a fruit smoothie. It's also very adaptable. Don't like kiwi? Leave it out. Can't find blueberries? Double up on the strawberries. Etc.

Serves 6

3 large ripe tomatoes, peeled and seeded

1 tablespoon sugar

3 cups orange juice

2 teaspoons grated orange peel

1 papaya, seeded, peeled, and cubed

1 cantaloupe, seeded, peeled, and cubed (about 2 cups)

1 small honeydew melon, seeded, peeled, and cubed (about 2 cups)

1 cup fresh strawberries, sliced

1 cup fresh blueberries

1 kiwifruit, peeled and sliced

1 large apple, cored but not peeled, cubed

Fresh mint, for garnish (optional)

1. Purée the tomatoes in a blender or food processor. Add the sugar, orange juice and peel, papaya, and half the cantaloupe and honeydew. Blend until smooth. Pour into a large bowl; stir in the reserved melon, strawberries, blueberries, kiwifruit, and apple.

2. Cover; chill 4 to 6 hours or until very cold. Garnish with fresh mint.

Make ahead? Yes, see step 2.

For large crowds: This lends itself well to making large batches because it is so adaptable. Depending on what's available on any given day, any fresh fruit in almost any combination works just fine.

Chilled Apricot-Orange Soup

This delicate fruit soup is a good one to have in your summer repertoire because it calls for ingredients you might have on hand already. It's perfect when you're between trips to the farmers' market. Any fresh fruit for garnishes is a sweet bonus.

Serves 6–8

2 (17-ounce) cans apricot halves in light syrup
1 teaspoon orange zest
½ cup orange juice, freshly squeezed if possible
¼ teaspoon ground cardamom
1 cup plain yogurt

Optional Garnishes
Raspberries
Blueberries
Orange slices

Make ahead? Yes. See step 3.

For large crowds: Easily and economically multiplied.

1. Drain the apricots, saving the syrup.

2. Combine the apricot syrup, half the apricots, the orange zest and juice, and the cardamom in a blender or food processor and purée until smooth. Add the yogurt, and blend until combined. Chop the remaining apricots into bite-size pieces.

3. Pour the soup into a bowl, stir in the chopped apricots, cover, and refrigerate for at least 1 hour.

4. Garnish with fresh raspberries, blueberries (a particularly nice color combination), or thin slices of orange.

Even cold soups seem to go better with hot-from-the-oven breads.

Blueberry-Orange Cornbread

It's almost like a dessert — a cornbread rich with orange and fresh blueberries. This is a wonderful accompaniment to any tomato-based cold soup.

Makes 8 (2- by 4-inch) pieces

1	cup all-purpose flour
1	cup whole-wheat flour
2	cups cornmeal
⅔	cup packed brown sugar
2	tablespoons baking powder
	Pinch salt
4	tablespoons butter, melted
2	cups milk
3	eggs
1	orange, seeded but unpeeled, chopped
2	cups fresh blueberries

1. Preheat the oven to 350°F; grease an 8-inch square baking pan.

2. Sift together the all-purpose flour, whole-wheat flour, cornmeal, brown sugar, baking powder, and salt.

3. Heat the butter and milk in a small saucepan, just warm enough to melt the butter; cool to lukewarm. Combine the eggs, orange, and milk mixture in a blender or food processor, and blend until well mixed. Add the liquid mixture to the dry ingredients, and stir gently; don't overdo it. Gently fold in the blueberries.

4. Pour the batter into the prepared pan, and bake 20 to 25 minutes until golden brown. Check the bread at 20 minutes by dipping a toothpick in the center; if it tests clean, your cornbread is done. Cool and cut into pieces.

Make ahead? Sure, if you have to. Rewarm at 300°F for a few minutes.

For large crowds: Baking can be tricky, so you're better off making this recipe two times than trying to double it.

Cheddar Drop Biscuits

Recipe from Albertina's Restaurant, Portland, Oregon (profile, page 55)

Warm cheese biscuits and cold soup — great combination.

Makes 10–12 medium biscuits

1	cup sifted all-purpose flour
1½	teaspoons baking powder
¼	teaspoon salt
2	tablespoons cold butter, cut into bits
6	ounces cheddar cheese, grated (1½ cups)
½	cup milk

1. Preheat the oven to 400°F. Grease a baking sheet.

2. Sift together the flour, baking powder, and salt. Rub the butter into the flour mixture. (A food processor is very handy for this.) Add the cheese, then stir in the milk to form a soft, sticky dough.

3. Drop the dough by rounded spoonfuls onto the prepared baking sheet. Bake 12 to 15 minutes until pale golden brown.

Make ahead? Yes, if you need to, but these go together so quickly and they're so wonderful straight from the oven, I hope you're able to make them just before supper's ready. I don't want you to miss all the swoons.

For large crowds: This recipe is easily doubled.

Ariana's Pink Potato Salad (photo, page 233)

Recipe from Ariana Jacob, Portland Stock, Portland, Oregon (profile, page 244)

Ariana says: I created this salad in 2000 for the Red Horse Secret Cafe in Olympia, Washington. We served it at the very first Stock dinner in July 2009 — and several times since, due to popular request.

Serves 6–8

4 medium yellow potatoes (such as Yellow Finn or Yukon Gold), unpeeled

4 medium red beets

¼ cup olive oil (or more to taste)

2–4 tablespoons umeboshi plum vinegar (see note)

1 red onion, finely chopped

3 tablespoons fresh tarragon, minced, or 2–3 teaspoons dried

Freshly ground black pepper (optional)

Note: Ariana says, "Umeboshi vinegar, so delicious and so essential to this recipe, is made with salted plums, which turn the vinegar pink and give it a salty taste. That hint of salt makes the beets taste lightly pickled, which is delicious! This Japanese vinegar is available, under several brand names, in Asian markets and natural foods stores, but if you are unable to find it, I think you could make the recipe with another vinegar, such as apple cider vinegar or red wine vinegar, plus ½–2 teaspoons salt."

1. Bring 2 saucepans of salted water to a boil. Add the potatoes to one pan and simmer until tender but not falling apart, 10 to 12 minutes. Add the beets to the other pan and simmer until tender but not falling apart, about 15 minutes.

2. When the potatoes and beets are tender, drain and run cold water over them until they are cool enough to handle. Peel off the skins, cut into large bite-size chunks, and put them in a large bowl.

3. Pour the olive oil and umeboshi vinegar over the warm potato mixture; mix well. Stir in the onion, tarragon, and pepper to taste. Mix everything together well, cover, and chill; the salad tastes best after sitting overnight in the refrigerator.

Make ahead? Yep — it's best if chilled overnight.

For large crowds: Since Ariana serves this salad at Portland Stock events (see page 244), which draw up to 100 people, I think it's safe to say her recipe can be expanded.

Spinach and Strawberry Salad

Stan Adler, a writing colleague from years ago, says this salad, created by his wife Carol, is "everybody's favorite." Sometimes Carol uses a blend of romaine and red-leaf lettuce in place of some or all of the spinach. The dressing is unusual and marvelous.

Serves 6

2 bunches spinach
¾ cup pecans, cut in half
2 cups fresh strawberries, cut in halves or quarters depending on size of the berries
8 scallions, sliced

Dressing
3 tablespoons confectioners' sugar
½ teaspoon dry mustard powder
½ teaspoon salt
½ cup olive oil
¼ cup vegetable oil
2 tablespoons raspberry vinegar
2 tablespoons poppy seeds (or more to taste)

1. Wash the spinach, remove the stems, and slice the leaves into smaller bite-size pieces.

2. Toast the pecans in a dry skillet for 3 to 4 minutes, stirring often to prevent burning.

3. Combine the spinach and strawberries in a salad bowl, along with the scallions and pecans.

4. Make the dressing: Mix the sugar, mustard, salt, olive oil, vegetable oil, vinegar, and poppy seeds together in a jar with a tight-fitting lid and shake well.

5. Toss the salad with the dressing at serving time.

Make ahead? You can prepare the greens, the toasted nuts, and the strawberries, but don't combine them. Refrigerate separately and toss together at serving time. Carol says, "I usually do a double batch of dressing for another salad some other day."

For large crowds: Easy to expand — limited only by the size of your salad bowl.

Cornbread Salad

This salad is a lot like Lou Brown, the woman who created it — colorful, zesty, and good for you. A few things to keep in mind: Because the onions are raw, it's important to search out a sweet variety, such as Vidalias from Georgia or Walla Wallas from Washington State. If you can't find either, substitute scallions. The pickle relish is essential to the overall taste of this fantastic salad, but it can easily overwhelm the vegetables, so go easy. And finally, presentation. Lou suggests making this in a glass bowl, to display the pretty colors. I happen to own a clear glass bowl with straight sides, and it was spectacular served in it. A trifle bowl — a glass bowl on a stand — would be even better.

Serves 6–8

1	package cornbread mix (such as Jiffy)
8–10	bacon strips
¼	cup vinaigrette, or more as needed
¼	cup sweet pickle relish
3–4	tomatoes, peeled and chopped
1½	cups chopped celery
1	sweet onion (such as Vidalia or Walla Walla), diced
1	red or yellow bell pepper, seeded and chopped
1	green bell pepper, seeded and chopped

1. Bake the cornbread according to the directions on the package. Cool and set aside.

2. Fry the bacon in a skillet over medium heat until very crisp. Drain on paper towels, crumble, and set aside.

3. Break the cornbread into chunks that will fit easily into the bottom of your round bowl, and use half the pieces to line the bottom of the bowl. Sprinkle the cornbread lightly with vinaigrette, just enough to moisten, and then spread the pickle relish over the cornbread in a very thin layer.

4. Keeping the layers separate, add the tomatoes, celery, onion, and bell peppers. Organize them in whatever sequence is visually pleasing to you. Spread the reserved bacon crumbles over the top vegetable layer.

5. Cover the bacon with the remaining cornbread chunks, and sprinkle the whole thing with more vinaigrette. You want to lightly moisten the cornbread without making it soggy.

6. Cover the bowl tightly with plastic wrap and refrigerate for at least 1 hour, for the flavors to meld.

Variations: The recipe you see here is already a variation. Rather than vinaigrette, Lou's original recipe calls for mayonnaise mixed with pickle juice. A jar of pickle juice is quite likely in the refrigerators of many a Southern home, but perhaps not elsewhere, so I used vinaigrette instead, and it lightens up the dish in a good way.

Make ahead? Of course — see step 6.

For large crowds: I don't see any reason why you couldn't double this. Going the other direction, I made a half-recipe for three hungry people and had some left over.

For vegetarians: Substitute cheese, such as sharp cheddar or Gorgonzola, for the bacon.

Steel Magnolias

Lou Brown, now of Lewisville, North Carolina, may be the original steel magnolia. She is tough, fearless, smart, kind, loyal, and Southern to the bone. Her family and mine were next-door neighbors many years ago in Columbia, South Carolina, and it is my good fortune that she has remained in my life. The Browns moved in next door when I was about 10. Soon after, my mother answered a knock on the door one day, and there stood Lou. "I've just made chocolate icing for cupcakes," she announced, "and I need a little boy to lick the spoon. Got one I can borrow?" (She meant my baby brother, now of the Stanton Street Soup Night, then not yet old enough to be in school.) That was the beginning of a friendship between the two women that lasted for 50 years.

Chilled Paella Salad

Recipe from Albertina's Restaurant, Portland, Oregon (profile, page 55)

Round out a summer meal of refreshing soup with this entree salad that carries the flavors and main ingredients of the fabulous Spanish rice-seafood dish usually served hot.

Serves 6–8

2	cups canned pineapple chunks
¾	teaspoon curry powder (or more)
2	tablespoons juice from pineapple
⅓	cup minced scallion
1¼	cups mayonnaise
⅓	cup finely chopped green bell pepper
¼	teaspoon garlic powder
3	cups warm cooked rice
1¼	cups frozen peas
6	ounces cooked shrimp
1½	cups cooked, cubed ham
1	tablespoon lemon juice

Garnishes

Marinated artichoke hearts, quartered

Chopped scallions

Chopped parsley

1. Drain the pineapple chunks, reserving 2 tablespoons of the juice. Set the pineapple aside in a mixing bowl.

2. Combine the curry powder, pineapple, pineapple juice, scallion, mayonnaise, bell pepper, and garlic powder in a medium mixing bowl. Fold in the warm rice. Combine thoroughly, cover, and chill at least 1 hour (overnight is fine).

3. Thaw the peas; drain and toss with the shrimp and ham. Sprinkle the lemon juice over the shrimp mixture. Chill in the refrigerator.

4. About an hour before serving, gently combine the shrimp mixture (after draining the liquid) with the rice mixture. Serve mounded on large lettuce leaves. Garnish as desired.

Variations: Paella, the hot dish, also features sausage, chicken, and other shellfish like scallops, mussels, and clams. Any of those would be wonderful in this salad.

Make ahead? Yes, up through step 2 or, depending on your schedule that day, through step 3.

For large crowds: Easy to expand, but if budget is a concern, use a lesser amount of shrimp; it will still be wonderful.

Double Blueberry Tart

Recipe from Albertina's Restaurant, Portland, Oregon (profile, page 55)

The combination of cooked and fresh blueberries is an inspired idea. If you don't have a springform pan, a regular pie pan is fine.

Serves 6–8

Crust

- 1 cup all-purpose flour
- 2 tablespoons sugar
- ⅛ teaspoon salt
- ½ cup (1 stick) cold butter, cut into small chunks
- 1 tablespoon white vinegar

Filling

- 5 cups blueberries
- ⅔ cup sugar
- 3 tablespoons all-purpose flour
- ⅛ teaspoon ground cinnamon
- ½ cup heavy cream, whipped and sweetened

1. Preheat the oven to 400°F. Grease a 9-inch springform pan or pie pan.

Make ahead? Sure.

For large crowds: Make the recipe multiple times, rather than trying to double the ingredients.

2. Make the crust: Pulse the flour, sugar, and salt in a food processor. Add the butter, and pulse until the dough resembles coarse crumbs. (Or, rub the butter into the dry ingredients in a mixing bowl.) Sprinkle vinegar over the top and pulse until a ball starts to form. Remove the dough and press it into a ball.

3. With lightly floured fingers, press the dough into the prepared pan. It should be about ¼ inch thick on the bottom and extend 1¼ inches up the side.

4. Make the filling: Put 3 cups of the blueberries into the crust. Combine the sugar, flour, and cinnamon, and sprinkle this mixture evenly over the berries. Bake the tart in the lower third of the oven for 25 minutes, until the berries have cooked enough to release some juice.

5. Remove the tart from the oven and gently stir the filling. Reduce the oven temperature to 350°F and bake for 15 to 20 minutes longer, until the crust is brown and the filling is bubbling.

6. Scatter the remaining 2 cups berries over the tart and cool on a wire rack. Serve with whipped cream.

Marionberry Cobbler

Marionberries are unique to Oregon. They were created by one of the talented horticulturists at Oregon State University, who crossed two blackberry hybrids (Chehalem and Ollalieberry) to create a brand-new cultivar that he named after Marion County, where the experiments took place. The berries are large (about the size of the first joint of a man's thumb) and unbelievably sweet. I understand they are sometimes shipped to other regions, but if you can't find them, any type of blackberry will be as good. Almost.

Serves 6–8

2 tablespoons cornstarch
¼ cup cold water
1 tablespoon lemon juice
1 cup sugar
4 cups marionberries or blackberries
1 cup all-purpose flour
1 teaspoon baking powder
½ teaspoon salt
4 tablespoons butter, cut into small bits
¼ cup boiling water

1. Preheat the oven to 400°F.

2. Make the filling: Combine the cornstarch, water, and lemon juice in a saucepan, and stir until the cornstarch dissolves. (Incidentally, cornstarch dissolves *only* in cold liquids, so don't even try to add it to something hot.)

3. Add ½ cup of the sugar and gently fold in the berries. Simmer the filling until the juices thicken, about 5 minutes, then transfer to a 9- by 12-inch baking pan. (Or make the cobbler in a cast-iron skillet; see note.)

4. Make the dough: Combine the flour, baking powder, salt, and remaining ½ cup sugar in a mixing bowl. Cut in the butter, and then add the boiling water and stir together into a soft dough.

5. Place spoonfuls of the dough evenly over the hot berry filling. You don't have to cover every inch, but gently smooth out the dough so it's more or less flat, not mounds as if you were making drop biscuits.

6. Place the baking pan on a cookie sheet that you have covered with foil (to catch the inevitable drips), and bake until the dough is golden, 25 to 30 minutes.

7. Serve the cobbler warm with whipped cream, vanilla ice cream, or just a Cheshire Cat smile.

Note: It's simpler to make the whole thing in a cast-iron skillet, if you have one. Blend the cornstarch mixture right in the skillet, add the berries, and simmer. Mix the dough ingredients separately, place on top of the bubbling berries, and put the skillet directly into the preheated oven, again using the foil-covered baking sheet.

Variations: Add ½ teaspoon vanilla extract to the berry mixture. Add ½ teaspoon allspice or ground cardamom to the biscuit dough. A sprinkle of organic sugar over the biscuit top is nice too.

Make ahead? If you must, but it's so much better warm from the oven.

For large crowds: This recipe doubles quite nicely.

QUICK COBBLERS

Impromptu dinner party (the best kind): friends drop by. *Please stay for supper. Oh no, we couldn't. Sure you could, there's plenty. But what shall we do about dessert?*

From common freezer and pantry ingredients, I developed this quick-and-easy version of cobbler (check the Marionberry Cobbler recipe on the facing page for guidance on measurements). Use whatever berries you have in the freezer, toss with cornstarch and sugar, add a splash of lemon juice, then simmer in a cast-iron pan until the fruit defrosts and the juices start to flow. Continue to simmer the filling until the juices thicken. For the dough, use commercial biscuit mix (such as Bisquick) but stir in *twice* as much liquid as you normally would; add some sugar and a few drops of vanilla extract. Pour this thin batter all over the berries, and carefully press individual nuts, such as pecans, walnuts, or sliced almonds, into the batter. Bake at 400°F until the dough is golden, about 15 minutes. Serve warm with vanilla ice cream.

Raspberry-Lemon Pie

Recipe from Elizabeth Newland, Civano Soup Supper, Tucson, Arizona (profile, page 46)

Elizabeth says: This is my brother-in-law's favorite pie. If I serve anything else for dessert, he's disappointed. He's too polite to say anything, but I can tell by the look on his face. I always serve this with real whipped cream on the side, and if the pie is going to a fancy affair, I spread whipped cream over the top, and decorate it with blue borage blossoms and a few extra raspberries. Red, white, and blue — beautiful!

Serves 5–6

1	unbaked single pie shell (ready-to-bake from the grocery store is fine)
1½	cups sugar
⅓	cup cornstarch
1½	cups water
3	egg yolks, lightly beaten
3	tablespoons butter
1	tablespoon lemon zest
¼	cup lemon juice
	About 1 pint fresh raspberries, more for garnish
	Heavy cream, whipped and sweetened
	Borage flowers, for garnish (optional)

1. Preheat the oven to 350°F.

2. Fit the pie shell into a pie plate and bake for about 7 minutes, until lightly browned. Set aside to cool.

3. Make the lemon filling: Combine the sugar and cornstarch in a saucepan and gradually whisk in the water. Cook over medium heat, stirring constantly, until the mixture thickens and comes to a boil. Boil, still stirring constantly, for 1 minute longer.

4. Gradually stir half of the thickened mixture into the egg yolks, mixing well. Then blend the egg mixture back into the remaining hot filling mixture in the saucepan. Boil for 1 minute longer, stirring constantly. Remove from the heat and stir in the butter, lemon zest, and lemon juice.

Make ahead? Yes — see step 6.

For large crowds: If you have enough berries, you could make this in a large baking pan with a crumb crust, and cut it into squares for serving. Alternately, make the original recipe multiple times.

5. Spread the hot filling in the cooled pie shell, and then cover the filling with a single layer of raspberries, pressing berries slightly into the filling, upside down (with the rounded berry bottoms facing up). It will take a little more than a pint to cover the pie, depending on the size of the berries.

6. Cover and chill the pie in the refrigerator. Serve with whipped cream and borage flowers, if using.

CHAPTER SIX

Start Your Own Soup Night

When my kids are in their 50s, sitting on their own front porch and thinking back over their lives, the main thing they will remember about their childhood is Soup Night.

— *Alex, Stanton Street*

If you are excited about the idea of Soup Night and would like to see one on your block, you will find plenty of help from the hosts whose stories are described in this book. Several of them took the extra step of outlining some of the things they have learned over the years about how to orchestrate Soup Night and keep it going. I have grouped them together here, along with my sincere thanks for their generosity. I have supplemented their accumulated wisdom with the following step-by-step outline of what it takes to start a Soup Night in your neighborhood.

Recruit one other neighbor as a partner. If you don't already know all your neighbors, ask someone who knows the people you don't to be your partner in this adventure.

Pick a date one or two weeks away to host your first neighborhood Soup Night. Weekends are generally the best.

Write a short letter, explaining the idea and giving the specifics of the first Soup Night, to be held at your house. List your address and phone number, along with the date and time in big letters. Make enough copies for all the houses on the block.

Go door to door with your partner, introducing yourself if need be and explaining your idea. Leave a copy of the letter.

Note the addresses where no one is home, and make a second effort. If they're still not home, leave your letter with a handwritten P.S. asking if they would please call you.

Prepare a colorful reminder invitation two or three days before the event and distribute it to everyone. Add a handwritten line for those you have not yet heard from, saying you hope they will come.

Soup Night Wisdom from Across the Country

One thing you may have noticed, reading through this book, is that the best ideas show up more than once. So you might not be surprised to see that some of the Soup Night hosts have hit upon similar strategies to keep their events running smoothly. As you read through their ideas here, feel free to pick and choose the ones that fit your own circumstances.

Barbara Rice, Chantilly, Virginia, see page 52

1. Establish a regular day and time, such as the third Monday of the month from 6 to 7:30 PM.

2. In the beginning, deliver invitations in person so you can explain your idea. Drop off reminders a few days ahead.

3. Invite everyone. That's really the whole point — so that people get to know each other.

4. Make it easy for people to attend. Don't ask them to bring food contributions; don't ask them to RSVP; set an end time so people know they're only committing for the dinner hour. I even have disposable coffee cups that people can use for "to go" containers if they need to. This is definitely hospitality rather than entertaining. It's a simple welcome and sharing, and that simplicity makes it easier for folks to come.

5. Do as much in advance as possible. Many soups can be made ahead, either completely or partially. Garnishes can be prepped ahead too. You don't want hours of last-minute work, or else how you would survive to do the next Soup Night?

6. Keep the soups warm on the stove, label them, and let people help themselves. I used disposable paper bowls but found we needed to double them because soup is hot!

Grace Martin, Aurora, Illinois, see page 108

On Organizing a Soup Night

1. Someone takes responsibility to set dates, sign up host families, and notify the neighbors. There needs to be a leader.

2. Our Soup Night is always on the same night at the same time of year for eight weeks. Whatever schedule an organizer/group picks, it works well to have a routine of some sort that people can count on.

3. We distributed creative invitations for a number of years, but a neighborhood directory which includes e-mail addresses has moved the invitations to the electronic level of communication and makes it a lot less expensive and a lot less work.

4. There needs to be a committed partnership of a few to attend and support soup supper. Our Soup Night was small at first, and always hosted by Kate, but it has grown because, I believe, a couple of other families with the gift of hospitality moved to the neighborhood and began to share hosting. This increased the radius of contacts with neighbors and broadened the enthusiasm, which sparked even greater interest. It also made it easier on Kate. Finding committed partners is important.

5. We live in a small historic district with defined boundaries. Having a clearly defined area also makes our Soup Nights successful as we have an identity as neighbors. Identifying and defining a geographical area is important even if there isn't a ready-made target area.

6. Keeping it simple makes it easy. A pot of soup by the host family can be put out for self-service or dished up by the hostess. The guests bring

any kind of finger food to add to the meal (breads, crackers, cheeses, veggie trays, deviled eggs, fruit, cookies, etc.). Our Soup Nights have been around long enough that folks have started to branch out with salads and desserts, which need plates and utensils. This is wonderful, but not necessary. The drinks are usually ice water and tea or coffee.

On Entertaining Large Groups

In the 42 years that we've been married, my husband and I have hosted many large gatherings. During that time I've come up with a couple of things that make it easy and inexpensive, and I rely on them when we are the soup hosts.

1. I have a couple of crock containers in which I keep utensils that are strictly for large group use. One has more than 40 soup spoons of random patterns, which I picked up at garage sales or thrift shops. The other container has more than 40 forks gathered the same way. When a crowd comes over, I just pull out these crocks from a convenient shelf and I'm all set for utensils. After the utensils have been washed, they are put away in the appropriate crock ready for next time.

2. I like blue-and-white dishes, so I've collected many blue-and-white bowls from garage sales and thrift shops; this collection can also be pulled out in

a hurry. Because they all have the same color scheme, there is a cohesive look to the ensemble. It also happened that over the years I've found about two dozen of the same pattern. I'm always on the lookout.

3. For beverages I use plastic cups, but wash them for reuse until they break and then I recycle them. If the crowd is really big, then a permanent marker lets people put an identifying mark on their cups. Coming up with crazy titles can be fun, such as "My parents' favorite child" and other silliness.

> I really believe that if everyone had a Soup Night to go to, there would be no more crime, no more wars.
> — *Regina Roberts,*
> *Loveland, Colorado*

4. I look for seasonal napkins/plates after the season and save them for use next year. I have a shelf in the basement dedicated to the plastic cups, napkins, and plates, so I always know where to find them.

5. I bought myself a large soup pot of good quality from a seconds store so I can make a very large pot of soup and walk away to do other jobs without worrying about the bottom scorching.

6. I put lemon, lime, berries, or cucumber slices in the water pitcher just to add a touch of flavor and elegance.

7. I always boil the holiday turkey bones and put the broth in the freezer. I often make a soup that calls for chicken broth but use the turkey broth first before using purchased chicken broth. I also use my freezer to keep vegetable broth or anything else that might go to make a tasty pot of soup. In the "anything else" category, veggies in the vegetable bin that are getting a little old can get chopped up and frozen to be thrown into a pot of soup for added flavor and richness. My kids laugh at me, but I'll even scrape the good bacon meat gel off of the bottom of the bacon fat once it has hardened and save that in a container in the freezer for use as a secret ingredient. Any meat gel is good to keep.

8. I keep a file for soup ideas to get me launched, but of course, adapt according to what I have on hand or what's on sale. It's good to give yourself permission to be flexible.

The Robbins Family, Grayslake, Illinois, see page 154

Soup Night Checklist

- ○ Put bowls and spoons out
- ○ Cups for water and wine-glasses ready
- ○ Soup made
- ○ Soup serving spoons out
- ○ Bread plate and knife out
- ○ Butter soft and out
- ○ Paper plates out
- ○ Feed dogs and let out
- ○ Plastic forks out
- ○ Napkins out
- ○ Garbage in kitchen dumped

- ○ Dishwasher unloaded
- ○ Both bathrooms cleaned
- ○ Move dog gates
- ○ Outside lights turned on
- ○ Dust house
- ○ Clean off kitchen and dining table
- ○ Put shoes away
- ○ Sign-in book set out
- ○ Pick up basement
- ○ Put rugs by front door out

Soup for a Good Cause

If you are involved in a nonprofit organization, or have kids in school, or know someone who does, you surely know all about special-event fund-raisers. And you know how easily even the most loyal supporters get to the point of fundraiser fatigue. I know people who say to their spouses or partners, "Can't we just give them some money and *not go* to the dinner/auction/costume party/whatever?"

Here's an idea: Host a soup supper. In researching this book, I came to know several organizations that use soup as the main mechanism of their fundraising activities, and always to great success. Because soup is casual and homey, it has a way of putting people at ease. A bowl of soup is comfortable in a way that a fancy dinner never can match. One participant explains it this way, describing her organization's annual Soup Cookoff: "It's so much nicer than the usual auction, which is — let's face it — bo-*ring*. Plus you get to eat something good" (Jennifer, SE Works, see page 80). Even neighborhood groups can add a "giving" component to their event; the Neelys' Big Soup dinner in Pittsburgh (page 118) is especially inspiring.

So if you are searching for ideas for your organization, take a look at the experiences of these groups below. And if you are invited to one of their events, go!

- ○ Empty Bowls, page 198
- ○ SE Works, page 80
- ○ Portland Stock, page 244
- ○ Logan Square, Chicago, Soup Night, page 212
- ○ Chicago Soup and Bread, page 139
- ○ Project MANA, page 208
- ○ Hiram College's Bread and Soup, page 263
- ○ Unity Church's Soup Sunday, page 216

CONTRIBUTORS

Carol Adler
Mill Valley, California

Nicole Adrian
On My Table
http://onmytable-nadrian.blogspot.com
onmytableblog@gmail.com

Albertina's Restaurant
424 NE 22nd Avenue
Portland, Oregon 97232
www.albertinakerr.org

Ann Armstrong
Salem, Oregon

Ann Bates
Civano Community
Tucson, Arizona

Dennis Battles
Long Beach, Washington

Martha Bayne
Soup and Bread
www.soupandbread.net

Lou Poole Brown
Lewisville, North Carolina

Anna Bueno
Bedford, Massachusetts

David Campiche
The Shelburne Inn
4415 Pacific Way
Seaview, Washington 98644
800-466-1896
http://theshelburneinn.com

Marilee Corey
Salem, Oregon

Julie Dahlberg
Grayslake, Illinois
Make of It What You Will
http://juliedahlberg.blogspot.com

Lisa Fine
Montpelier, Vermont
City Sprouts
www.lisafine.org

Heather Vogel Frederick
www.heathervogelfrederick.com

Lori and Paul Fredrich
Milwaukee, Wisconsin
Burp!
peefandlo@eatatburp.com
www.eatatburp.com

Rebecca Gagnon
Milwaukee, Wisconsin
CakeWalk
www.rcakewalk.blogspot.com

Renee Giroux
Portland, Oregon

Ariana Jacob
Portland, Oregon
publicwondering@gmail.com
http://publicwondering.wordpress.com
For stock grants
portlandstock@gmail.com
http://portlandstock.blogspot.com

Cheyenne Johnson
Aurora, Illinois
our lovely mess
www.ourlovelymess.com

Toni Kelly
Erie, Pennsylvania
toni@tonikellystudio.com
www.tonikellystudio.com

Rev. Mary Knight
Spokane, Washington
Community Minister, Hospital Chaplain

Mary Ella Kuster
Portland, Oregon

Trudy Ludwig
Portland, Oregon
Ludwig Creative, Inc.
www.trudyludwig.com
Children's Advocate & Author

Grace Martin
Aurora, Illinois

Diane Mermigas
Chicago, Illinois

Channing Meyer
Loveland, Colorado
Satori Grill
www.satorigrill.com

Kathryn and Eric Meyer
Cleveland Heights, Ohio
http://meyerweb.com

Sonia Montalbano
Portland, Oregon

Stephen and Melissa Neely
Pittsburgh, Pennsylvania

Elizabeth Newland
Civano Community, Tucson, Arizona
Marysville, Washington

Kennette Osborn
Ocean Park, Washington

Andrea Pedolsky
Washington, D.C.

Suzy and Philip Poll
Houston, Texas

Kathleen Pool
Portland, Oregon

Regina Wirsich Roberts, Intuitive Artist
Loveland, Colorado
Red Sun Studio
http://redsunstudio.com

Jennifer Rollins
Portland, Oregon

Maureen M. Ruddy
Fairfax, Virginia

Jennifer Sammons
Portland, Oregon

Elizabeth Schellberg
Portland, Oregon
easchell@comcast.net

Lewinna Solwing
www.lewinnasolwing.com

Sydney Stevens
Oysterville, Washington
www.sydneyofoysterville.com

Virginia Tackett
Hillsboro, Oregon

Patty Wood
Oysterville, Washington

Lexa Walsh
Oakland, California
lexawalsh@gmail.com
http://lexawalsh.tumblr.com

INDEX

Page references in *italics* indicate photos.

METRIC CONVERSION CHARTS

Unless you have finely calibrated measuring equipment, conversions between U.S. and metric measurements will be somewhat inexact. It's important to convert the measurements for all of the ingredients in a recipe to maintain the same proportions as the original.

General Formula for Metric Conversion	
Ounces to grams	multiply ounces by 28.35
Grams to ounces	multiply grams by 0.035
Pounds to grams	multiply pounds by 453.5
Pounds to kilograms	multiply pounds by 0.45
Cups to liters	multiply cups by 0.24
Fahrenheit to Celsius	subtract 32 from Fahrenheit temperature, multiply by 5, then divide by 9
Celsius to Fahrenheit	multiply Celsius temperature by 9, divide by 5, then add 32

Approximate Equivalents by Volume		Approximate Equivalents by Weight			
U.S.	Metric	U.S.	Metric	Metric	U.S.
1 teaspoon	5 milliliters	¼ ounce	7 grams	1 gram	0.035 ounce
1 tablespoon	15 milliliters	½ ounce	14 grams	50 grams	1.75 ounces
¼ cup	60 milliliters	1 ounce	28 grams	100 grams	3.5 ounces
½ cup	120 milliliters	1¼ ounces	35 grams	250 grams	8.75 ounces
1 cup	230 milliliters	1½ ounces	40 grams	500 grams	1.1 pounds
1¼ cups	300 milliliters	2½ ounces	70 grams	1 kilogram	2.2 pounds
1½ cups	360 milliliters	4 ounces	112 grams		
2 cups	460 milliliters	5 ounces	140 grams		
2½ cups	600 milliliters	8 ounces	228 grams		
3 cups	700 milliliters	10 ounces	280 grams		
4 cups (1 quart)	0.95 liter	15 ounces	425 grams		
1.06 quarts	1 liter	16 ounces	454 grams		
4 quarts (1 gallon)	3.8 liters	(1 pound)			